Georgia State Politics:
The Constitutional Foundation

Georgia State Politics
The Constitutional Foundation

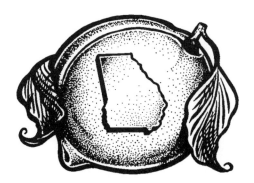

Lee M. Allen ☆ **Richard T. Saeger**
Valdosta State University

Third Edition
Revised Printing

KENDALL/HUNT PUBLISHING COMPANY
4050 Westmark Drive P.O. Box 1840 Dubuque, Iowa 52004-1840

Cover (peach) image provided by Corel.

Copyright © 1992, 1994, 1998, 2000 by Kendall/Hunt Publishing Company

Revised Printing

ISBN 0-7872-6738-4

All rights reserved. No part of this publication may be reproduced, stored in a retrieval system, or transmitted, in any form or by any means, electronic, mechanical, photocopying, recording, or otherwise, without the prior written permission of the copyright owner.

Printed in the United States of America

10 9 8 7 6 5 4 3 2

Contents

Photographs and Figures   viii

Cartoons   ix

Tables   x

Preface   xi

Acknowledgements   xiii

1. Introduction to Georgia Politics   1

    Introduction   1
       The Constitutional Basis of State Government   3
       State Constitutions   4
       Georgia's Constitution   5

    The Constitution of 1983   10

2. Civil Rights and Civil Liberties   13

    Introduction   13
       Civil Liberties   13
       Civil Rights   19

    Article I—Section II: Origin and Structure of Government   22
    Article I—Section III: General Provisions and Operations   23

3. Political Participation in Georgia   27

    Participation in Georgia Politics   29
       Georgia's Political Party System   31
       Georgia's Party Organization   34
       Interest Groups in Georgia   36

4. The Legislative Branch   43

    Composition of the General Assembly   43
       Legislative Leadership   46
       Legislative Tasks—Bills   49
       Local and Special Legislation   53

vi   Contents

    Legislative Politics in Georgia   55
        General Appropriations Bills   56

    Conclusion   59

5. The Plural Executive of Georgia   61

    The Governor of Georgia   61
        The Powers of the Governor   62
        Governor James E. Carter   64
        Vision and Policy Initiative   66

    The Lieutenant Governor   67
    Attorney General   69
    Educational Executives   69
    Other Elected Executives   70
    Conclusion   71

6. Administration and Agencies   73

    The Georgia State Administration   73
        Public Administrators   74
        Constitutional Boards   76
        Executive Commissions   78

    Intergovernmental Interactions   83
        Conservation of the Environment   84
        Other Regulatory Areas   85

    Conclusion   87

7. The Georgia State Judiciary   89

    The Vested Judicial Power   89
        The Unified Judicial System   91
        The Lower Court Jurisdiction   92
        The Higher Courts   94

    Judicial Vacancies and Removals   98
    District Attorneys   100
    Conclusion   101

8. Budgeting and Finance   103

    Introduction   103
    State Taxes and Revenues   103
    Georgia State Budget   110
    Educational Expenditures   112
    Local Government Expenditures   112
    State Income Sources   114

    State Income Sources and Budget   114
    Budgetary Increases   116
    Conclusion   117

9. State Education Policy   119

    State Educational Structure   119
        Local School Districts   120
        Higher Education in Georgia   125
        Educational Policy   127
        Educational Morality   128

10. Local Government   133

    Introduction   133
        County Government   134
        Georgia County Government   135
        City Government   137
        Local Government in Georgia   137
        The City Charter in Georgia   138
        The City of Atlanta   139
        Special District Funding   145
        Too Many Governments?   146

    Conclusion   147

11. The State Constitution   149

    Reflecting State Diversity   149
        The Constitution of 1983   151
        The Amending Processes   153
        Constitutional Changes   155
        Recent Amendments   158

    Conclusions   160

Appendix I: Questions by Chapters   163

Appendix II: The Georgia State Constitution   189

Bibliography   255

General Index   261

Photographs and Figures

1.1 Monument to James Oglethorpe   xiv
2.1 Civil Rights Shrine   12
3.1 Historical Legislative Photo   26
3.4 Political Party Organization   35
4.1 The Capitol Building   42
4.3 The General Assembly   47
5.1 The Governor's Mansion   60
5.3 Selected Governor's Appointments   68
6.1 Department of Transportation   72
7.1 Local Courthouse   88
7.4 State Court System in Georgia   98
8.1 Georgia Department of Revenue   102
8.3 Dividing the 1998 State Budget Pie   111
8.4 Origin of States Revenues   116
9.1 Children at Play   118
9.3 Educational Bureaucracies   124
10.1 Savannah City Hall   132
10.2 Strong Mayor Organization Chart   140
10.3 Council Manager Organization Chart   143
10.5 Special Purpose Government Chart   145
11.1 Statue of Herman Eugene Talmadge   148

Cartoons

1.2 Voice of the People   6
2.2 Sparticus   17
3.2 Leading the Campaign   32
3.3 Democrat Faces Republican   33
4.2 The Clowns Together   44
5.2 Choosing Today's Role   64
6.2 Bureaucratic Empire Building   75
7.2 We Have the Final Decision   91
7.3 Beneath the Robes   97
8.2 Juggling the Budget   107
9.2 Educational Burden   123
10.4 Local Government Promises Revealed   144
11.2 Safety Improved Baby Carriage   154

Tables

1.1　Georgia Constitutional Systems　11
3.1　Government Entities in Georgia　37
3.2　Georgia Interest Groups　37
3.3　Factors of Influence　38
4.1　Georgia Legislators　45
4.2　Standing Committees in the Georgia Legislature　50
4.4　How a Bill Becomes Law　52
6.1　Administrative Subdivisions　77
6.2　Examining and Licensing Boards—Selected Health Professions　79
6.3　Other Examining Boards　80
6.4　Types of Authorities　86
7.1　Exclusive Jurisdiction　94
7.2　Appellate Jurisdiction　95
7.3　Georgia Judicial Agencies　96
8.1　Georgia 1994 Fiscal Statistics　104
8.2　All States 1994 Fiscal Statistics　104
8.3　Allowable State Indebtedness　109
8.4　1998 Legislative Appropriations　111
8.5　Atlanta General Fund Budget: 1993　113
8.6　Georgia—1997 Budget Revenues　115
9.1　School Responsibilities　121
10.1　Municipal Responsibilities　134
10.2　County Commission Sizes　136
11.1　Changes Listed by Sections　156
11.2　Amendments Listed by Years　156

Preface

Many states, including Georgia, have laws requiring that public colleges and universities provide their students with a basic education about the practice and theory of state government. Usually textbooks are available to assist professors in satisfying the legal requirements.

The State of Georgia has had several textbooks in the past, but with the exception of a small pamphlet issued by the League of Women Voters they are out of print. This textbook you are holding in your hand has been written to fill the gap and to satisfy the state law. It is brief enough to remain interesting and long enough to build a solid understanding of Georgia State Government. It is also designed to be compatible with a joint State/American Government course.

Our approach is Constitutional, tracing the development of the various Constitutions of Georgia, linking the current Constitution to the existing institutions of government, and showing how the recent amendments to the Constitution reflect Georgia culture and politics. Government can be a difficult subject, but we believe that this book makes it easier. Several features were designed to increase interest and readability:

★ Figures and Graphs on the major agencies and institutions
★ Tables showing legislative interests, budget monies, and relationships
★ Cartoons to show the humorous side of Georgia State Government
★ Tables of Contents and Figures
★ Bibliographic references
★ An Index
★ New Chapters on:
   Civil Rights and Civil Liberties
   Political Participation
   Education

Acknowledgments

We are indebted to our colleagues for their advice, suggestions and occasional contributions. We acknowledge the support and assistance offered by the staff and administration of Valdosta State University, and we are grateful to our students for their perspectives and frank comments over the years. Most of all we thank our parents, who encouraged our educational endeavors.

Of course, we accept all the blame for errors of omission and commission which appear herein. Differences on matters of fact and interpretation have been compromised or left to the readers to decide. We believe we have written a readable book for a variety of audiences, and welcome your comments.

FIGURE 1.1. Monument to James Oglethorpe

Introduction to Georgia Politics

Introduction to Georgia Politics

Georgia is the largest state east of the Mississippi River. It contains 58,909 square miles of land area, which ranges from the Appalachian mountains of the northwest region to the rolling hills and plains of the Piedmont and its great pine forests, and down to the fertile river deltas and the Savannahs, the coastal beaches and the lush off-shore islands. This area is drained by two watersheds, one leading to the Mississippi River and then to the Gulf of Mexico; the other leading south and east, ending in the Atlantic Ocean. Georgia was founded in 1733 and today is inhabited by over seven million people, both rural and urban dwellers. Economically, raw materials and food are produced by an active population of farmers, ranchers and lumbermen; and the people in the Atlanta metroplex staff a world class center of trade, commerce and information. The state population, as of 1995, is estimated at over 7,200,000 people. The people of Georgia have created a dynamic and flexible system of public and private sector organizations to help them achieve their goals and aspirations. Until recently, Georgia was a one-party state, with a plural executive and a weak but sometimes influential governor. There are over one thousand government entities in Georgia (Hepburn, 138). Chief among these organizations is the State Government of the State of Georgia, and its agencies.

The Importance of State Government

The late U.S. Senator Everett Mckinley Dirksen of Illinois used to complain that the way things were going, pretty soon the only people who would care about state boundaries would be Rand-McNally (the mapmakers). What Senator Dirksen was lamenting was the transfer of power from the states to the national (federal) government in Washington, D.C. The Senator's complaint was that states were losing their very reason for existing as they allowed or encouraged the national government to become involved in more and more areas of public policy. And, to be sure, the states have given up a great deal of their power to the national government.

Since the 1930s, the relationship between the national government and the states has become much more cooperative, replacing the competitive federalism (the relationship between the national government and the states is known as federalism) that existed before President Roosevelt's New Deal (the name for the programs that F.D.R. proposed to get the nation out of the Great Depression). This cooperation frequently takes the form of the national government's identifying a problem, passing legislation to address that problem, and providing carrots (inducements often in the form of money) or sticks (threats to withhold money if the states don't comply) to tackle the problem. Normally, the states do not have the option of choosing to do nothing. Cooperation, then, really becomes coerced cooperation.

To draw the conclusion that this transfer of power to Washington has left the states powerless would be to go far beyond what the facts warrant. In fact, this is an error of thinking which assumes that there is a finite amount of power, and that if one side gains power, then the other side must lose power. In fact, the power of all governments to regulate their citizens, and to control nature and improve living conditions, has grown tremendously over the years. The states are hardly powerless; they just don't have the same kinds of power they used to have in relation to the national government. The national government started off small but has grown very large in recent years, in our complex federal system. Many people believe that the federal government has become *too* large, and much of its power should devolve to the states. The watchword of the Republican "revolution" that captured control of the 104th Congress in 1994 was, in fact, "devolution."

Also, other levels of government operate in the United States and Georgia, such as international treaties and organizations, multistate agencies, and sub-local neighborhood compacts, which work together well. The unity of federalism has been highlighted by studies which stress the increasing vertical bureaucratization of programs in the United States, created by the lobbying of special interest groups (Beer). In fact, every policy and program exists at every level, administratively integrated, with costs shared by all three levels.

States may no longer discriminate on the basis of race; they may, however, enact affirmative action guidelines that exceed federal guidelines. States cannot pollute the environment; they may, however, pass environmental protection laws that exceed (as Georgia's does) the national pollution standards. States have lots of powers. What they lack is the power to deprive their citizens of the equal protection of the laws, or to subject them to unreasonable dangers. In other words, the states' power to do evil is curtailed; their power to do good is limitless.

We look to state governments to provide us with education, with transportation, with police protection, with health care and sanitation, with jobs and economic development, with recreation, and with justice. The national government cooperates with the states in all of these areas. States, however, bear most of the responsibility. States then, are not merely important; in the areas that affect us most directly, states are the most important tier of our governments. And their strength is a protection against factions and special interest groups that dominate the nation (Madison).

The Constitutional Basis of State Government

Because some state governments existed prior to the writing of the Constitution of the United States, the national Constitution could not be said to have created the states. Nor did the states create the national government; rather, the people created both levels of government. And although each level of government has its own powers, ultimately some political authority has to decide which level has which powers. Article VI of the U.S. Constitution contains the "Supremacy Clause" which states that "This Constitution . . . the laws . . . and all treaties . . . of the United States, shall be the supreme law of the land." Therefore, any state constitution or state law (states can make treaties or compacts only with congressional approval) that contravenes the U.S. Constitution, federal law, or a U.S. Treaty is unconstitutional on the face of it.

If Georgia wanted a state constitutional provision or a law establishing a state church, the state could not do so because it would violate the federal laws, particularly the Establishment Clause of the First Amendment of the U.S. Constitution. If Georgia wanted to reestablish slavery, the Thirteenth Amendment to the U.S. Constitution would preclude the state from doing so. And if Georgia wanted a law prohibiting interracial marriage (in fact, such a law existed until fairly recently), provisions of the U.S. Constitution and federal law would invalidate such a blatant violation of personal freedom. In short, states are free to exceed federal constitutional protections; they are not free, however, to supersede those protections. They are not free to deny, disparage, or abuse peoples' rights. Thus states sometimes offer greater protections then does the federal government.

Sometimes government agencies or overzealous bureaucrats, both state and federal, do "ride roughshod" over rights and must be ordered to stop. Frequently, it is a state's Attorney General who offers the opinion that an action, law or constitutional provision is legally unenforceable. Occasionally, it is the state courts which rule that a law violates the state constitution or that a state law or the state constitution violates federal law or the U.S. Constitution. On even rarer occasions, it is a federal appellate court, exercising the power of judicial review (determining whether a law is consonant with the Constitution) that holds some state law or constitutional provision to be in violation of federal laws and the U.S. Constitution. Regardless of which legal authority reviews it, they all agree that the hierarchy of law in the United States is in the following order: 1) the U.S. Constitution; 2) Federal laws; 3) Treaties of the United States; 4) State constitutions; 5) State laws; 6) Local (City and County) ordinances. Each must be consistent with all the laws above it.

Relationships among the various levels of government in the United States are not always about power or high principles. Sometimes mundane business matters and strategies of economic growth at the local government level take center stage. In the Five Points Neighborhood in the City of Atlanta, the federal government proposed to operate a new office complex, the Atlanta Federal Center, and to relocate about 8,000 workers to that facility (land and building would be owned by the city). The consolidation would allow federal employees to work together with associated savings in amenities such as a cafeteria, day-care center and a clinic. One impact study estimated that the entire project would add $68.6 million to the local economy (Salter, C7). While the merchants in the area were optimistic about the proposed project, other merchants and politicians worried that the relocations and changes in work habits and transportation would injure existing businesses (Parker, C7).

In a democracy such as ours, politicians are always in the market for new ideas to impress the voters and to inspire other politicians to close ranks and pursue a mutually beneficial program. Such was the necessity facing Governor Zell Miller at the beginning of the 1994 legislative session. Although his previous legislative agenda, *Georgia Rebound,* could be considered a success (the economy *did* improve), every program has its critics and naysayers. Yet, at least theoretically new programs have one advantage: they lack a track record to be attacked by opponents during the heat of an election campaign. Usually the flag, mom, and apple pie are good old standbys, but in Georgia, the issues of the flag (confederate symbol or historical tradition?) and mom (affected by the gay rights problem) were tarnished; and apple pie is not a top priority in the Peach State. Governor Miller had been burned pretty badly during the flag controversy, so he needed some new issue (A.Press, 1-10-94, 1). Ah, how about anti-crime and educational issues? So suddenly there was a new agenda for the 1994 legislative session, a package the people wanted and needed, and the Governor could tie into the traditional conservative values of the state, and he and his fellow Democrats could face the Republican party candidates in the fall with a politically popular platform. In fact, this strategy worked so well, that Miller would continue to employ it throughout the rest of his second term. Roy Barnes, our new governor, has yet to settle his strategy.

State Constitutions

Although the theory of constitutional government has a long history, real constitutions were first created by colonists in North America. In addition to the national constitution, every one of the fifty states has a constitution. To a significant extent all are modeled on American revolutionary ideas and reflect a common pattern. They all reflect a belief in popular sovereignty and democracy, they all contain preambles, which state the basic purposes of the state government. They all have bills of rights, which largely mimic the original Virginia Bill of Rights written by Thomas Jefferson, although most expand on it. They all have articles outlining the organization, powers and selection procedures for the three branches of government: legislative, executive, and judicial. They all spell out the methods of selection for these branches.

But beyond these similarities there are also significant differences. One such difference is length. The U.S. Constitution is short, containing only about 8,700 words. State constitutions tend to be much longer (averaging 26,000 words), although the newer ones are much shorter than the older ones. One reason why they are longer is because they usually have articles pertaining to the specific duties of the state government. For example, they contain articles on taxation, boards and commissions, education, the environment, licensing, transportation, etc. Another reason why they are longer is that they tend to be amended more often. The U.S. Constitution has only twenty-seven amendments. Alabama's has around five hundred. Georgia has had forty-eight in thirteen years (as of 1996). Since Georgia does not have statewide elections in odd-numbered years, and since voters must ratify state amendments in statewide elections, the next amendments must be ratified in 1998.

Georgia's Constitution

The Constitution of the State of Georgia, unlike the national constitution, begins with a Bill of Rights. Georgia's Bill of Rights emphasizes the power of the people to alter or reform government, and it is often used. In fact, Georgia is second only to Louisiana in terms of the number of constitutions enacted. Louisiana has had eleven since 1812; Georgia has had ten since 1777. Nineteen states still operate with their original constitution, much amended. And one state, Massachusetts, still uses its colonial charter. In Georgia, the political tradition has been more dynamic, calling for periodic revisions to meet the needs of a changing society.

Georgia's ten constitutions reflect this alert response. Political changes at the national level justified new constitutions in 1777 and 1789. Popular dissatisfaction led to a new constitution in 1798, and the turmoil of the Civil War produced several controversial new constitutions; the Secession in 1861, the Lincoln Plan in 1865, the Reconstruction Era in 1868, and the Bourbon Coup or Restoration Constitution of 1877. More recently, the pressures of modern life led to Executive Reform in 1945, an Interim Constitution in 1976, and the contemporary Bureaucratic Constitution which went into effect on July 1, 1983.

In comparison, the federal Constitution has been amended (but not revised) over a dozen times during the same period, substantially altering the federal relationship and the tax structure between 1965 and the present. In another decade or two, new problems will probably result in a call for another modernization of the Constitution of the State of Georgia. Some critics say the people are apathetic and powerless. In Georgia, the people are like a slumbering giant; when they are jolted awake by scandals or hard times, the political system takes notice. Our state's people shape the constitution to their needs. In Georgia, the people rule.

FIGURE 1.2. Voice of the People

The 1983 Constitution reflects the modern trend in state constitutions: it is short (only 25,000 words); it is less specific and its language is much less legalistic. The Georgia Constitution consists of a preamble and eleven articles. The preamble is similar to that of the U.S. Constitution except that Georgia's invokes divine protection and guidance, a common feature of preambles to state constitutions. Forty-eight amendments have been added to the present Constitution as of 1996.

The people of the State of Georgia enjoy the protection of a Bill of Rights which is in many ways more libertarian than that of the federal document. The Georgia Bill of Rights is in Article I, Section I of the state Constitution, and included within it are several provisions which provide protections beyond those of the federal government. Paragraph VI expressly allows us to assert 'truth' as a defense against charges of libel; paragraph XII is the right to prosecute or defend lawsuits in person (although lawyers are recommended); and in paragraph XIV we find the right to an attorney whenever charged with a criminal offense. The Georgia Bill of Rights also, in paragraph XXVI protects the separate property of spouses, a modern note of gender sensitivity. And finally, the Constitution of Georgia, like that of the United States, has a reserve clause which protects the inherent rights of the people even if those rights have not been articulated, like the penumbral right of privacy. The Georgia Bill of Rights is more extensive than the federal provisions.

While few persons will deny or protest that the civil liberties movement (limiting government encroachment on all citizens' lives) is alive and growing in Georgia, the area of civil rights (whether different people have the same rights) continues to be contentious and provocative. Should minors be allowed to drink alcohol, or ex-convicts be allowed to vote, or homosexuals be allowed to marry? Among these groups, the National Gay and Lesbian Task Force is one of the most active in attempting to change political and cultural beliefs and customs. On the other side of the issue are political entities like conservative Cobb County, which passed legislation saying *"homosexuality is incompatible with community standards"* (Watson, 3A). The issue was highlighted as both sides moved in a series of demonstrations and marches to take advantage of the spotlights thrown on Georgia when the national media converged on the state for the 1996 Olympic Games.

Article II continues the theme of popular sovereignty, by providing for voting and elections and detailing procedures for suspension and removal of public officials. This section also provides for secret ballots, first used in Australia. Article III is the legislative article, its position in the constitution reflects the legislative primacy established after the Revolutionary War. This illustrates the importance of the representatives of the people in framing the laws of the state. The Third Article describes the composition of the legislature, called in Georgia the General Assembly; it also identifies the officers of the General Assembly, and outlines its organization, procedures, and its powers.

Georgia does not have a unitary chief executive like the presidency of the federal government. Instead, it has a complex array of independent agencies and a plural executive. Indeed, the increasing complexities of modern life have led to a strengthening of bureaucratic structures. This is reflected in the Fourth Article, dealing with constitutional boards and commissions, some of which are elected by the people, one of which (the State Transportation Board) is elected by the members of the General Assembly, and some of which are appointed by the Governor, subject to confirmation by the State Senate. The relationship between the Governor and the state bureaucracy is often subtle, held together as much by personal charisma and by politics as by Constitutional provisions.

Article V describes the executive branch *per se*. Unlike Article II of the U.S. Constitution, which is the federal executive article, and which describes the methods of election (the Electoral College) and the powers of the Chief Executive officers (the President and Vice-President), Georgia's Constitution addresses the election and powers of Georgia's various separately elected executive officers. Most states have more than two popularly elected executive officers. Georgia has eight, which places it in the middle range of states in terms of the number of independently elected executives required. These executive officers in Georgia include the Governor, the Lieutenant Governor, the Secretary of State, the Attorney General, State School Superintendent, Commissioner of Insurance, Commissioner of Agriculture, and Commissioner of Labor.

Article VI completes the establishment of the major officials of the state, by outlining the judicial branch of government. It also identifies the types of courts, their jurisdiction, and the procedures for selection of judges, their compensation, and discipline. The article creates a network of specialized courts to deal with the complex problems presented to a modern society. It also includes district attorneys, who are major players in the legal system. And in Article I of the Constitution, the state courts are specifically given authority of judicial review over legislative acts.

Just as the creation of a national income tax required a separate federal Constitutional Amendment (the 16th), Georgia also deals with taxation policy at the constitutional level. Article VII is the taxation article, granting the power to tax, the power to exempt from taxation, and discusses the purposes for which debt may be incurred. Since education is the most important function of state government, it has its own article in the State Constitution. Article VIII is the public education article, providing for the governance, bureaucratic structure and for the financial support of education at the elementary, secondary and college levels.

Local city governments do not merit mention in the national Constitution; these governments are creatures of the states. Because counties and cities derive their powers from the state, a separate article is necessary to address the legal status and duties of substate governments. Article IX of the Georgia Constitution describes the structure, powers and governance of city and county governments. It also concerns the many special districts, and relations among these and between the state and its substate governments.

Article X is the amending article. It allows amendments to the Constitution to be proposed either by the General Assembly or by a constitutional convention. It is based on the Madisonian idea that frequent elections to facilitate change is superior to suppressing dissent and risking violent change. It provides for amendments to be submitted to the voters, with a majority of those voting necessary for ratification. Finally, Article XI is the implementing article. That is, it provides for the effectuation of the Constitution, concluding in Paragraph VI: "this Constitution shall become effective on July 1, 1983; and except as otherwise provided in this Constitution, all previous Constitutions and all amendments thereto shall thereupon stand repealed."

Georgia's Politics

Georgia's government is based on its Constitution which delegates and limits powers. Understanding that Constitution is a necessary condition for understanding the Peach State's government. But it is not a sufficient condition. To truly understand its government, one must examine Georgia politics. To understand the political system, that is the operation of political parties, belief systems, and patterns of political participation, we must understand the political culture of the state. Of course, the complex economic system and the variety of ethnic and racial groups in Georgia means that there are lots of different perspectives in the state. But there is a pattern, a political culture defined as the general collection of political beliefs, practices and behaviors of a people.

The dominant political culture in Georgia can be described as traditionalistic. Political scientist Daniel Elazar has identified three major patterns of political culture in the United States. These are the traditionalistic, individualistic, and the moralistic cultures. He describes Georgia's political culture as a blend of traditionalistic and individualistic, with a trace of the moralistic political culture in the mountains of North Georgia. The individualistic and traditionalistic political cultures are alike in that persons active in politics are expected to benefit personally from their activity, although not necessarily by direct pecuniary gain. (Elazar, 1984, 118–119).

> The traditionalistic political culture accepts government as an actor with a positive role in the community, but it tries to limit that role to securing the continued maintenance of the existing social order. To do so, it functions to confine real political power to a relatively small and self-perpetuating group drawn from an established elite who often inherit their right to govern though family ties or social position . . . .
>
> The individualistic political culture emphasizes the conception of the democratic order as a marketplace. In this view, government is instituted for strictly utilitarian reasons, to handle those functions demanded by the people it is created to serve. A government need not have any direct concern with questions of the good society, except insofar as it may be used to advance some common conception of the good society . . . .
>
> The moralistic political culture emphasizes the commonwealth conception as the basis for democratic government. Politics, to the moralistic political culture, is considered one of the great activities of humanity in its search for the good society . . . ..Good government . . . .is measured by the degree to which it promotes the public good and in terms of the honesty, selflessness, and commitment to the public welfare of those who govern (Elazar, 1984, 115–19).

An understanding of Georgia's political culture as being traditionalistic helps us to understand why Georgia for so long had a one-party system, why voter turnout in Georgia is among the lowest in the nation, and also why Georgia has had so many Constitutions in her history. It also helps to explain Georgia's political conservatism. That conservatism is also explained, in part, by ethnicity, which is tied closely to political culture. Indeed, as political scientist Thomas R. Dye writes:

> The location of . . . political subcultures throughout the American states is largely determined by the migration patterns of different ethnic and religious groups . . . {W}hile Elazar himself fails to trace the origin of these subcultures, it appears that: the *moralistic* subculture is a product of northern European, English, and German liberal Protestantism; the *individualistic* subculture is a product of southern and eastern European and Irish Catholicism; the

traditionalistic subculture is a product of fundamentalist white Protestantism in potential conflict with large black populations (Dye, 1991, 14–15).

The Constitution of 1983

Georgia is governed constitutionally. Although common today, Constitutional government is a recent innovation in human civilization. It grew out of British social contract theory, which asserts that government rests on the consent of the governed, evolving to cope with the conflicts and tensions that arose among the various ethnic groups and political factions within those small but energetic island nations. The theory of a government of laws, instead of a government of autocratic monarchy, took root in the British colonies, and has become a venerable tradition in the area now known as the State of Georgia. In the new American nation, the older idea of Parliamentary supremacy became the normal standard instead of deviation from monarchical rule, and legislative government came into its own. In the new world, Constitutional government is limited government, a restraint on politicians, bureaucrats and special interest groups.

Georgia began as a tiny colony on the southern fringes of the British Empire, near rival Spanish Florida. The new land of Georgia, and its sister colonies, eventually grew industrially, socially and politically, far beyond the wildest dreams of its founders, due in large part to the flexibility and fairness of constitutional government. This limited government framework still governs Georgia today.

By convention, the original operating British charters are not thought of as constitutional *per se,* but they served the same purpose: a fundamental outline of official powers and official limits. Scholars differ on whether Georgia and the other colonies became independent nations after the Revolutionary War. But by the simple language of the Articles of Confederation, they claimed themselves to be sovereign states, and Georgia's first Constitution was therefore a national one. However, after Georgia joined the Union in 1788, with its broadened constitutional system, claims of sovereignty became muted, and finally ceased a hundred years later.

While the people of the United States as a whole have adopted only two constitutions since the Revolutionary War, the people of the State of Georgia have adopted ten. These ten constitutions can be divided into three groups: the founding era, the federalizing era, and the modern era; these are displayed in Table 1.1.

In the founding era, legislative primacy was the rule of the day, and constitutions adopted in that period reflected the common revolutionary bias against the excesses of monarchical or executive rule. At both the national and state level, constitutions exalted the representative legislature. During the federalizing

TABLE 1.1
Georgia Constitutional Systems

Founding Era
Legislative Primacy Constitution (1777)
Union Constitution (1789)
Reform Constitution (1798)
Federalizing Era
Confederal Constitution (1861)
Reconciliation Constitution (1865)
Reconstruction Constitution (1868)
Restoration Constitution (1877)
Modern Era
Executive Reform Constitution (1945)
Interim Constitution (1976)
Bureaucratic Constitution (1983)

Source: Compiled by authors.

era, regional and ethnic strife mingled with bitter debate over the extent and legitimacy of states' rights, and the great amount of constitutional revision of that time period shows the stresses and strains of the Civil War era.

Going into modern times, the executive branch has seen a revival of its historic strength, but the most modern trend endangers the chief executive system itself, with the burgeoning growth of modern administrative agencies (bureaucracy) eclipsing it. According to some scholars, the world is experiencing an emerging bureaucratic government (Nachmias, 14). Georgia goes with the general trend. In 1945, Georgia Governor Ellis Arnall sponsored constitutional reform, including a new Article Three insulating the Public Utilities Commission from interference by political hacks (Pound & Saye, 55–56).

The latest Georgia Constitution, adopted in 1983, continued to follow the emerging global pattern, and created a large number of independent commissions, agency boards, and local authorities that largely operate outside of the formal control of the chief executive. In Georgia, the modern trend towards bureaucratic government has blended nicely into the state's traditionalistic and individualistic culture. The feudal plantation systems of the past have evolved into the functional fiefdoms of the present. The result is a continuation of a venerable way of life, localistic and decentralized.

FIGURE 2.1. Civil Rights Shrine

2

Civil Rights and Civil Liberties

Introduction

Our civil rights and our civil liberties are two of the most fundamental features of Georgia's state constitution. After all, the original purpose of the new Georgia colony was to provide a haven for people in debt and for the unemployed poor, although in fact the majority of the actual settlers were ordinary working people. Our civil rights and civil liberties include such important political values as our religious liberty, the popular rights of free speech, freedom of assembly and freedom from imprisonment for debt. Both Oglethorpe and the King supported this effort.

Many other rights and privileges are part of the traditional political culture of the state, rooted in a historical tradition that dates back over two hundred years. This makes Georgia one of the leading developers of democracy at a time when monarchy and elite privilege was the rule in most of the world. This chapter focuses on describing the scope and extent of the civil liberties and civil rights enjoyed by the citizens of the State of Georgia, but of course students are directed to read the exact wording of the constitution after they have read this chapter.

The first article of our Georgia State Constitution, sometimes referred to as the Georgia Bill of Rights, has three parts. The first part describes and enshrines some of our most basic civil liberties and civil rights, which are two different concepts. The second part explains our primary conception of the origins and purposes of popular government. And the third part sets forth other general provisions which control the structure and operation of the state and its political institutions. These general provisions include limitations on official powers, basic patterns of intergovernmental relationships among state institutions, and protection for private property rights.

Civil Liberties

Section I of Article I of the Georgia Constitution contains twenty-eight different paragraphs, of which the great majority concentrate on protection of our liberty.

Civil liberties issues focus on the question of the general degree and limits of freedom allowed by society, and whether or not some types of activities will be forbidden to everyone. Twenty-one of the paragraphs, as described below, detail the liberties enjoyed by the people of the State of Georgia. Another four paragraphs discuss libertarian topics as well as civil rights issues. In civil liberty issues the concern is over the limits on liberty and the boundaries between our freedom and the power of government.

The first paragraph of Article I guarantees that no Georgian shall be deprived of three of the most important possessions of a free citizen: life, liberty, or property; unless a government agency deliberately acts to deprive a person of these things. These freedoms are also explicitly provided for in the national constitution. But if the government perceives a need to act in such a fashion, it must move carefully, by an official and formal proceeding marked by all of the requirements of due process of law. Due Process of law usually requires that the person be notified in advance of the intended action, that an official public hearing shall be held, and that the person shall have opportunity to dispute the state's action, including calling witnesses and having the benefit of legal counsel during the process.

Another civil liberty is found in the third paragraph, which provides for freedom of conscience and guaranteeing that each person has the natural and inalienable right to worship God in their own way, and that no human authority should control or interfere with anyone's right of conscience. Similarly, the next paragraph guarantees that we all shall enjoy freedom of speech and of the press. So in Georgia, every person may speak, write, publish sentiments on all subjects. But of course everyone shall be responsible for the abuse of that liberty, such as inciting to riot or falsely shouting "fire" and thus threatening the lives and safety of other citizens.

What if you call someone a thief, and that person says you are lying? Well, paragraph six covers that situation, under the provision governing libel lawsuits. In all civil or criminal actions for libel, the defendant may offer evidence that the matter is true, and if a trial determines that the matter charged as libelous is in fact true, then the defendant shall be discharged. Of course citizens are well advised to be soft spoken, and not to "shoot off their mouths" unless they are prepared to back up everything they say with hard evidence.

One of the most controversial liberties possessed by all Americans is the right to keep and bear weapons, including firearms. Currently it is disputed whether this right belongs to each individual citizen or only to organized and approved militia companies. It is clear that this right originated as a result of the successful American Revolution against the tyrannical British government. These revolutionaries in Georgia and the other twelve colonies insisted on their right to use weapons to protect themselves. But nowadays some political action groups think that times have changed, and that since the problem of controlling violent criminals is greater than problems of abusive government, the liberty should be re-interpreted and severely restricted. Currently, the right of the people to keep and bear arms remains intact, subject to the power of the General Assembly to prescribe the manner in which arms may be bought and sold, carried and used. Today firearms of all types are closely regulated.

The ninth and tenth paragraphs describe several relatively non-controversial liberties. These include the rights of people to assemble in groups, and to circulate petitions calling for redress of their public grievances. The people have the right to assemble peaceably for their common good or pleasure, and to sign petitions to send to officials of their government so that their problems can be attended to. Sometimes laws do not attract attention simply because they are good laws and are working well. Examples of this are found in the next paragraph, which prevents several of the most favorite abuses by bad governments. These include: bills of attainder (legislative targeting of individuals); ex post facto laws (punishing someone for something he or she did which was legal at the time); also known as retroactive laws. This section also prohibits any laws impairing the obligation of contract, or voluntarily surrendering or recanting any of their special privileges or immunities.

The Jury System

Paragraph XI focuses on the important matter of citizen juries. It is a prime tenet of our culture that when the government accuses people of crimes that they should be tried by a jury of the citizen peers, and not by a government official. It specifies that the right to trial by jury shall remain inviolate, except perhaps in where a jury is not demanded in writing by either party. But in all criminal cases, defendants are guaranteed the right to a public and speedy trial by an impartial jury; and the jury shall be the judges of the law and the facts. While in extremely rare cases a judge may set aside a jury verdict, the system of review by higher courts and public opinion ensures that this possibility is not abused.

Usually a trial jury will consist of 12 persons, especially in important felony cases. However, to save time and money the General Assembly may prescribe any number, not less than six, to constitute a trial jury in the smaller courts of limited jurisdiction and in the state superior courts in misdemeanor cases. The General Assembly regulates by law for the selection and compensation to persons to serve as grand jurors and trial jurors. The monetary compensation for jury duty is not very high; the major reward for citizens comes in the satisfaction of knowing that they have helped to maintain our rights and liberties.

Paragraph XII of the Georgia Constitution makes sure that all Georgians have full and unrestricted rights of access to the state courts. More specifically, it provides that no person shall be deprived of the right to prosecute or defend his or her legal causes, either in person or by representation by an attorney. It would be unfair if a person was not allowed to defend himself if charged with a crime. Our continued liberty depends on being able to defend ourselves in such circumstances. This concern is also the subject of the next constitutional paragraph, which limits the government's use of searches, seizures, and warrants.

The people have a right to be secure in their persons, houses, papers, and effects against unreasonable searches and seizures. Generally a judge or magistrate will issue a search warrant only if witnesses make an oath or affirmation asserting that there is probable cause to suspect criminal activity, and if the warrant particularly describes the place or places to be searched by the official officers, and if it specifies the persons or things to be seized.

Paragraph XIV outlines the rights and liberties that people have if they are charged with an offense against society, a crime or other risk to their freedom such as imprisonment for contempt of court. These include having the benefit of a defense lawyer, which is almost essential if a person is to be able to defend herself in a modern court of law. Other elements of this section include being furnished with a copy of the accusation or indictment and, on demand, with a list of witnesses on whose testimony such charge is founded. Accused persons also have the right to use compulsory process to obtain the testimony of their own witnesses; and the right to be confronted with the witnesses testifying against such person.

In our modern society, two new issues have arisen which have caused considerable debate over our cherished right to be confronted by our accusers. First, society's mounting concern over child abuse cases and the sensitivity of underage witnesses to intimidation have raised questions of the right of confrontation in those kinds of cases. Prosecutors will sometimes demand that a child's testimony be pre-recorded, and that cross-examination will not be conducted in open court. Also, sometimes an agency will leak accusations against persons to the mass media, and in effect conduct a trial that leaves persons unable to defend themselves against supposition, rumors and innuendo. Under these conditions, innocent people may be fired from their jobs, turned out by their families and hounded by their neighbors.

Case Study: Richard Jewell

Most people, especially idealistic young adults just beginning their careers, will often hope to accomplish great things. This was true of one campus security guard at an educational institution who occasionally dreamed of becoming a peace officer and maybe even someday of being hailed as a hero. Sometimes dreams come true, and for Richard Jewell it meant being hired to help with security at the Olympic Games in 1996. As a security guard, it represented a significant step in his professional career. Just when the city of Atlanta was at the center of attention of the entire world Richard Jewell spotted a suspicious package and raised the alarm and thus helped to limit the damage and injuries caused by a terrorist bomb and was called a hero. But his dream turned to nightmare when, in the days following the bombing, a sensationalist media and over-zealous investigators who could not find any other suspect tried to pin blame on him before all the facts were fully checked out. Many people rushed to judgment and assumed he was guilty, although he was later cleared of wrongdoing and initiated several lawsuits. Among the civil liberty protections in the constitution are the presumption of innocence, the right not to be judged guilty without a fair trial.

Civil Rights and Civil Liberties 17

In modern Georgia, few if any people have been secretly thrown in jail without a public trial, but that used to be a real problem in historical times. The remedy for this abuse of government power was for someone to go to a regular judge and seek a Writ of Habeas Corpus, which is an order to the jailer to produce the prisoner and to show proof that the person was being lawfully detained. This protection is provided in paragraph XV of the first Article of the Georgia Constitution. It is still used a lot today however, as a procedure where a defendant can claim that there was some serious defect in their original trial, and to request an appeals court to let them have another chance to demonstrate their innocence. The constitution provides that this writ of habeas corpus shall not be suspended unless the public safety may require it, as in the extremely unlikely event of rebellion or invasion. Of course, rebellion is unlikely in our democratic society where people are free. It is only when people are severely mistreated by their government and their leaders that they begin to think about using force and violence to secure their liberty. Ever since the days of Sparticus, in ancient Rome, tyrants have learned not to push people too far.

The next two paragraphs in Article I, Section I provide further protections for persons accused of crimes. Because we disapprove of torture, and because we know that persons can sometimes be forced to confess to crimes that they did not commit, the Georgia Bill of Rights ensures that no person shall be compelled to

FIGURE 2.2. Sparticus = The Gladiators

give testimony tending in any manner to be self-incriminating. Furthermore, the constitution provides that excessive bail shall not be required, nor excessive fines imposed, nor cruel or unusual punishments inflicted; nor shall any person be abused in being arrested, while under arrest, or in prison. While there are occasional reports of such abuses occurring, the criminal justice system is closely watched, and proven incidents of beating of inmates will result in the punishment of the guards and officials involved.

Paragraph XVIII ensures that no persons shall be put in jeopardy of life or liberty more than once for the same offense. There are exceptions however, such as when a new trial has been granted after conviction, or in case of mistrial. Because of the over-crowding of our prison systems in Georgia, it has become common for prosecutors to charge defendants with every possible offense arising from a criminal activity. Thus someone who hits a victim several times might be charged with several counts of battery. Faced with the prospect of several trials and several possible convictions, many criminals may plea bargain, plead guilty to one charge in return for less time in jail. In some states, prosecutors may even have the right to appeal a jury verdict of not guilty, and try a defendant again for the very same crime!

The next section, paragraph XIX, concerns the rare problem of someone accused of treason against the State of Georgia. Treason against the State of Georgia is defined as insurrection against the state, adhering to the state's enemies, or giving them aid and comfort. No person shall be convicted of treason except on the testimony of two witnesses to the same overt act or confession in open court. Many government officials and state agency employees are required to take a loyalty oath asserting their faith and loyalty to the State of Georgia.

The consequences of being convicted of a crime in Georgia are described in the next few paragraphs, limiting the kinds and effects of punishment. Number twenty guarantees that no conviction shall work corruption of blood (punishing a criminal's relatives as well as the criminal); or allowing the courts to engage in forfeiture of a criminal's estate (although stolen property, or property used for criminal activity, or purchased with tainted funds can be confiscated. Paragraph XXI forbids using banishment and whipping as punishment for crime. The next paragraph provides that there shall be no involuntary servitude within the State of Georgia except as a punishment except for crime after legal conviction thereof or for contempt of court. This outlaws slavery within the State of Georgia. Similarly, number XXIII prohibits imprisonment for debt. And paragraph XXIV, the last of the sections dealing with civil liberties per se, guarantees that no person shall be compelled to pay costs in any criminal case except after conviction on final trial.

Georgia thus has a long list of guarantees for persons which prevents many of the old abusive actions that historically were used to limit the liberties of the people. However, there are some civil liberties which exist in some states, but not in Georgia. Of these, perhaps the most significant is whether citizens have the right to initiate new laws and policies without the approval of the state government? In some states, such as California, the people have the liberty to circulate petitions for new laws which, if signed by a sufficient number of voting citizens, puts the proposed new laws directly on the ballot for popular approval, completely bypassing the ordinary legislative role in enacting new laws. The Georgia Constitution does permit ballot initiatives in some local government matters. Civil liberties, protections against over-zealous government officials, are traditionally important and protected elements of our state constitutional system.

Civil Rights

Civil Rights are a closely related but different concept. Civil Rights focuses on egalitarian issues. In other words the question is whether or not all people are treated equally by the government. Interest and participation in the full extent and scope of civil rights is arguably among the most controversial issues in any democratic society, including Georgia. The major questions sparking our lively debates include asking about the distribution of rights of equality and privilege among the people. Should all citizens have exactly the same rights and opportunities under government and its agencies? Does discrimination exist and when should the powers of government be used to ensure that no one has unfair advantages under the policies and operations of state government? Are all ethnic groups guaranteed equal opportunity, and are both genders provided with equal treatment in educational and occupational settings? The Georgia Constitution addressed these important civil rights matters.

The political culture of Georgia has often supported advances in civil rights. Perhaps the most significant inequality in human history has been the different treatment of men and women. Perhaps in early history primitive conditions made it advisable for society to channel women into domestic servant roles, with low status. But the modern technological revolution, and its requirements for a highly trained intelligent work force, do not allow us to exclude fifty percent of our human resources from full access to skilled employment opportunities. Georgia has been a leader in women's rights. For example, in 1802 the Georgian Sarah P. Hillhouse became the first woman to own and edit a newspaper. And Wesleyan College in Macon, in 1836, became the first college in the world to be chartered to confer degrees to women. Similarly, in 1866 Georgia became the first to allow women to have full property rights, and in 1922 Georgia chose Rebecca Felton as the first elected United States Senator. Civil rights and equal opportunity is as important to Georgians as making sure that government does not infringe on our liberties.

The second paragraph of Article I provides protection to persons and their property by guaranteeing equal protection under the law. It proclaims that protection to persons and property is the paramount duty of government, and that the state government shall be impartial in its administration of the laws. In Georgia no person shall be denied equal protection of the laws. No individual or group can be denied rights which are granted to other citizens. Similarly, paragraph IV specifically orders that no inhabitant of this state shall be molested in person or property or be prohibited from holding any public office or trust on account of religious opinions. However, it takes the precaution of ensuring that the right of freedom of religion shall not be constructed as to excuse acts of licentiousness or justify practices inconsistent with the peace and safety of the state.

Echoing the national constitution, the Constitution of the State of Georgia in paragraph VII proclaims that all citizens of the United States, resident in this state, are hereby declared citizens of this state; and that it shall be the affirmative duty of the General Assembly to enact such laws as will protect them in the full enjoyment of the rights, privileges, and immunities due to such citizenship. And paragraph XXIV was inserted to make sure that the social status of any citizen shall never be the subject of legislation. This reflected the national constitution, which prohibits the federal government from proclaiming any elite individuals being granted any title of nobility. Thus Georgia cannot declare that anyone is either a peasant or an aristocrat. And, in line with modern practice to guarantee that women are treated equally, the state constitution prohibits the practice of putting wives and their property under the control of their husbands. Paragraph XXVII says that the separate property of each spouse shall remain the separate property of that spouse, except as may otherwise be provided by the laws of the state, such as prenuptial agreements, contracts and divorce decrees.

One major reason for the adoption of the present Georgia Constitution was disenchantment with the antebellum treatment of the issue of civil rights, particularly freed slaves, in many states following reconstruction. Civil rights are always the subject of debate and controversy, partly because of prejudice and partly because social progress creates new inventions and customs which raise or revive questions of claims for privilege for the elite few. During the turmoil of the 1960s' civil rights movement in Georgia, great pressure grew to modernize the constitutional wording to reflect the new social and political conditions of the Twentieth Century. During the political struggles that ensued, the Reverend Martin Luther King, Jr. became the leader of the civil rights movement in the 1960s.

Case Study: Martin Luther King

Individuals participate in politics or seek political careers for many reasons, and sometimes they may become great leaders who effect great changes in politics and society. One such individual was the Reverend Martin Luther King, Jr. Probably nothing makes people more active and politicized than being subjected to bias and discrimination, especially when it interferes with their rights and opportunities, or results in their being treated as second class citizens. Following the second World War, an increased sensitivity to equality and equal rights resulted in the great civil rights movement that culminated in an end to racial segregation and the passage of important civil rights acts. Martin Luther King became the leader of the civil rights movement in the 1960's, and his dedication and sacrifice to that cause has earned him recognition as one of the most important and progressive figures of the twentieth Century. His "I have a dream" speech will long be remembered as one of the most eloquent statements of human civil rights.

Both Liberty and Rights

Some of the sections of the Georgia Bill of Rights concern issues which touch on both civil rights and on civil liberties. For example, Paragraph XI deals with operation of the state's jury system. The provisions here are oriented to making sure that civil liberties and civil rights are not just handled by government officials, who may have institutional agendas, but rather by ordinary citizens chosen at random. This is designed to make sure that people have their cases decided by a jury of their peers.

Felony trials always require a jury of twelve persons. And further protections against arbitrary government specifies that grand jurors, who issue complaints charging people with crimes and the trial jurors who decide guilt, will operate separately.

Paragraph XXVI has a homestead exemption. The basic idea is that a person's home should not be taken away just because they owe a lot of money and cannot repay it in a timely fashion. The current homestead exemption is set at not less than $1,600.00; and gives the General Assembly the authority to define when any additional exemptions shall be allowed and to specify the amount of such exemptions. The assembly is also required to provide for the manner of exempting such property and for the sale, alienation, and encumbrance thereof; and it should be noted that the law actually provides for the waiver of the homestead exemptions by a debtor. So if someone wants to waive their homestead exemptions, to obtain a mortgage loan for example, they can do so, if they want to take the risk.

22 Chapter Two

Finally, the last part of Section I of Article I, paragraph number XXVIII, has a reserve clause for civil liberties and civil rights. It provides that the enumeration of the rights described above shall not be interpreted as meaning that there is an automatic denial of other rights. The enumeration of rights herein contained as a part of this Constitution shall not be construed to deny to the people any inherent rights which they may have hitherto enjoyed. To use a somewhat humorous example, suppose that our legislature imposed a tax on the air we need to breathe. Under the reserve clause, a citizen could go to the courts for a ruling that the new tax violated our inherent right to use the atmosphere.

Article I—Section II Origin and Structure of Government

The second section of Article I, concerning the origin, foundations and structure of government, focuses on the basic political concepts underlying our state government. Paragraph I proclaims our fundamental belief that all government, of right, originates with the people, is founded upon their will only, and is instituted solely for the good of the whole. Public officers are considered to be the trustees and servants of the people and must at all times be answerable to them. The second paragraph concerns the object of government. It reflects our value system, asserting that the people of this state have the inherent right of regulating their internal government. Government is instituted for the protection, security, and benefit of the people; and at all times they have the right to alter or reform the same whenever the public good may require it.

Paragraph III concerns the separation of legislative, judicial, and executive powers. The legislative, judicial, and executive powers are intended to forever remain separate and distinct; and no person discharging the duties of one shall at the same time exercise the function of either of the others except as herein provided. The following paragraphs put particular limits on the powers of the government institutions by what can be called a check and balance system. In paragraph IV, the power of the courts to punish for contempt shall be limited by legislative acts. As detailed in paragraph V, if the General Assembly enacts legislation in violation of this Constitution or the Constitution of the United States, the judiciary branch shall be required to declare them void. And paragraph VI declares that the civil authority shall be superior to the military.

The next two paragraphs deal with narrower topics. Paragraph VII prevents the government from trying to favor the establishment of a religion. It definitely asserts that no money shall ever be taken from the public treasury, directly or indirectly, in aid of any church, sect, cult, or religious denomination or of any sectarian institution. And paragraph VIII deals with gambling and lotteries. All lotteries, and the sale of lottery tickets, are therein prohibited; and this prohibition shall be enforced by penal laws, except that the General Assembly may by law provide that the operation of a nonprofit bingo game shall not be a lottery and shall be legal in this state. The General Assembly may by law define a nonprofit bingo game and provide for the regulation of nonprofit bingo games.

Under the old British system of monarchy, the King could do no wrong, and therefore people could not sue the King for any misdeeds; there was sovereign immunity. But in our democracy, it is understood that state government may sometimes inadvertently injure someone, and that person should be able to sue for compensation. Lawsuits filed to get repayment for injuries are called tort actions, and we believe that everyone should have the right to sue anyone who injures them. Accordingly, paragraph nine provides that the General Assembly may waive the state's sovereign immunity from suit, and that the General Assembly may provide by law for procedures for the making, handling, and disposition of actions or claims against the state and its departments, agencies, offices, and employees.

There are limitations designed to protect the state treasury. The General Assembly is allowed to provide by law for the processing and disposition of claims against the state which do not exceed certain maximum amounts. And the state's traditional defense of sovereign immunity is also generally waived for the breach of any valid written contract entered into by the state or its departments and agencies. So state agencies are required to honor their contracts with the state's citizens and businesses. Therefore, unless otherwise specifically provided for by the General Assembly, all officers and employees of the state or its departments and agencies may be subject to suit and may be liable for injuries and damages caused by their negligent performance of, or even of a negligent failure to perform, their official functions.

And state employees may be personally liable for injuries and damages if they act with actual malice or with actual intent to cause injury to persons during the performance of their official functions. But otherwise, with some exceptions, officers and employees of the state or its departments and agencies are not subject to suit or liability, and no judgment shall be entered against them, merely because someone is injured or doesn't like the approved actions or duties of these government officials. The provisions are further strengthened by other parts of the state constitution, which students are advised to read in their entirety.

Article I—Section III General Provisions and Operations

In our capitalist society, the lure of wealth and the acquisition of private property is used to encourage people to work hard to create new inventions and to improve the general economy. But sometimes the public good requires that the state take or damage property, as for example for building roads or bridges. The last section of Article I sets out some basic rules controlling such state action. Generally, the state is allowed to appropriate property, but it is required to pay people for their property. The first paragraph of this section sets out some fairly complicated and detailed language on this complicated area of private property rights.

When a government body asserts its right to take property, the legal term used may be *eminent domain* or condemnation. The first paragraph says that: (a) except as otherwise provided, private property shall not be taken or damaged for public purposes without just and adequate compensation being first paid. However, part (b) says that when private property is taken or damaged by the state (or by counties or municipalities), for public road or street purposes, or for public transportation purposes, or for any other public purpose as determined by the General Assembly, that just and adequate compensation therefor need not be paid until the same has been finally fixed and determined as provided by law; but such just and adequate compensation shall then be paid in preference to all other obligations except bonded indebtedness.

This means that people whose property is taken get paid first, even before people who lent money to the public body. Of course, the fiscal system in the State of Georgia is very well administered, and the chance that Georgia might fail to repay any of its debts is extremely remote. Other parts of this paragraph specify that: (c) the General Assembly may by law require the condemner (such as a local government) to make prepayment against adequate compensation as a condition precedent to the exercise of the right of eminent domain. This is to make sure that all parties with claims to the property are protected. And in part (d) the constitution provides that the General Assembly may provide by law for the payment by the condemner of reasonable expenses, including attorney's fees, incurred by the property owner in determining just and adequate compensation.

The framers of the Constitution of the State of Georgia were also concerned about other problems that might happen to people whose property has to be taken for the public good. So in part (e), the law provides that notwithstanding any other provision of the Constitution, the General Assembly may provide by law for relocation assistance and payments to persons displaced through the exercise of the powers of the government and that tax money may be spent for that purpose.

In a related but different problem, government is sometimes called upon to settle disputes between two private landowners, particularly if one person's property is surrounded by another person's property. If a court or other government agency determines that someone should have a right to go across someone else's private property, then paragraph II of this last section of Article I provides that in case of necessity, private ways may be granted, but only if just and adequate compensation is first paid by the applicant.

Finally, because the State of Georgia borders on the Atlantic Ocean, there have been disputes about the ownership of beach front property. Throughout history there have been a lot of different laws about the ownership of waterfront property. In some countries, private citizens are forbidden to own property near the ocean. In America, citizens are allowed to own such property, and sometimes even to build houses right next to the water. But on oceanfront property, the tides move in and out, and the land between high tide and low tide may be considerable.

In California, property can only be owned to the high tide level, and other citizens are allowed to walk on the low areas. But in Texas, property may be privately owned down to the low tide mark. The last paragraph in this section follows the latter example, and provides that the Act of the General Assembly approved back in December 16, 1902, extending the title of ownership of lands abutting on tidal water to the low water mark, is ratified and confirmed by the Constitution of Georgia.

The Georgia State Constitution emphasizes the importance of our civil rights and our civil liberties, as should be expected given the state's history and traditions. Our civil rights focus on our belief that people should be treated equally whenever possible, and our civil liberties reflect our determination that government should not be abusive or tyrannical. Our traditional beliefs have made Georgia one of the leading developers of democracy, starting over two hundred years ago when monarchy and elite privilege dominated government in the world. But in order to ensure that our liberties and our rights are protected, government institutions and agencies have to be designed to protect these values.

FIGURE 3.1. Historical Legislative Photo
Source: Courtesy of Georgia State Department of Archives and History

3

Political Participation in Georgia

Popular participation in politics and government is essential to a successful democracy. But because of the dangers of overbearing majorities, we prefer a representative system instead of a pure democracy. And by creating a complex network of local, state, and federal governing bodies, we maximize the routes that individual citizens and interest groups can use to gain access to power and to influence public policy.

Decisions concerning political participation, particularly voting, including the setting of times for elections, the eligibility of voters, and the offices to be filled by elections, traditionally have been considered state and local governmental prerogatives. However, the national government has been gradually encroaching on this territory. The Fifteenth Amendment to the United States Constitution prohibited states from denying anyone the right to vote "on account of race, color, or previous condition of servitude," although many states, including Georgia, found numerous ways to evade those prohibitions.

The Nineteenth Amendment guaranteed to women the right to vote, although in many states, again including Georgia, that right was not exercised by women nearly to the same extent as it was by men (until recently). The Twenty-sixth Amendment to the U.S. Constitution gave eighteen, nineteen, and twenty-year olds the right to vote in all elections. But this merely did for the nation what Georgia had been doing since 1943, when it granted people in that age group the franchise.

Federal statutes as well as Constitutional Amendments have required the states to alter their electoral procedures, where procedures and laws may have the effect of discriminating against local minorities. The Voting Rights Act of 1965, as extended in 1982, requires Georgia and other so-called Section Five states (those with a history of racial discrimination against African Americans or other minorities, e.g., Mexicans in Texas) to seek preclearance from the Civil Rights Division of the U. S. Department of Justice or from the Federal District Court for the District of Columbia before they are allowed to make any change in voting districts or voting procedures. Even if such a change might purport to enhance rather than dilute minority voting strength, such as changing city council or county commission elections from an at-large to a ward or district basis, federal approval must still be sought and granted.

Article II of the Georgia Constitution addresses the matter of voting and elections. It requires voting to be by secret ballot and to be open to all persons over the age of eighteen who meet certain residency requirements, and who are neither convicted felons involving a crime of "moral turpitude" nor mental incompetents.

Owing to its one-party tradition, Georgia requires candidates for public office to win a majority of the votes cast in a primary election. If no candidate does so, a run-off election between the top two vote-getters is provided for. Legislation passed by the Georgia General Assembly in 1998, however, requires only a forty-five percent plurality to win general elections.

The only constitutional restrictions placed on the right to run for public office are that a candidate must be a registered voter and may not have been convicted of a felony involving moral turpitude, unless his or her rights have been restored. Of course, a candidate may have to have access to money, may have to have ideas, may have to have charisma (you can't make a silk purse out of a sow's ear), but those are political restrictions, not constitutional ones.

Article II also requires candidates for local, state or national office to resign their current offices, if any, "if the term of the office for which such official is qualifying for (sic) begins more than 30 days prior to the expiration of such official's present term of office."

Most of Article II deals with getting rid of public officials, or "unelecting" them, if you will. Public officials may be recalled, meaning that the general assembly may enact a procedure whereby the people can remove an officeholder from office if they feel that he or she is not performing satisfactorily. An elected state official—Governor, Lt. Governor, Secretary of State, Attorney General, State School Superintendent, Commissioners of Agriculture, Insurance, and Labor, and members of the General Assembly—*can* be suspended from office if he or she is indicted for a felony. If he or she is convicted of a felony, that official *will be* suspended.

In politics, the will of the people usually determines the substantive policies and procedures of the state. This chapter focuses on the major political linkages between the participation of the citizens, the two political parties, and a wide variety of interest groups. In 1988, Georgia had the somewhat dubious distinction of ranking dead last among all fifty states in terms of voter participation in the presidential election held that year. Only about thirty-eight percent of the eligible electorate turned out to cast its votes for either George Bush or Michael Dukakis. That is a fairly terrible statistic for a democratic state. It was a little better in 1992 but fell again in 1996.

Normally turnout in presidential elections is much higher than turnout in other elections where a presidential nominee does not head the ticket. That is true in Georgia too. Sadly, the average person's lack of interest in national politics is generally surpassed only by apathy about international, state and local politics. In the gubernatorial election of 1994, for example, voter turnout was only 29.9 percent of the eligible electorate. Why is the level of public interest and participation so poor?

Participation in Georgia Politics

If by participation we mean voting only, participation *per se* is not as poor as it seems. In the United States we measure voter turnout according to the number of eligible voters, not by the number of registered voters. Registering to vote can be made easy or difficult. In Georgia, as in much of the United States, voting is a two-stage process—registering first and then actually voting—so that there are more obstacles in the U.S. than in other countries. If we were to measure voter turnout by the number of registered voters who vote, Georgia would be in the seventieth, not the thirtieth, percentile. Compared to other countries and states, that's not good, but it's not as terrible as it looks at first blush.

The fact stands, however, that voting is the form of political participation engaged in most frequently by those who engage in any form of political participation. Activities such as running for public office, membership and participation in party activities and in political campaigns, giving campaign contributions, sporting a campaign button or a bumper sticker, or writing or calling a public official, are much less likely to attract participants than the act of voting.

People don't participate simply because it is easier not to. Registration requirements, as noted above, still serve as an effective barrier to voter participation, even though national "motor voter" law now requires Georgia and other states to facilitate registration by allowing persons to register when they obtain or renew their drivers' licenses or when they visit the welfare office. Otherwise, one must present himself or herself at the county courthouse to register to vote. In some jurisdictions, voting registrars will travel to schools, colleges, senior citizen centers and other locations to facilitate the registration process, but all such activities are optional. A birth certificate, or naturalization papers, or even a driver's license may be all the documentation required to prove citizenship and residency. Since Georgia has permanent rather than periodic registration, once one is properly registered and votes at regular intervals, his or her name remains inscribed on the rolls. In contrast, a requirement for periodic registration means that rolls are regularly purged after a certain time whether the voter votes or not. In fact, where that is the procedure, such as in Texas, registration is far more of a barrier than it is in Georgia.

Another reason for low levels of participation is that some people doubt that their vote will make a meaningful difference. When the winner is certain, or if competition for office is weak or non-existent, potential voters may remain non-voters. Thus, in states with weak interparty competition, voter turnout tends to be low, especially in general elections where the opposition party either runs no candidate at all or a mere token candidate.

Often the quality of party competition depends on the extent of cleavages within the community, based in turn on degree of urbanization, income, education and the percent of resident minorities (Hy & Saeger, 53). This may have been a factor in Georgia, which has traditionally been a one party (Democratic) state.

That is, until recently, the Democratic Party, while seldom carrying the state in presidential elections, nevertheless won virtually all other elections. Democrats currently control both houses of the General Assembly, have controlled the Governor's office since the reconstruction era, and usually won nearly every other state executive office (only the Public Service Commission had seen Republicans among its members), and only five Republicans had been elected to Congress from Georgia between the end of Reconstruction (in 1876) and 1992. These were Mack Mattingly in the Senate from 1981 to 1987; Howard (Bo) Callaway from 1965 to 1967; Ben Blackburn in the House from 1969 to 1975; Pat Swindall in the House from 1985 to 1989; and currently Newt Gingrich, who has been serving in the House since 1979. The year 1992, however, was particularly fruitful for Republicans in Georgia. They gained eighteen seats in the State House of Representatives, six seats in the State Senate, one U.S. Senate seat (Paul Coverdell) and three U.S. House seats (Reps. Linder, Kingston, and Collins). Many of these victories resulted, at least in part, from legislative redistricting, which could have been expected to benefit the Democrats, who controlled the General Assembly.

Occasionally, however, the result of a legislative redistricting effort is nullified by partisanship at the federal level. One rigorous statistical study of the federal review of Georgia redistricting efforts hypothesized that the Department of Justice under the Bush administration pursued a Republican oriented strategy of packing legislative districts with a maximum number of voting age black Americans to increase the potential number of Republican districts (Lauth and Reese, 3). The subsequent research supported the view that a federal Justice Department, dominated by Republicans, was able to use the Voting Rights Act to partisan advantage.

That partisan advantage bore precious fruit in the 1994 and 1996 congressional elections. Joining Gingrich, who would become Speaker of the U.S. House of Representatives following the Republican takeover of the Congress in 1994, and Representatives Linder, Kingston and Collins, were three newly elected Republican congressmen—Saxby Chambliss, Charlie Norwood, and Bob Barr,—with Congressman Nathan Deal switching from the Democratic to the Republican Party. Republicans now hold a majority, controlling eight of the eleven Georgia congressional seats. Interestingly, all eight Republicans are white. The three Democratic members of Congress—Sanford Bishop, Cynthia McKinney, and John Lewis—are all African-American.

Of course, not everyone favors divisive politics or bitterly fought elections. In Louisiana in the 1991 Governor's race between former Ku Klux Klansman David Duke and the former (and then re-elected) Governor Edwin Edwards, the struggle was very divisive. However, there is little doubt that when the competition becomes keen or when the stakes are high, as they were in Louisiana, dormant voters may become more actively involved, thus swelling the turnout to extraordinary proportions; but at the cost of bitter feelings. Conversely, much perceived apathy may in fact represent a basic contentment with the political status quo.

A third reason why people don't participate is because they lack faith in the political system, or feel that it is too complex for them to understand. Ignorance of candidates, parties, or issues serves as a barrier to participation. Thus, turnout in states with low levels of educational attainment is usually quite low. Georgia is, unfortunately, such a state, ranking at or near the bottom of the list of states in terms of educational attainment. The result for Georgians is high dropout rates, poor scores on standardized tests, poor performance on the Armed Forces Literacy Test, low percentages of students pursuing higher educational opportunities, and low voter turnout.

Several other factors positively associated with political participation include a high degree of urbanization, high median family incomes and small percentages of disadvantaged minority groups. As a whole, Georgia strikes out on all three counts. Georgia is largely a rural state (some people count Atlanta as a separate state) still fairly poor in terms of income, especially outside the Atlanta metroplex, and has very high numbers of minority group members who have not been incorporated into the middle class. The largest minority group, blacks or African-Americans, constitute about 28 percent of the total population, and historically have not been able to achieve the economic or educational levels of other ethnic groups. The effect of these demographic factors is obvious. However, well-educated, well-to-do urban minorities actually participate more than do whites from poor rural areas.

Thus a large number of factors have a synergistic impact that dampens voter participation. As we have seen, however, this is not necessarily bad; our analysis suggesting that imaginative change-oriented people are the most active voters supports the idea that much perceived apathy in Georgia may in fact reveal basic contentment with the political status quo.

Moreover, voter turnout in Georgia is actually improving rather dramatically. Some of the improvement can be explained by falling turnout across the nation, so that Georgia doesn't look as bad as it used to. But there is also evidence that Georgia's voter turnout is improving absolutely as well as relatively. One study shows that from 1960 to 1996 the convergence of Georgia and national turnout in presidential election years has been nearly inexorable. That is, in nearly every year Georgia turnout improved both absolutely and relatively, while national turnout declined in the same absolute and relative way (Mishou and Ellinger, 1997). Nevertheless, national politics will continue to be very active.

Georgia's Political Party System

State party systems can be classified as two-party, modified one-party, or simple one-party structures, depending on the strength and number of victories the opposition party gets or the number of votes it usually gets. On this basis, Georgia has been classified as a noncompetitive one-party democratic state. That means that the Democratic Party won virtually all of the elections in the state

32   Chapter Three

FIGURE 3.2. Leading the Campaign

(except Presidential) and in fact won them by substantial margins, frequently by votes of more than 60% (Gray, 149). Why was this so?

There are many reasons why any state has the party system it does. The history of a state or region often reveals the significant factors, and in this context the Civil War continues to have an influence on Georgia's political parties. With regard to political party affiliations, states tend to "vote as they shot." Along the eastern Atlantic seaboard, both the northern states, and the more southern states, established their prevailing political patterns more than a hundred years ago. All of the states of the southern Confederacy, except Florida, have had either one-party Democratic dominance or modified one-party Democratic systems. Georgia can be described as the most Democratic, or perhaps as the least Republican, of all of them.

However, there certainly are some Republican counties in Georgia. These mostly tend to be located in the north Georgia mountains, remnants of communities that opposed secession and have largely remained Republican since the Civil War days. In addition, there are other communities in Georgia which, influenced by economic growth, transportation corridors, federal military bases or transplanted Yankee retirees, today tend to vote along Republican party lines.

Aside from historical events, population growth and migration patterns offer significant explanations for the modern configuration of any particular state's political party system. Aside from the "mountain Republican" counties, such as Catoosa, Fannin and Whitfield, the most other important Republican strongholds in Georgia are found in the Atlanta metropolitan area and its

FIGURE 3.3. Democrat Faces Republican

surrounding counties, especially Cobb, DeKalb and Gwinnett—with large numbers of transplanted managers and professionals from northern and midwestern states who arrived in Georgia with Republican affiliations and have kept them intact.

Other urban counties, such as Bibb (Macon), Muscogee (Columbus), Chatham (Savannah), Richmond (Augusta), Lowndes (Valdosta) and more affluent counties—Glynn (St. Simons, Jekyll and Sea Islands) have growing numbers of Republicans and have experienced the growth of a viable two-party system. There is a third group of Republicans in Georgia: Goldwater Republicans. These are former Democrats who so admired former Senator Barry Goldwater (Rep., Arizona) and his stand on the 1964 Civil Rights Act (he was one of the few non-southerners to vote against it) that when he became the GOP presidential nominee in 1964, they converted to his party. Thus ideology is also a reason for a state's party system being what it is.

But ideology is usually more significant a factor in presidential politics than it is in state or local politics. Georgia Democrats are quick to point out that they are just that: *Georgia* Democrats. The emphasis on "Georgia" is intended to let other people know that they do not necessarily approve of the national Democratic Party, or its leaders, its presidential candidates, and certainly not its liberal ideology. Georgia Democrats are conservative, both fiscally and socially, and are proud of it. They elect conservative Democrats to the U.S. Senate and to the U.S. House, to the General Assembly, to the Governor's mansion, to other state posts, to county commissions, to sheriff's posts, to city councils (even when they are officially non-partisan), and to virtually every other office filled by election. The relatively few Democrats in Georgia who are national Democrats are intellectuals or members of minority groups, residing usually in Atlanta. Blacks outside Atlanta tend to be almost as conservative as their white counterparts.

The distinctive existence of the Georgia Democratic Party illustrates well the dictum uttered by Tip O'Neill, a former Speaker of the House of Representatives of the United States Congress: "all politics is local." In the United States, there really is not a unified national Democratic party system, no real national

Democratic party. What appears to be a national party system is really a collection of state party systems, and in turn what appears to be a state party system is actually little more than an amalgam of local (mostly county) party systems. In fact, the repeated use of the word "system" by the authors may be misleading. American party politics is a lot less than systematic.

Different authors use different typologies for classifying state party systems, but virtually all of them consider Georgia's party system as one-party dominant or as modified one-party Democratic. However, most of those assessments are dated, even in those general State and Local Government texts published as late as 1998. The gains that Republicans have made in Georgia since 1994 are nothing short of phenomenal. It is true that Georgia is the only deep South state that has not elected a Republican Governor since Reconstruction, although by the time you read this that may have changed. It is true that Georgia is the only deep South state that has had neither chamber of the General Assembly controlled by the Republican Party since Reconstruction, although that too may have changed by the time you read this chapter.

A gain of twelve seats for the GOP in the State House and seven in the Senate would give them majorities in the General Assembly. And given the fact that they picked up eighteen seats in the House in 1992, fourteen in 1994, and eight in 1996, an additional pickup of twelve seats is not beyond the realm of possibility. Gaining a majority in the State Senate, however, is a more daunting task. Republicans gained four seats in 1992, six seats in 1994, and only one seat in 1996. Thus, a seven seat gain, while not impossible, is not a probable scenario.

The state's constitutional officers were all Democrats before 1994. Then Republicans won elections for State School Superintendent and Insurance Commissioner, and with then Attorney General Michael Bowers's defection from the Democrats prior to the election and his victory as a Republican, half of the constitutional officers were members of the GOP (Bowers has since resigned as Attorney General to run for governor and has been replaced by a Democrat, Thurbert Baker). Four of the five current members of the Public Service Commission, who are also elected, are Republicans. Thus, one would have to question the classification of Georgia as a one-party state. It seems to have moved rather into the ranks of the two-party states.

Georgia's Party Organization

Both the Democratic and the Republican parties have state executive committees that meet periodically, and recommend policies and procedures for their respective parties. Members of these committees are chosen in local caucuses by their fellow partisans for long terms. The duties of these committees include fund-raising, policy-making, and approving choices for membership in the Electoral College (a reward for faithful service). Each of the state organizations elects officers, including a chairperson, a vice-chairperson, and an executive board. Each of the state party committees has a paid staff headed by an executive director who coordinates the day-to-day activities of the state party. Given the increasing candidate-centeredness of political campaigns, the state executive committees have relatively little to do with directing campaigns. Moreover, while fundraising may be numbered among the committee's duties, they never collect enough, and the resulting dearth of funds to distribute forces candidates to rely on their own devices to raise money.

If one were to think that the state executive committees were answerable to the Democratic and/or Republican National Committees, one would be making a natural mistake, but a mistake nonetheless. Samuel J. Eldersveld described our party system as "stratarchical" not hierarchical, so as to emphasize that each stratum—federal, state, and local, is largely independent of the others (Eldersveld, Chapter 5). Thus the National Committees do not dictate to the state committees, and the state committees do not (although they may try) dictate to the various county committees. Insofar as there is any action in the party organization, the county organization is where the action is.

Perhaps the main reason for this local based party system is the fact that the vast majority of elected officials in the United States are locally based, paid, and organized. Although it varies somewhat from county to county in Georgia (and with 159 counties that is a lot of room for variation), Georgians elect the following officials to county offices: county commissioners and county sheriffs; judges of state and superior courts, probate courts, juvenile courts; magistrates and district attorneys; various clerks of the courts; school board members and school superintendents. While some of these—particularly the judges—are elected on nonpartisan ballots, the parties still play a role in endorsing them for office.

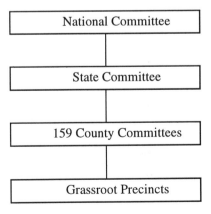

FIGURE 3.4. Political Party Organization
Source: Compiled by authors.

Each of the county committee members is elected in the primary elections, and each appoints a chairperson and such other officers as are called for in their party charters. The electoral base of all of this activity is the precinct. In a state-by-state ranking of the strength of local party organizations (basically the county committees), Georgia's Republican committees were the weakest of all fifty states, and the Democrats were not far behind; their rank was 46th in the nation (Gibson, 154-155). It would appear, therefore, that local "party organization" in Georgia may be a bit of an oxymoron, a contradiction in terms; there is precious little organization in either of the two political parties. However, that too may be changing. While the Democratic party organization appears to be somewhat demoralized and moribund, anecdotal evidence suggests that the Republican organization is optimistic and invigorated, sensing that majority party status is just over the horizon.

Interest Groups in Georgia

Power abhors a vacuum. In states where political parties are weak, as in Georgia, political interest groups are strong (Froman, 956–94). Variously called interest groups, special interest groups, or pressure groups, political interest groups are organized associations created to affect or effectuate public policy. They differ from political parties in that their members do not seek public office as such, but rather desire to influence policy outcomes and outputs. The more and varied the regions, industries, peoples and purposes that a state government encompasses, the more and varied the interest groups will be. Georgia has a lot of such varied interests, and hence, a lot of interest groups.

In fact, reflecting its large size and diverse economy, Georgia has an awful lot of interest groups. They cannot all be described here, because even identifying the basic groupings would be a long list. Interest groups can be business associations and labor unions, farmers and fishermen, sportsmen, professional and trades groups; that is, they are often organized around the various occupational or economic groups found in Georgia. On the other hand, they can be established on the basis of achieved religious preferences such as the National Council of Churches (NCC); or ascribed racial groupings, such as the National Association for the Advancement of Colored People (NAACP).

Interest groups may be built up from shared experiences leading to a desire to participate in policy making. The League of Women Voters (LWV) and the American Legion (AL) are examples of such groups. Furthermore, ideological interest groups may organize to shape general policies; the liberal Americans for Democratic Action (ADA) or the conservative Eagle Forum (AF) are two such groups. Many interest groups represent recipients (or hopeful recipients) of government services, such as welfare, student loans, and business subsidies. Curiously, because of the complexities of the over 1270 governments in the State of Georgia alone, the actual governments themselves, and their agencies and officials, often find it necessary or expedient to try to lobby each other to influence the course of public policy in Georgia and in adjoining states, and across the nation. Groups of government entities band together for such purposes, such as the nationally based State Municipal Association, the National Association of Counties, and the National Association of Chiefs of Police (Dye, 109).

TABLE 3.1
Government Entities in Georgia

Government Units	Number
State Government	1
Counties	159
School Districts	187
Special Districts	391
Municipalities	533
Total:	1,271

Sources: Compiled by authors, including Hepburn, Lawrence R. "Politics and Government" in *Contemporary Georgia* (Athens, Georgia: University of Georgia, 1987).

To determine which interest groups were the most powerful in Georgia Politics, professors Ronald J. Hrebenar and Clive S. Thomas asked knowledgeable persons both within and without the state to put together two lists of interest groups: the first identifying those which were consistently influential, and the second to list those which were either rising or falling in power, or which were only occasionally active (Dye, 117–124). On the second list were the Board of Regents of the University System, The Georgia Municipal Association, the Association of County Commissioners, and the Georgia Trial Lawyers Association. Influential Georgia organizations of the first rank are depicted on Table 3.2.

TABLE 3.2
Georgia Interest Groups

Nation's Bank	Medical Assoc. of Georgia
Suntrust Bank	Georgia Assoc. of Educators
Wachovia Bank	St. Dept. of Transportation
Coca Cola	Business Council of Georgia
Delta Airlines	

Assembled by the authors from various sources including Dye, Thomas R. *Politics in States and Communities*, 9th Ed. (Englewood Cliffs, N.J.: Prentice-Hall, 1997), and Gray, et al, *Politics in the American States: A Comparative Analysis*, 5th Ed. (Washington, D.C.: CQ Press, 1996)

In Georgia, and in much of the United States, business organizations certainly do dominate. They have both the means and the determination to influence policy to their advantage, or at least not to the disadvantage, of their interests. But the Georgia Association of Educators is also a force to reckon with. It represents a significant number of well-educated, well-informed professionals located in every state House and Senate District, who vote and who are largely united in their goals, objectives and concerns. And that description is a formula for political success.

A number of factors affect the ability of an interest group to influence public policy. Former Georgia Southern University President Nicholas Henry, a political scientist, identifies seven such factors (Henry, 65–68). These factors include not only the size of the membership and their financial wealth, but also intangibles such as leadership qualities and the effectiveness of their organization. The various factors are listed below on Table 3.3.

TABLE 3.3
Factors of Influence

1. The size of the group
2. The group's cohesiveness
3. Its geographical spread
4. Member's social status
5. Its leadership and organization
6. The features of its program
7. The political environment

Based on results alone, The Georgia Association of Educators (GAE) appears to score highly on each of these factors. These factors, along with the importance of education for economic competitiveness, probably goes far to explain why the proportion of Georgia's state budget spent on education (over 50%) is as high as it is. Another highly rated group is the Medical Association of Georgia (MAG), which scores highly enough on these factors to cause its success rate to exceed its failure rate in its policy initiatives. In other words, what the MAG lacks in size it makes up for in other areas, particularly in money. And money, once described by Jesse Unruh, former speaker of the California House of Representatives as "the mother's milk of politics," can be influential indeed. Money alone is no substitute for all of the other factors, but in conjunction with the other factors it tends to give great power to those influential groups which have plenty of it to spare. In contrast, the organization calling itself Queer Nation/Atlanta ranks low on all of these factors and has correspondingly little influence in the State of Georgia.

Interest groups have two major political functions: lobbying and campaign financing. The term "lobbying" derives from the practice of interested parties contacting Members of the British Parliament (who had no individual offices) in the lobby of the Parliament Building (Westminster). The image evoked by the term is one of a petitioner sidling up to the very buttonholes of legislators to solicit support. While a bit simplistic today, the fundamental relationship described is still accurate.

The variety of techniques interest groups use to influence government almost matches their variety of interests. Often, they conduct public relations campaigns to persuade the public to their points of view. In our representative system, if they can get the public on their side, the legislator will soon follow. In addition, they encourage, campaign for, and fund the campaigns of, elected executive officials. They also pressure appointed bureaucrats, seeking special rules, regulations, and strict or lax enforcement of standards. Interest group lawyers threaten litigation in the courts, seeking and obtaining injunctions, mediation, settlements, decisions, and appeals. But most obvious of all, hundreds of their representatives, known as lobbyists, can be seen during each session of the General Assembly, and in smaller numbers at county commissions and city council meetings. They attempt to 'buttonhole' legislative policy makers in the halls of government, and wine and dine our elected representatives in fancy restaurants and plush hospitality suites set up in hotels and at sporting arenas.

The reputation of lobbyists for bribing legislators is based partly on historical fact, the Yazoo Land Fraud, but it is not a particularly common practice in the modern era. For a number of reasons, attempts at bribery are chilled by fears of detection and the consequences of disclosure, leading to the lobbyist's loss of effectiveness and loss of office for the legislator. Indeed, legislators who pride themselves on their integrity are prone to "blow the whistle" on lobbyists who attempt to buy their votes.

What lobbyists really want is *access* to decision-makers, and today that access is "bought" with information, not with money. Faced with a dizzying array of issues, most beyond the comprehension of a single legislator, our representatives cry out for information about problems: what are the real goals of a bill, what effect will it have on the legislator's constituents, and how will it affect their own districts? The legislative committee system, the state bureaucracy and the limited research facilities of the General Assembly all welcome lobbyists who have thoroughly studied a bill and who are in a position to explain it. Of course, the information provided by some may be biased, but it is a place to start, and by weighing it against other sources of information, often from opposing lobbyists, the legislators can make a more informed and better decision.

Sometimes it seems as if everyone is lobbying everyone else, especially during the annual sessions of the General Assembly. Actually, lobbying was illegal in Georgia before 1992. Under this quaint fiction, an ancient law made lobbying akin to bribery and a misdemeanor. Indeed, lobbyists were called "registered agents" in the State of Georgia and had to pay a $5.00 fee to the

Secretary of State at the start of each legislative session. They were then free to go about their "registered agent" business, unhampered by any additional laws, rules or regulations.

Prior to passage of the 1992 ethics legislation by the General Assembly lobbyists in Georgia did not have to declare publicly which bills they were working to pass or defeat; nor did they have to report the amounts they were spending on their efforts. Nor did they have to report any meals, drinks, gifts or entertainments they provided to their legislative friends, except for their formal monetary campaign contributions. The Secretary of State's Office received $5.00 from each of 1,229 individual registered agents for the 1990 legislative session, almost five for each legislator (Pettys, 2).

The 1992 ethics law was perhaps the most hotly debated issue at that session of the Georgia General Assembly. In its final form it made lobbying legal, but it actually regulated it much more closely than it had been before. Instead of a nominal one-time fee, lobbyists were required to pay an annual $200.00 registration fee to the State Ethics Commission plus an additional $15.00 for supplemental registration and a lobbyist identification tag. However, the fees were rescinded in 1994, although registration with the Ethics Commission is still required by law. All lobbying expenditures must be reported, along with the names of the legislators whom the lobbyists were trying to influence. The law sets a maximum of $1,000.00 that an interest group can give in campaign contributions for local offices and for the General Assembly seats, and a maximum of $2,500 to candidates for statewide office.

Perhaps the main reason why lobbyists don't have to illegally bribe legislators is that there are two perfectly legal ways to transfer money directly. In Georgia, legislators are allowed to engage in business ventures with lobbyists. However, the real return here is long term future benefit. The other technique is quick up-front money, and is called a campaign contribution. The transfer is usually handled by specially created groups called political action committees (PACs). While these PACs are limited in the amount they can contribute to any one candidate (Pettys, 2), there is no limit on the number of candidates they may contribute to, and more importantly there is no limit to the number of PACs that can be formed by any one interest group. As a result, PACs are becoming increasing influential, especially as the costs of political campaigning escalate. With this complex system, a particular PAC will be unable to "buy" a legislator, but it can certainly get a legislator to return its telephone calls whenever it deems necessary. That's access. That's influence. That's power.

What about those who are not members of organized interest groups? Do they have access? Certainly they can write or call their legislators. They can attend the periodic town meetings and pre-legislative forums that some legislators hold. But unless they organize, their interests and concerns are unlikely to be heeded. People who lack the factors of political influence, and who are unable to create effective organizations to pursue their goals in the political system, have little or no influence (Parenti). Increasing the share of the state's budget, gathering more political influence, and changing the law and the state's Constitution are most effectively done by organized special interest groups. Georgia ranks tenth in the nation in terms of the number of interest groups it has. It also ranks as a dominant/complementary state in terms of the overall impact that interest groups have. That means that political interest groups are more powerful than political parties in the state, but the interest groups are not so powerful that they eclipse or subordinate the parties (Thomas and Hrebenar, 1996). Considering the fact that in 1987 the Georgia General Assembly was ranked second in the nation in terms of its accountability to interest groups, or forty-ninth in its accountability to the unorganized public, the Peach State seems to be becoming more democratic (the ideology) as it becomes less Democratic (the Party). That is, as party competition increases, interest group dominance decreases.

FIGURE 4.1. The Capitol Building

4

The Legislative Branch

Composition of the General Assembly

The legislative power of the State of Georgia is vested in the General Assembly. Although the state legislature is no longer the dominant state institution, it remains very, very powerful. The General Assembly is a bicameral body composed of an upper house, the Senate, and a lower house, the House of Representatives. Each year, on the second Monday in January, the old hands and the newly elected legislators convene in the sprawling city of Atlanta for the first session of the state legislature.

While we each tend to love our own local Representative or Senator, love is not the word to use to describe the peoples' attitude toward everybody else's state legislator. Our representative is a statesman; theirs is a politician. Ours is an astute fiscal manager; theirs is a spendthrift. Ours tends to the people's business; theirs plays around. The legislative circus would be really funny, except for the fact that this odd collection of other peoples' representatives controls the state's purse strings, the taxing and spending policies.

Elections for the 236 members of the General Assembly are held on the Tuesday after the first Monday in November of even numbered years. Members of both houses are elected to two year terms of office. The Senate is a smaller body, consisting of 56 Senators, each of whom is from a single member district. The House of Representatives has 180 Representatives, who are elected from smaller districts. The General Assembly is responsible for apportioning the state into the appropriate Senate and House districts. To reduce gerrymandering, or redrawing district lines into strange shapes for political or racial advantage, these districts must be drawn to contiguous territorial boundaries and be based on the results of each United States decennial census.

At the time of their election, the members of the Senate must be citizens of the United States, at least 25 years of age, citizens of Georgia for two years, and residents within their districts for at least one year. The members of the House of Representatives must meet similar requirements, except that they need to be only 21 years old when elected to office. Each Senator and Representative, before taking his or her legislative seat, must take an oath or affirmation as required by law. But some people who meet these qualifications are still not eligible for office, such as persons recently convicted of felonies; or persons holding civil offices under the United States, or who are on active duty with any branch of the armed forces of the United States. The latter provision is to avoid conflicts of interest and competing loyalties. Opening day is almost literally a circus. Owing to the differences in the legislators' geographical districts, their religious, racial and ethnic diversity, and their differences in occupations and their preoccupations, observing the opening day is a studied contrast in representation. The image can be amusing, as shown in Figure 4.2.

During their terms of office, legislators may not hold another state office. Except for a few leadership posts, they can not be elected by the General Assembly or appointed by the Governor to any office or appointment having any "emolument annexed thereto" (salary or stipend), unless they resign their seat. And they may not be appointed to any civil office created during their term of office. Each house is the sole judge of the elections of their members. When a vacancy occurs, it is filled by the governor as provided by the Constitution and by statute. Some of the characteristics of the members of the 1998 session of the Georgia General Assembly are shown on Table 4.1.

FIGURE 4.2. The Clowns Together

TABLE 4.1
Georgia Legislators

Characteristic	House of Rep.	Senate
Party		
Democratic	101	34
Republican	79	22
Gender		
Male	147	49
Female	33	7
Ethnic/Race		
White	147	49
Black	33	11
Occupation		
Business	47	16
Attorney	31	9
Retired	20	7
Real Estate/Insurance	16	8
Consultant	11	1
Banking/Finance	6	1
Farmer/Agribusiness	9	1
Airline Pilot	2	0
Pharmacist	6	1
Engineer	1	1
Teacher/Professor	2	1
Veterinarian	1	1
Nurse	1	1
Clergy	3	0
Accountant	2	0
Funeral Director	3	1
Physician	0	2
Architect	0	1
Other (inc."legislator")	19	1

Source: Compiled by the authors.

As shown by the table, the Democratic Party dominates the Georgia State Legislature, although Republicans are rapidly gaining seats and are almost certain to capture at least one chamber within the very near future, perhaps as early as 1998. Most members are protestant (about half Baptists); businessmen and lawyers are well represented; and there is a sprinkling of farmers, teachers, health professionals, and two pilots. The pay of the members of the General Assembly is set by the legislature itself, but no increases in salary can take effect until the next session. Currently, legislators receive $11,125 per year, plus per diem pay of $75.00 while the legislature is in session and $4800 per year for expense reimbursement. Each house is the sole judge of the elections of their members. When a vacancy occurs, it is filled by the governor as provided by the Constitution and by statute. While the typical state legislator is a white male businessman, there are black female lawyers and a wide variety of other types of members. Some may be simple freshman spectators, others profit seeking advertisers, reluctants, or true lawmakers (Barber, 1965), but once gathered together, they represent all the people of the state.

Because of fears of interference by political opponents, state legislators are free from arrest during sessions of the General Assembly or during committee meetings, and while they are traveling to or returning from these meetings. This is not an absolute protection. Of course, they may still be arrested for serious crimes such as treason, felony, or breach of the peace. But they do enjoy one special privilege: the Constitution specifies that no member is liable to answer in any other place for anything spoken in either house or in any committee meeting. This special right of unlimited free speech is necessary for candid discussion about political issues.

Legislative Leadership

In addition to unofficial political party posts such as the majority leaders, The Constitution of the State of Georgia creates three major legislative officials in each chamber. In 1999 the presiding senate officer was the Lt. Governor, Mark Taylor, officially titled the President of the Senate. The Senators also elect a President Pro Tempore, to preside when the Lt. Governor is absent and to act as President in case of the temporary or permanent disability of that official. If Democrats retain control of the Senate, there will also be a new President Pro-Tem, as the holder of that office in the 1998 session, Sen. Sonny Perdue (Bonaire) announced after that session that he was switching to the Republican side. Since each house must keep and publish an official journal of its proceedings, a Secretary of the Senate is also selected to maintain its official records. The organization of the General Assembly is depicted on Figure 4.3.

The primary officer of the House of Representatives is called the Speaker of the House of Representatives. In 1998 Thomas B. Murphy was the Speaker, as he has been since 1973, making him the longest serving Speaker in the United States. Speaker Murphy is elected by the other Representatives to be their presiding officer. Because of the large size of the House of Representatives, the Speaker has to be able to assert a certain amount of control during

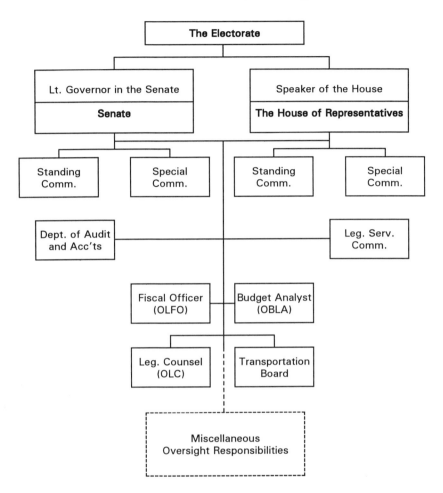

FIGURE 4.3. The General Assembly
Source: Compiled by authors.

legislative sessions. Although politics can be a nasty business, it is easier to paint a negative image of a politician than it is to get the legislature or an ethics committee to press charges or to punish a member for alleged transgressions. When the House Speaker was accused by a state employee of an ethics violation, some critics were surprised at the ease with which the matter was buried by the House ethics committee. One defender said: *"he's just one of 180 legislators, how could he pressure anyone"?*

A profile of the Speaker is presented in the following sidebar.

Some years ago, the Speaker was the target of negative press coverage, oftentimes shallow and sensationalistic, such as when Speaker Murphy was being accused of pressuring a state agency to remove a business client's name from a

Chapter Four

Tom Murphy, Speaker

Mr. Thomas B. Murphy was elected to the Georgia House of Representatives from House District 18, representing in part three state counties: Haralson, Paulding and Polk. Murphy has been the indisputable ruler of the House for two decades, since he was selected Speaker in the 1970's. UGA Professor Charles Bullock indicated he was a firm hand in control of the House. Of course, life at the top is often uneasy, and with ill health, some heart by-pass surgery, and after a few increasingly nasty attacks on his ethics and friends, both allies and critics began wondering who could replace him.

---

list of child abusers (A. Press, 10–5–94, 3B), and being too lenient on a legislator playing with sex toys on the House floor (AJ/AC, 1–14–94, C4), and even of being cruel to blind children and to pet animals (A.Press, 2–23–94, 1A). To House Democrats, fearing the loss of their majority status as the Republican Party gains strength, Murphy seems to have become something of a political liability. But he has not yet decided to step down. Uneasy is the head that wears the crown.

Other house legislative officers include a Speaker Pro Tempore, elected to preside when the Speaker is absent; and a Clerk of the House who is chosen to oversee the maintenance of the records of that chamber. Legislative proposals for new laws, (bills) must go through a complex process before becoming law. Many bills never make it. The majority of bills are sponsored and introduced in the House, but the General Assembly may provide by law for the joint sponsorship of bills and resolutions.

The Georgia General Assembly meets in regular session on the second Monday in January of each year, and reorganizes itself each odd-numbered year after elections. Usually the crowd under the Gold Dome continues in session for a period of 40 working days; the 1992 session set a modern record by meeting from January 13th until March 31st. By concurrent resolution, the General Assembly may adjourn during any regular session to later dates at its own convenience, but neither house may adjourn during a regular session for more than three days or meet in any place other than the state capitol without the consent of the other house.

During special sessions, neither house may adjourn more than twice, or for more than seven days at a time. If after thirty days of a session one house adjourns without similar action by the other house, the governor may adjourn both houses for up to ten days. However, if an impeachment trial is pending at the end of any session, the House can adjourn while the Senate remains in session until the trial is completed.

Legislative Tasks—Bills

Two major tasks of the legislature are to consider legislation and to enact law. In order to transact official business a quorum is necessary, which must consist of a majority of the members of each chamber. However, a smaller number may adjourn from day to day and compel the presence of its absent members. Each house determines its own rules of procedure and regulates its own employees. Because legislation is so complex in modern society, the real work of the legislature is done in interim committees instead of on the floor of the legislative chamber. Legislators can then specialize in areas which interest their constituents. In 1998 the Senate had 25 committees, and the House had 32 committees. Table 4.2 lists the standing committees in the Georgia General Assembly.

Committees exist to facilitate the passage of bills. These committees include standing committees to perform routine tasks, special committees for unusual problems, and joint committees. Joint committees have members from both houses, usually for conference committees to reconcile chamber differences in versions of bills. Bills must be drafted, sponsored, introduced, assigned to committees and then assigned to sub-committees for their research and hearings. This is perhaps the crucial stage where a bill is most likely to be killed. But even after clearing these hurdles, a House bill still must be assigned to a calendar, be read on the floor, be debated upon if they are controversial, and then voted for by a majority of the House membership present. Then the entire process must be repeated by the Senate. It might also be necessary to have a conference committee iron out differences in the two versions of the resulting bill.

Politics is often called the *"Art of the Possible."* Very often well intentioned but naive people ask the state legislature to pass a law that is either realistically impossible, politically unfeasible, or simply stupid. Since legislators cannot tell their constituents that they are unwise or unintelligent, they have devised ways to *"kill"* a bill without triggering a confrontation with the voters. Two time honored ways of doing this are to bury it in a committee, or to send it to some other group for study and evaluation. Each session of the Georgia legislature creates dozens of these so-called study commissions or task forces whose real job is to bury the new ideas. In 1994, the General Assembly created at least twenty-three of these bodies (Whitt, 1). Sometimes they will issue reports, but often the proposed material simply vanishes without a trace, and the legislators are off the hook.

Legislative bills can be enacted only if they are approved by a majority vote of all the members of both houses. In either house, when ordered by the presiding officer or at the desire of one-fifth of the members present, a roll-call vote on any question must be taken and officially recorded in the journal. For appropriation bills, or on any issue requiring a two-thirds vote, each separate yea and nay vote is recorded. After a general bill has cleared the committee process, and reached the floor for debate, its title must be read three times and on three sepa-

TABLE 4.2
Standing Committees in the Georgia Legislature

Senate	House of Representatives
Agriculture	Agriculture and Consumer Affairs
Appropriations	Appropriations
Banking and Financial Institutions	Banks and Banking
Consumer Affairs	Children and Youth
Corrections, C. Institutions and Property	Defense and Veterans Affairs
Ethics	Education
Defense and Veterans Affairs	Game, Fish & Parks
Economic Development, Tourism and Cultural Affairs	Governmental Affairs
Health and Ecology	Human Relations and Aging
Education	Industrial Relations
Ethics	Industry
Finance and Public Utilities	Insurance
Health and Human Services	Interstate Cooperation
Higher Education	Intra-Governmental Coordination
Insurance and Labor	Journals
Interstate Cooperation	Judiciary
Judiciary	Legislative and Congressional Reapportionment
Natural Resources	Metropolitan Atlanta Rapid Transit Overview Committee
Public Safety	Motor Vehicles
Reapportionment	Natural Resources and Environment
Retirement	Public Safety
Rules	Regulated Beverages
Science, Technology, and Industry	Retirement
Special Judiciary	Rules
State and Local Governmental Operations	Special Judiciary
Transportation	State Institutions and Property
Youth, Aging and Human Ecology	State Planning and Community Affairs
	Transportation
	University System of Georgia
	Ways and Means

Source: Senate Public Information Office and House Public Information Office, Members of the Georgia General Assembly (January 1996), 28-32,101-9.

rate days in each house before it can be voted on; and the third reading of such bill and resolution must be in the entirety when ordered by the presiding officer or by a majority of the members voting on the bill.

Once a bill has been passed by both houses it must be signed by both the President of the Senate and the Speaker of the House of Representatives before being sent to the Governor. No bill can become law unless the Governor signs it or fails to act upon it within six days from its transmission to the Governor, except where it is passed over the Governor's veto. Sometimes the General Assembly adjourns *sine die* or adjourns for more than 40 days prior to the expiration of the six day period. In such cases, the bill becomes law if approved or not vetoed by the Governor within 40 days from the date of any such adjournment. There is no pocket veto in Georgia.

If the Governor does veto a bill and if the legislature is still in session, the bill must be returned within three days, along with the reasons for the veto, to the presiding officer of the house where it originated. But if the General Assembly had adjourned *sine die,* or adjourned for more than 40 days, the Governor has sixty days to return it. However, in modern times the legislature has never lasted that long.

During legislative sessions, any vetoed bill or resolution may upon receipt be immediately considered by the originating house for the purpose of overriding the veto. If two-thirds of the membership do vote to override the veto, and the other house does the same, it becomes law despite the Governor's opposition. In the rare cases where bills and resolutions are vetoed during the last three days of the session and not reconsidered for overriding, the General Assembly can consider the issue at its next yearly session.

Georgia is especially sensitive to the desires of the citizens for open government. The state Constitution requires that sessions of the General Assembly and all standing committee meetings shall be open to the public, except where reasons of public policy justify. Each house has power to punish members for disorderly behavior or misconduct. This punishment can include censure or monetary fines, and in extreme cases even imprisonment or expulsion. However, no member can be expelled except by a vote of two-thirds of their fellow members. Just prior to the opening of the 1998 session of the General Assembly State Senator Ralph David Abernathy III, the son of the civil rights leader whose name he shares, was arrested for attempting to smuggle a small amount of marijuana into the country through Hartsfield Airport in Atlanta. The Customs Service confiscated the substance and imposed a small fine on the Senator, which reports indicated was a routine punishment for a first and minor infraction. However, the Senate moved to censure the Senator, and Republicans, particularly in the House, moved to impeach Abernathy, arguing that he had brought disrespect to the entire General Assembly. By the end of the session nothing had come of the impeachment attempt.

TABLE 4.3
How a Bill Becomes Law

1. The Idea
   a. Conceived by individual legislator.
   b. Conceived by Study Committee, agencies.
   c. Conceived by citizen or special interest group.
2. Drafting the Bill
   a. Drafted by the above or by legal specialists.
   b. Drafted by Legislative Counsel for Legislator(s).
   c. Copied after legislation in other states.
3. Introduction
   a. Filed with Clerk of House of Representatives.
   b. First Reading to entire House.
   c. Assigned to committee by Speaker.
   d. Second Reading automatically next day.
4. Committee Action
   a. Chairman sets dates, notify interested parties.
   b. Holds hearings for testimony for and against.
   c. Committee holds bill, delays, votes "do not pass."
   d. Committee amends, recommends, votes "do pass."
5. Bill Returned to House?
   a. Placed on Calendar.
   b. Called by Speaker for third reading and vote.
   c. Floor debates, amends, vote to defeat or pass.
   d. 2/3 vote required for appropriations, amendments.
6. Send to the Senate **ENTIRE PROCESS REPEATED**
7. Return to the House?
   a. Senate amendments approved, or
   b. Conference Committee (3 + 3) reconciles bill.
   c. House & Senate vote on reconciled bill
8. Bill goes to the Governor
   a. Has 6 days during, 40 days after, session to act.
   b. The Governor either vetoes or signs bill.
   c. If no action, bill automatically becomes law.
9. Vetoed Bill Override
   a. By a 2/3 vote, the legislature may override a veto.

Source: Office of the Legislative Counsel.

Local and Special Legislation

As might be expected according to the individualistic side of its culture, Georgia has a strong commitment to home rule. The General Assembly can enact laws for considering local legislation. But in addition to the usual reading requirements, no such bill or resolution can be voted upon prior to the second day following the day of introduction, and the General Assembly must advertise a notice of intention to introduce specific local bills. This reflects our localistic traditions.

A local bill on a subject which is required by the Constitution to have a referendum election conducted before it becomes effective can be handled in an expedited fashion by immediate transmittal to the Governor. This responsiveness to local issues is characteristic of Georgia's concern for local needs. Laws of a general nature always have uniform operation throughout the state, and preempt the enactment of local and special laws, except that the General Assembly may by general law authorize local governments to use their powers of local ordinance or resolution to exercise police powers, as long as they do not conflict with the general laws. This encourages flexibility.

The duties of the Georgia General Assembly include not only legislation but responsibility for the general welfare of the people of the state. Because of the obligation of each branch to maintain separation of powers, the Constitution requires the legislature to protect its prerogatives. The General Assembly cannot abridge its own powers, nor can any law enacted by the General Assembly be construed by the courts as acting to limit its powers.

Among the specific powers granted to the legislature by the Constitution are: (1) to restrict land use in order to protect and preserve the state's natural resources and environment; (2) to maintain and regulate a state militia in cooperation with the Governor as commander in chief; (3) to tax, spend money, zone and condemn property to comply with federal law and grant-in-aid requirements; (4) to ensure the continuity of state and local governments in periods of emergency resulting from disasters caused by enemy attack; (5) to act in concert with any county, municipality, nonprofit organization, or any combination thereof for promoting tourism; and (6) to tax, spend money and regulate outdoor advertising near federal highways.

On the other hand, various specific limitations are placed on the law making power. Some of these are geared to economic activities. For example, the General Assembly does not have the power to grant incorporation to private persons except by formal enactment with standardized procedures, and modification of corporate charters and debts are specifically restricted. And it lacks the power to authorize any contract or agreement which may have the effect of defeating or lessening competition, or encouraging a monopoly. In addition, monopolies are declared to be unlawful and void in the State of Georgia. The General Assembly does not have the power to regulate the fees or charges of public utilities owned or operated by counties or municipalities except as authorized by the Constitution.

The interesting case of the *Yazoo Land Grant Fraud* resulted in specific prohibitions against corrupt practices. Prior to ceding its territorial claims to the lands reaching to the Mississippi River, successive Georgia legislatures made and then canceled millions of acres of land grants to the Yazoo Land Company (Current, 211). When the 1796 legislature attempted to void the land grant, the United States Supreme Court used the case of *Fletcher v. Peck (1810)* to void the state law, on grounds of "no impairment of contracts (Current, 271). Since then, except as specifically permitted, the General Assembly may not grant any donation or gratuity or forgive any debt or obligation owing to the public, and it can not grant or authorize extra compensation to any public officer, agent, or contractor after the contract has been formalized or performed. Similarly, Article III of the Constitution specifically invests the power to issue insurance licenses to the Commissioner of Insurance instead of to the legislature *per se*.

No personal or population bills can be passed. Partly because of fears of rural versus city politics, and partly out of fears of favoritism, the state Constitution prohibits any bill using classification by size of population as a means of determining the applicability of any bill or law to any political subdivision, or as a means of using size to amend or repeal the general law. Similarly, no special law relating to the rights or status of particular private persons can be enacted.

The drafters of the Georgia Constitution were careful to include checks and balances to ensure that state government officials would remain accountable to the people. So on occasion, the legislature may act to remove other officials from office via the impeachment process. The process starts in the House of Representatives, which has the sole power to vote impeachment charges against any executive or judicial officer of the state or any member of the General Assembly.

The Senate has the sole power to try impeachments. When sitting as a court during impeachments the Senate is presided over by the Chief Justice of the Supreme Court. But no official can be impeached, or removed from office, unless convicted by two-thirds of the full membership. Upon such conviction, the defendant is removed from office and disqualified to hold and enjoy any office of honor, trust, or profit within the state or to receive a pension, but no other penalties are attached. However, impeachment does not relieve any party from any other criminal or civil liability.

Legislative Politics in Georgia

In presidential election years, the second Tuesday in March has become known as Super Tuesday because many states hold their primary elections on that date. But in 1992, with the approval of the Justice Department of the United States Government, Georgia lawmakers separated from the pack and Georgia became a bellwether state for the South when it moved its presidential primary date up one week to the first Tuesday in March. Georgia now joins that group of states which have decided to hold their primary votes on "Junior Tuesday". State Rep. Calvin Smyre (D-Columbus) touted the merits of the date change (Sherman, A1). He and other veteran Georgia Democrats indicated that the change could make Georgia a necessary must-win state for candidates. To vote in the party primaries, voters must register a month in advance.

Few things so engage the attention of a legislator as the necessity for redrawing electoral district boundaries after a national census. Because Georgia's population is increasing, it recently qualified for a new 11th Congressional District. Many people are concerned about re-districting changes, and the state lawmakers are not often given a free hand. Georgia is one of fifteen states whose proposed election law changes are reviewed by the U.S. Justice Department. In January of 1992, Georgia lawmakers where shocked when the U.S. Justice Department rejected the proposed redistricting maps for Georgia, which had been drawn up nearly seven months earlier. The rejection letter, signed by Assistant Attorney General John R. Dunne, said that the state's pattern of "racially polarized voting . . . appears to be exacerbated" by the proposed plans (Cook, A1). As a result of this federal bureaucratic decision, State House and Senate district maps, as well as U.S. Congressional district maps, were thrown back on the drawing board.

The reasons for the rejection were two: that they worked to benefit incumbents and that the proposed districts minimized black voting strength. The problem areas involved southern rural Baldwin, Dougherty, Houston and Peach Counties; and growing minority areas in suburban Atlanta Counties such as Clayton, Cobb and Fayette. Overall, the Justice Department found fault with the legislative plans for almost all of Georgia south of Interstate 20. Since the Georgia Legislature was in session, the House and Senate reapportionment committees immediately scheduled action on the matter. One prominent politician agreed that some white incumbents had benefitted from the legislatively crafted districts (Cook, A1).

While state Rep. Tyrone Brooks (D-Atlanta) a critic of the proposed redistricting proposal, said voters should be angry with the legislators, not the

Justice Department; another legislator took a different view. State Sen. Gene Walker (D-DeKalb), chairman of the Senate Reapportionment Committee, said "I'm disappointed in the kind of tone they used. I'm black, and I'm not a racist." The Lt. Governor, Pierre Howard, also was disappointed at the federal bureaucratic ruling, saying that the legislature had tried to follow the federal Voting Rights Act (Walston, A8).

One state legislator took the high moral ground. State Sen. Don Johnson, announced candidate for the proposed new 10th Congressional District seat, said he would ask Lt. Governor Pierre Howard to take him off the map-drawing reapportionment committee to avoid potential conflicts of interest. He also chaired the Senate Appropriations Committee (Staff, A5). The authors are forced to conclude that charges of gerrymandering are perhaps an inescapable part of Georgia politics. The constitutionality of gerrymandering the new 11th Congressional District was challenged in 1994. The case was brought for a decision to a federal panel of three judges and alleged that this majority black district, stretching from Stone Mountain to Savannah (approximately two hundred and sixty miles) was neither compact nor contiguous as the high court had required. In 1996, the U.S. Supreme Court in *Miller v. Johnson* held that the 11th District, which had been drawn with racial politics in mind, was unconstitutional, and its boundaries must be redrawn.

Another issue raises almost as much smoke and fire, the appropriation and budgeting process. Funding for education, the biggest single expenditure of Georgia State Government, also engages the avid attention of dutiful legislators. The complex funding formulas are a ripe area for legislative debate. Rep. Dubose Porter, a legislative floor leader and point man for Governor Miller, indicated that Quality Basic Education (QBE) formulas may overlook some of the advantages of small schools. As criticism mounts that school mergers and consolidation do not work, the formulas may have to be adjusted to allow flexibility and the elimination of incentives to merge schools. Community based schools and less busing may be needed (Roberts, A4).

General Appropriations Bills

Since the British barons forced King John to sign the Magna Carta, it has been truly said that the power of the legislature is the power of the purse. As is traditional in former British colonies, all bills for raising revenue, or appropriating money, originate in the most representative body of the legislature; in Georgia this is the House of Representatives. More is presented on this topic in Chapter Eight: Budgeting and Finance.

However, the power of the purse is somewhat restricted in Georgia, which gives some strong budgetary powers to the Chief Executive. An important feature of the Georgia Constitution is that it requires the Governor to play a major legislative role. Within five days after the legislature convenes, the Governor must submit a budget message and a budget report, accompanied by a draft of a general appropriations bill. This bill must provide for the appropriation of the funds necessary to operate all the various state departments and agencies, and to meet the current expenses of the state for the next fiscal year.

In addition, the Constitution strictly prohibits riders on appropriation bills. Every bill must have a descriptive title, and no bill which refers to more than one subject matter can pass. Furthermore, no law or section of the State Code can be amended or repealed by mere reference to its title or to its number. The Constitution places precise restrictions on the way the legislature handles the finances of state government. The most important provision is that no money can be drawn from the treasury except by appropriation made by law.

Ultimately, the General Assembly is responsible for annual appropriation of state funds necessary to operate the state government. In addition, the state budget must include federal funds as well. To the extent that federal funds received by the state for various programs and projects exceed the amount appropriated in the general appropriations Act, these federal funds are appropriated by the state according to federal rules. The fiscal year of the state begins on the first day of July of each year and terminates on the thirtieth day of June in the following year. The budget for State Fiscal Year 1999 (SFY1999) is $12.6 billion dollars.

The scope of the general appropriations bill is strictly defined by Constitutional provision. Revenues appropriated by this bill can include only (1) materials fixed by previous laws; (2) the ordinary expenses of the executive, legislative, and judicial branches and bureaucratic departments; (3) payment of the public debt and interest thereon; and (4) support of the public institutions and educational interests of the state. All other appropriations must be made by separate bills, and each such bill can only embrace one subject.

Each annual general appropriations Act can continue in effect for only one fiscal year after adoption, after which it expires and a new one must be enacted. There is no perpetual funding in Georgia. In brief, the State of Georgia is required to balance its operational budget. The General Assembly can not appropriate funds for any given fiscal year which exceed anticipated revenues and on-hand surpluses, as estimated in the Governor's budget report. Supplementary appropriations, if any, also cannot exceed these limits unless based on a tax base and collections, and these appropriations expire along with the annual appropriations. Neither house can pass a supplementary appropriation bill until the general appropriations Act has been finally adopted by both houses and approved by the Governor.

All such appropriations must be made for specific sums, and no appropriation can allocate to any object the proceeds of any particular tax or fund unless the Constitution permits an exception. One major exception is money derived from gasoline and motor fuel taxes, which are set aside for providing and maintaining an adequate system of public roads and bridges in the state. Of course, in times of emergency, these rules are relaxed. In the event of invasion of the state by enemies, or in case of a major catastrophe, state funds may be utilized for defense or relief purposes according to the Governor's Executive Orders.

Other exceptions to the annual appropriations bill include the creation and administration of a trust fund for workers' compensation injuries and disabilities. And in any case in which any court imposes a fine or orders the forfeiture of any bond, the proceeds may be allocated for the specific purpose of providing training to law enforcement officers and to prosecuting officials. Another exception allows the General Assembly, by a three-fifths' vote of both houses, to designate any part or all of the proceeds of any state tax on alcoholic beverages to be used for prevention, education, and treatment relating to alcohol and drug abuse.

Public funds may be expended for the purpose of paying benefits and costs of retirement and pension systems for public officers and employees and their beneficiaries; and to establish or modify local retirement systems covering employees of county boards of education. The General Assembly may pass appropriations bills for the purpose of paying for a firemen's pension system. In these cases, the legislature must define funding standards which will assure the actuarial soundness of these retirement or pension systems.

In addition to the power of drafting the initial general appropriations bill, the Governor of Georgia has an item veto over appropriations bills passed by the General Assembly. The Governor may approve any appropriation and veto any other appropriation in the same bill, and any appropriation vetoed is eliminated unless the General Assembly overrides the item veto. Despite the powers of the Governor, the General Assembly remains very powerful.

Conclusion

At the beginning of every year, the old experienced hands and the newly elected freshmen converge on the Gold Dome in the sprawling city of Atlanta. They assemble with fire in their eyes, missions in their hearts, and IOU's in their pockets. As a group, they represent diverse economical and geographical interests. When one considers the vast differences in the legislator's occupational backgrounds, and their religious, racial and ethnic diversity, it is a wonder that they can get together on anything. But when they do act, exercising the power of the purse, they are a potent force in Georgia's state politics.

FIGURE 5.1. The Governor's Mansion

5

The Plural Executive of Georgia

The Governor of Georgia

Roy Barnes, the Governor of the State of Georgia is the heir to untold generations of tribal chieftains and to the doubtful assertions of several royal Spanish Viceroys. While earlier leaders of the area now known as Georgia would have based their personal power on might of arms or sycophancy, modern Georgia chief executives owe their positions to popular elections. The modern Governor is the ultimate successor to James Oglethorpe, Proprietor and Trustee of the British colony of Georgia, and after him to the three Proprietary Presidents, three Royal British Governors, and to seventeen post-colonial and pre-federal state Governors.

In addition, the Georgia Governor is the inheritor of the legacies of twenty-five pre-civil war Governors, five wartime Governors, and to thirty-five Governors since the Civil War. In short, the modern chief executive is the latest of a long and distinguished line of Georgia Governors, and presides over the most prosperous, largest population that the State of Georgia has ever had. But unlike many of his predecessors, and unlike the federal President, the Governor of the State of Georgia is not an all-powerful unitary Chief Executive.

Instead of presiding over a responsive bureaucracy directed by their personal appointees, Georgia Governors must contend with a pluralistic structure directed by a variety of separately elected officials and a variety of appointed administrators. Thus, instead of a simple pyramidal power structure, culminating in one person, the apex of the Georgia state government structure resembles an oval crown with many points and no center of gravity. The other elected officials often contest the power of the Governor. How can the Governor effectively initiate policy?

These other elected executives include the Lt. Governor, who presides over the Senate; The Secretary of State, who has widely ranging administrative duties; the Attorney General who presides over the Department of Law; the State School Superintendent; and the Commissioners of Agriculture, Insurance and Labor, each presiding over their own departments. These officials are separately elected by the people and do not have to belong to the same party or share the same political philosophy as the Governor. The result is often a lack of coordination, administrative headaches and political conflict. How can a Governor cope?

To make things more complex, in addition to the individual elected officials, there are various constitutional boards and commissions which run their own specialized agencies. These include the state's Public Service Commission, the State Transportation Board, the State Board of Pardons and Paroles, The State Personnel Board, the Veterans Service Board and the Board of Natural Resources. Generally, the boards function as committees with administrative powers defined in the constitution and therefore largely independently of the Governor's formal control. Each board has its own chairman, who presides over meetings and who has the power to break tying votes. Some of these boards are separately elected by the people of Georgia in general elections, some are elected by legislators, and some are appointed by the Governor with the advice and confirmation of the Senate. What is the Governor to do?

The Powers of the Governor

With such a wide variety of executive officers sharing power, it may be surprising that the Governor of Georgia is ranked among the more influential Governors in the U.S.A. But although the formal powers are only moderate (Gray, 202), the Governor of Georgia enjoys high prestige (Hepburn, 147). There are two reasons for this ranking. In one classical analysis of power, an Italian scholar suggested that when a ruler can rely on strong formal powers and resources to solve problems, those powers should be used vigorously. But when the formal powers of the ruler are insufficient, a wise ruler will use guile to achieve goals. In short, a prince must sometimes act like a Lion and sometimes like a Fox (Machiavelli, 91). The key to the success of a Georgia Governor is how well he can balance these two sources of power.

In Georgia, with its history of suspicion of strong chief executives, its oppressive historical experiences, and its many reform Constitutions restricting the Governor's formal powers, guile became a necessary qualification for the job. But there was an additional pillar of support for a wily Governor: Georgia's strong element of consensus politics in its long-time one party system. The prestige of the Governor, both as titular head of government and chief of the dominant political party, enabled the incumbent to influence events even when the formal powers were inadequate.

The Constitution of the State of Georgia specifies that the chief executive powers shall be vested in the Governor. These formal powers enable the Governor to exploit several avenues of power and influence. The power and influence of Governors depends on their facility in playing various political roles. Perhaps most important of all these roles is his visibility as a mythical and symbolic leader, linked with the expectations of the general public. In this capacity, the

Governor interacts with other state leaders and agencies, with cities and other states, and with the federal government and sometimes foreign powers. In fulfilling these roles, the Governor is acting as a intergovernmental middleman, a fulcrum of power and a center of political gravity.

In our federal system of government, the middleman role is complex. In the beginning, the system could be described as dual federalism, with separate spheres of responsibilities for state governments and the federal government, a sort of *layer cake* model. Until the Civil War, there was little overlap. But in time, a more complex cooperative federalism, with commingling spheres developed, like a *marble cake* (Wilson, 67).

This cooperative federalism is characterized by a vertical bureaucratization of programs in the United States (Beer). In fact, every policy and program exists at every level, and they are all functionally integrated, with costs shared by all three levels, federal, state and local. One author suggested a picket fence model, in which the three "rails" of local, state and federal government are crossed by a variety of policy arena "slats" (Wright, 83). However, this model does not support the "middleman" concept.

The authors suggest an *apple pie* model of government, emphasizing the unity of the federal system. In this model, we start with a foundation of dough, filled with nuts and fruits and sweets, criss-crossed on top with more dough, some horizontal to reflect the various levels of government, and some vertical to reflect the varied organized interest groups. This mixture is put under heat and pressure, and the result is government like *apple pie.* In this cooperative model, the governor is the only state official with the power and visibility to influence the mixture, and to determine the consistency of the final product.

The Chief Executive of a state has various roles to play, and one of the most important of these is *Head of State,* ceremonial and ritual leader, serving as the focus of identification of all the people of the state. Therefore it came as a bit of a surprise when Governor Miller attacked the state flag during the State of the State speech to the 1993 legislative session. In Georgia the flag issue has much symbolic importance to various groups. Miller argued that the flag was changed in 1956 to include the Confederate battle cross in opposition to court rulings for school desegregation (Winder, 5). This raised a storm of controversy: does the flag exist for internal purposes of uniting and representing people within the state or for the external purpose of representing the state to the outside world?

Miller's proposal to change the flag was introduced into the state Senate which decided that so potent an issue would be referred directly to the voters and passed Senate Bill 71 calling for a public referendum on the issue. But with an increasing level of anxiety, House Speaker Murphy and other leaders could not support the measure. Especially troubling to many powerful state politicians was the decision by various local government bodies, some controlled by African American representatives, to refuse to fly the state flag, the first being the Atlanta-Fulton County Recreation Authority, which voted to remove the flag from the Atlanta-Fulton County Stadium, then the home of the Atlanta Braves baseball team (Salzer, D1). Finally Governor Miller requested that the House take no action on the matter, citing constitutional issues and costs. He summarized the issue by declaring: *"I made the fight and I lost the fight"* (Winder, 8). Politically, it had become a "no-win" situation, and the Governor would never bring it up again.

The Governor has several other important roles. Since the State of Georgia existed before it joined the United States, the governor has some of the prerogatives of a nation state leader. While these include the role of commander of the military and law enforcement arms of the state, the Highway Patrol and the National Guard, these are not a major concern of Governors today. More important are the political roles of the governor as the chief legislator: setting the agenda, initiating the budget, and signing or vetoing legislative bills. There are two major parts to this latter role, the first with regard to legislation itself, and the second involving the convening of the legislature and the filling of vacancies in it. A good Governor analyzes situations and figures out which roles would maximize political influence and power.

Governor James E. Carter

One recent Georgia Governor, James Earl Carter, succeeded in applying his understanding of the role of the chief executive to the Presidency of the United States. After serving in the United States Navy, Jimmy Carter returned home to

FIGURE 5.2. Choosing Today's Role.

manage the family's peanut farm business, and to engage in public service. After serving in the state Senate, he became Governor in 1971 and established a reputation as an honest political reformer. In the wake of the national Watergate scandal, he built a national organization and became President of the United States in January, 1977. In addition to his role as a peacemaker in foreign affairs, he is perhaps best known domestically for his successful congressional initiatives to reorganize the federal civil service system (Allen).

As we saw in Chapter Four, the Governor's law making role is significant. The Governor can convene special sessions, and always writes the annual appropriation bill. The Governor can set the agenda of each session by giving the opening speech: the State of the State Address. Governor Zell Miller has used this forum to give the General Assembly information on current problems of the state and to recommend legislative measures. Governor Miller had a notable record of prior public service, as a citizen, college professor and as a Lt. Governor. In 1992, the *Georgia Rebound* Program offered by the Governor demonstrated his grasp of the legislative options. In addition, the Governor used his appointment powers and political power over his party and over public opinion to influence the members of the General Assembly to support his policies. And finally, the Governor reviews each proposed bill or resolution and decides whether to approve and sign it, or to veto it. The governor can use the veto power as a tool to reward or punish members of the General Assembly for their support of or opposition to his legislative agenda. Following the 1997 legislative session, Miller used his item veto to veto several legislators' pet projects ("pork barrel") for which appropriations had been voted as a way of "paying back" legislators who had opposed several of his favorite projects. Members were not happy with this turn of events, but they realized that, although a "lame duck" governor, Miller was still in control, and with an approval rating of over 70%, could and would make good on his threats. However, having made his point, Miller relented, and most of the money was ultimately restored.

Parallel powers exist vis-a-vis the administrative apparatus of the state. The appointment of individuals to vacant positions is a significant tool in the administration of state government. When constitutional public offices such as the Attorney General become vacant, the Governor usually fills the vacancy. In most cases the appointment will be for the remainder of the unexpired term unless otherwise provided for by the Constitution. However, many appointments are conditional upon the confirmation of the State Senate.

The Governor is the top bureaucrat in the state system, and has the power to require information in writing from the other constitutional officers, as well as from all other officers and employees of the executive branch. The Governor may inquire into any subject relating to their duties. Along the same lines, the chief executive is charged with the responsibility to take care that the laws are faithfully executed, and he is the conservator of the peace throughout the state. The Governor must take an oath or affirmation to fulfill these duties as prescribed by law.

The terms of office, compensation and allowances of Constitutional Officers are set by the current Georgia Constitution. Elections for Governor are held once every four years, beginning in 1986, on Tuesdays after the first Monday in November. The elections occur in the same way as for the state legislators, and by the same voters. The Governor-elect is installed in office at the next session of the General Assembly, and serves a four year term with the possibility of one succession.

If Georgia Governors want a third term, they have to wait four years after their second term before they can run again. In order to qualify for the office of Governor, a person must have been a citizen of the United States for at least 15 years and a legal resident of the state for at least six years preceding the election, and must be at least 30 years old when assuming office. These requirements ensure that the Governor is familiar with the state, and can make informed decisions and appointments. But governors should be able to do more than make decisions, they should be able to provide their people with a vision of a better future.

Vision and Policy Initiative

Georgia has had lots of leaders with vision. Jimmy Carter's adroit ability to gauge the public mood led him all the way to the White House. Martin Luther King's "I Have a Dream" speech was an example of a leader's vision and ability to motivate followers. In the early 1990's the depressed state of the American economy cracked even Georgia's well run economy. Beset by rising unemployment, reduced growth, and economic shortfalls, Governor Zell Miller, in 1992, created the *Georgia Rebound* proposal as the centerpiece of his budgetary and policy recommendations. The basic program goals were to anticipate and spur economic recovery and competitiveness in the state of Georgia. The plan balanced expenditures primarily with a slight increase in user fees, usually in areas where the fees were not sufficiently self-sustaining. The total estimated cost of his annual budget proposal was over 8.3 billion dollars.

In his first term, the four point expenditure program focused on economic development, educational improvements, environmental planning and public safety. By increasing support for capital improvements and teacher salaries, the state workforce was better able to exploit economic opportunities such as new environmental technologies. At the conclusion of the 1992 legislative session, Governor Miller proclaimed the legislative session a success, with most of the *Georgia Rebound* approved and funded (LoMonte, B1). But in politics a governor can only rarely afford to rest on their laurels, and stiff competition in his campaign for a second term in office led to his offering of a new vision, and a new message for the people and a new agenda for the legislature.

Whereas in his first term his plan had relied heavily on public construction projects, such as transportation facilities, waterways and airways development; his new plan focused on education. Georgia had been a southern leader in educational progress, but had in recent years slipped back and lost ground. Governor Miller's new vision centered on building hope for better schools. Awakening to the financial problems of schools and students alike, the *Hope Scholarship Program* linked the idea of government scholarships and educational appropriations to a risky new revenue source: a state sponsored lottery which promised to bring millions of new dollars into state coffers. The *Hope Scholarship* program basically pays the college tuition of any Georgia student who maintains a "B" or better grade point average. It all came together: a politician's vision, a legislative agenda, a constitutional amendment, and in 1998 the legislature was able to draw upon over five hundred million new dollars ($500,000,000.00) for education. This supports several different educational grant and loan programs, all expected to expand as lottery revenues increase, which ensures better grade schools and that every college student can pursue their educational dreams and be able to compete in the emerging global marketplace. And of course in the modern world no one person can do it all. A good governor must create a good management team, and be able to put strong and active managers who share a common vision onto all of the boards and commissions over which a governor has appointive authority or political influence.

The Lieutenant Governor

Like most states, Georgia elects a Lieutenant Governor. This is a relatively new position in Georgia, created for the first time in the 1945 Constitution (Pound & Saye, 60). Governor Roy Barnes' Lieutenant Governor, Mark Taylor, was elected at the same time, for the same term, and in the same manner as the Governor. While the Lt. Governor's job is basically to replace the Governor if necessary, he also serves as the President of the Senate. This is a powerful position in its own right, almost as powerful as the Speaker of the House of Representatives.

Lt. Governors have such various other executive duties as may be prescribed by the Governor or by law. Primarily, in case of the temporary disability of the Governor, the Lieutenant Governor exercises the powers and duties of the Governor, until such time as the disability ends. But in case of the death, resignation, or permanent disability of the Governor, the Lieutenant Governor becomes the new Governor until a successor is elected at the next general election.

But if such death, resignation, or permanent disability occurs within 30 days of the next general election, or if the term expires 90 days after the next general election, the Lieutenant Governor becomes Governor for the remainder of the unexpired term. When that happens, the office of Lt. Governor remains vacant, since the Georgia Constitution does not provide for a new Lt. Governor to be appointed. On those rare occasions where both the Governorship and the Lieutenant Governorship are vacant, the Speaker of the House of Representatives exercises the powers and duties of the Governor until a special election can be held within 90 days.

68 Chapter Five

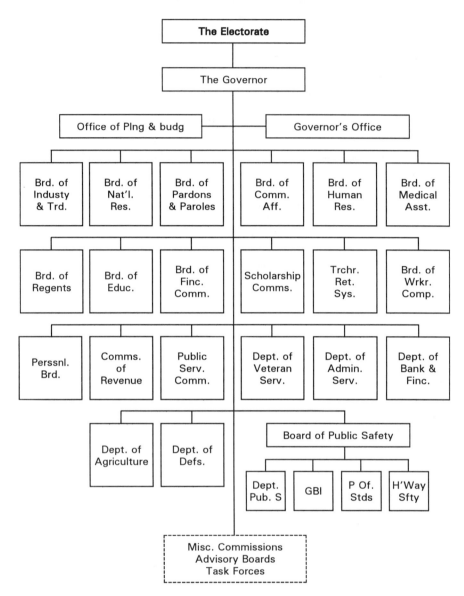

FIGURE 5.3. Selected Governor's Appointments
Source: Compiled by authors.

Attorney General

Another important Constitutional Official in Georgia is the Attorney General. The Attorney General acts as the legal advisor of the Department of Law, and represents the state in the State Supreme Court for all capital felonies, and performs such other legal duties as may be required by the Governor or by law. One of the most important of these is authoring legal opinions on problems of interpretation of law for other state officials and agencies. No person can be Attorney General unless he or she has been an active-status member of the State Bar of Georgia for seven years. The Attorney General is a vital link between the executive branch and the judicial branch of government.

The Attorney General of Georgia is the Constitutional Executive Officer whose administrative duties include presiding over the Department of Law. As the state's lawyer, he or she provides legal opinions to other state agencies. The formal powers of the various state Attorneys General throughout the United States have been rated in a comparative analysis by scholars. The Office of the Attorney General of the State of Georgia rates slightly above the average for the fifty states (Winder, 67–92). The office is further discussed in the judiciary chapter.

Educational Executives

The State School Superintendent is the chief executive officer of the State Board of Education, but she is not appointed by the Board. The Constitution specifies that the Superintendent shall be elected at the same time and in the same manner and for the same terms as that of the Governor. Only sixteen states elect their School Superintendent. In the other thirty-four states s/he is either appointed by the Governor or by the Board of Education itself. Some consideration has been given to having the Georgia Superintendent appointed and incumbent Superintendents have endorsed that suggestion. However, Georgia citizens like to elect as many of their public officials as possible, and once a position is elective it is hard to change; the General Assembly has not yet made the change to an appointive state Superintendent.

The members of the Georgia State Board of Regents, like the Board of Education, are appointed by the Governor of Georgia and confirmed by the Senate. However, in addition to representatives chosen from the congressional districts, there are also five more Regents who are chosen at large; all Regents serve seven-year terms. Among state agencies, the Board of Regents is unique in the sense that its budget is not line-itemed. To insulate the University System from politics, the General Assembly appropriates monies to the Board of Regents in a lump sum, and the Constitution instructs the regents to allocate these monies as the Board sees fit.

This peculiar insulation of the Board of Regents was initiated during the administration of Governor Arnall in the 1940s as part of a strategy to secure educational re-accreditation for the university system, whose accreditation had been lost. The withdrawal of accreditation originally occurred when the previous Governor, Eugene Talmadge, had tried to manipulate and intimidate the Board and the entire university system for partisan purposes. In an attempt to prevent similar problems in the future, Governor Arnall and the legislature placed the system of higher education out of the budgetary reach of both the executive and the legislative branches.

Other Elected Executives

The Secretary of State is another vitally important official but is dealt with primarily in the next chapter. The other major constitutionally elected officials include the Commissioner of Insurance, the Commissioner of Agriculture, and the Commissioner of Labor. These officials are elected in the same manner as the members of the General Assembly, and hold their officers for the same term as the Governor. Together with the other officials discussed above, these officials have another power in addition to their departmental duties. Any four of these elected constitutional officers can petition the Supreme Court of Georgia to declare that another elected constitutional executive officer (including the Governor) is unable to perform the duties of their office. When the grounds are properly based on physical or mental disability, the Supreme Court will provide a speedy and public hearing on the matter. This is a formal process that includes notice of the nature and cause of the accusation, process for obtaining witnesses, and assistance of counsel. Evidence at such hearings must include testimony from at least three qualified physicians in private practice, one of whom must be a psychiatrist.

If, after hearing the evidence on disability, the Supreme Court determines that there is a disability and that it is permanent, the office will be declared vacant and a successor to that office will be chosen according to the Constitution and the laws of Georgia. But if the disability is not permanent, the Supreme Court must later determine when the disability has ended and when the officer can resume the exercise of powers of office. During the period of temporary disability, the powers of such office will be exercised according to law, usually by an assistant administrator.

Conclusion

How is a Governor to cope with such a complex and decentralized system of government and administration? How can a Governor be evaluated? Some researchers suggest that a good Governor can identify the needs of the people of the state, develop intergovernmental strategies to meet these needs, and persuade at least half the people (or their legislative representatives) to adopt his proposals (Gray, 1983, at 230). The Governor must be foxy enough to understand the problems and aggressive enough to act on the information.

FIGURE 6.1. Department of Transportation

6

Administration and Agencies

The Georgia State Administration

What do a female tourist, a group of senior citizens and a County Commissioner have in common? They have all had negative experiences with modern bureaucracy. When the government machinery runs well, we call it an administration; when it runs badly, we call it a bureaucracy. In today's mass society, composed largely of alienated strangers, bureaucracy can be a nightmare. Administration can be defined as a complex rationally designed system of organization that relies on training, specialization, division of labor, record keeping and hierarchical control to meet the needs of a technological mass society. Its evil twin brother, bureaucracy, can be defined simply as a nightmare of impersonal government. This chapter describes some of the major administrative organizations and how they fit into the governmental system of the State of Georgia, and how they affect the lives of its citizens.

The tourist, a 300 pound woman returning from a bus trip to Ft. Lauderdale, was arrested in Macon Georgia for disturbing the peace when she objected to being kicked off the bus because the bus company driver was attempting to squeeze in a maximum number of passengers (Ass. Press, 3–29–92). The senior citizens were playing their usual game of bingo at McDonalds in Lavonia Georgia when the Georgia Bureau of Investigation closed the games down because they were not properly run by a non-profit, tax-exempt organization with a bingo license (Ass. Press, 4–2–92). Jimmy Helms, Chairman of the Paulding County Board of Commissioners, announced that he wanted to hire a professional manager to cope with the demands of modern growth, because amateurs such as he could not adequately run the county bureaucracy as efficiently as a professional public administrator (Ass. Press, 2–23–92).

Article IV of the Georgia Constitution establishes an administrative branch of government. Just as the principle of legislative primacy has yielded to executive dominance, so in turn the executive model is being replaced by an administrative model of government organization and policy making. Most of the administrative machinery of the State of Georgia is run by various Constitutional Boards and elected and appointed officials whose names are largely unknown to the average citizen. Generally, these officials are not formally subordinate to the Governor, except for reporting obligations, as we saw in the last chapter.

Public Administrators

Administrators are basically people. State government is one of the largest employers in Georgia. Including higher education personnel, over 114,000 people work for the State of Georgia (Fleischmann, 146). They are headquartered in buildings in Atlanta and their basic job is implementing the state's laws and policies. Together, these state employees constitute the muscle and nerve systems of the state. Small in the beginning of the state's history, their numbers have increased every time new programs and policies were created to cope with the increasing complexity of everyday life.

The growth of population has led to modern mass organization and an increasingly complex interdependent society. Few people really like the system, preferring the more individualistic lifestyles of the past, but rational organization is necessary today. When the invention of the railroad created jobs for conductors and engineers, it also required a Railroad Commission, (the forerunner of the Public Service Commission); and the invention of the airplane created a need for both pilots and the employees of the Atlanta Airport. In fact, in every major policy area, such as education, law enforcement, health care, welfare, and economic regulation, a new bureaucracy has had to be created to ensure that the general public good will be protected. In addition, bureaucratic proliferation occurs in five technical areas of bureaucratic activity: information, service, regulation, licensing, and promoting. The result is an expanding administrative structure which in its size, complexity and impersonality sometimes takes on a bureaucratic aspect in the minds of some citizens.

The stages by which modern societies have come to rely on mechanical bureaucracies can be traced. In the beginning, individuals and families took care of their own needs. But as society progressed, people learned that specialization and division of labor in a free market were more productive. Slowly, private organizations evolved which better satisfied peoples' needs. Except for taxation to support charities for the poor and disabled, monarchical governments encouraged these organizations with a minimum of interference, a laissez-faire approach. But as private organizations increased in power, adapting bureaucratic structures to profit making enterprises, some became too self-serving and a few created destructive monopolies. Entering the industrial revolution, western democratic societies attempted to retain their sense of community by curbing monopolies and by creating welfare agencies.

As populations grew, the western societies created ever larger bureaucratic institutions to deal with large masses of people: armies, schools, social work

FIGURE 6.2. Bureaucratic Empire Building

agencies and even prisons. But these facilities are very expensive to operate. Reforms and modification of the institutional society led to attempts to directly subsidize individuals. Poorhouses were closed, mental institutions were emptied, and individuals were given government pensions and welfare checks to take care of themselves, but bureaucracies continued to grow. Even recent suggestions to cut costs and bureaucracy by passing regulations requiring families to provide child support and for employers to provide family and health care, envision new enforcement bureaucracies. Truly, we live in a bureaucratic age.

In one year the various agencies of the Georgia State Government make millions of phone calls, process over a million driver's licenses, almost two million vehicle titles, almost two and a half million income tax returns, close to six million vehicle registrations, and handles fifty million criminal justice inquiries (Christenberry, 19). Over one hundred thousand state employees carried on a bewildering array of activities. They administered the largest self-insurance program in the state, maintained real estate leases in almost two hundred cities, provided services for seventy-eight thousand telephones, and managed over six hundred thousand procurements transactions (Ibid). The state's workforce is big business.

Constitutional Boards

Decades ago, Leonard White, a political scientist, predicted an eventual shift from legislative based government to bureaucratic based government (Nachmias, viii). In fact there is a long history of such predictions; most of the serious scholars who have contemplated the issue have agreed that a new locus of bureaucratic power is developing. This is reasonable, because bureaucratic government has several advantages over legislative and executive government. Some of the major ones are rational planning, specialization and division of labor, record keeping, and a career orientation (Weber, 196-199. Perhaps the major one is that it avoids what Max Weber called the 'succession crisis'. Max Weber identified a typology of historical change in government organization. According to that typology, new *charismatic* governments created by gifted individuals would experience a crisis when the leader died; much energy and effort would be diverted to solidify gains and create *traditional* governments based on the leader's ideas. But these governments too often hardened into rigid forms; and western political systems developed *legalistic* means of choosing new leaders and new policies. These legalistic procedures are the fundamental basis of bureaucratic organization (Weber, 1913, at 112).

Of course, researchers have found some instances of this system of bureaucracy to be dysfunctional. It has been suggested that the Reagan Administration, which succeeded the Carter Administration, acted on assumptions that regulatory agencies and commissions were often harmful to society. These assumptions are that such organizations create contradictory policies with heavy compliance costs, perceive regulations as ends in themselves, and tend to devote resources to advance their own interests (Friedman, 24).

Perhaps the most influential of the anti-regulatory studies was the one conducted by Murray Weidenbaum, who calculated that the total economic impact of federal regulations was more than $100 billion dollars (Cooper, 253). This report was cited in Congress, and charged regulatory agencies with being staffed by overly zealous and impractical officials. However, analysis of the Weidenbaum report by Mark Green showed that it was seriously flawed, that it was largely "puffing" for partisanship purposes, and that it exaggerated the costs of regulation and completely neglected the economic benefits of regulatory activity (Cooper, 254–45). The reason that bureaucratic techniques and regulations are so pervasive is that they are superior to other forms of mass organization.

The old mold of traditionalistic monarchical government was broken in the new world. In America, new states and new governments were created by charismatic individuals with the vision and energy to implement their ideas. Colonial Georgia's Oglethorpe is a good example of a charismatic visionary. The creation of constitutional government, influenced by John Locke and Jean Rousseau, traditionalized many of Oglethorpe's principles for a new social order, and the American Revolution solidified them. Georgia's political evolution has largely been a continuation of the legalistic and bureaucratic transformations identified and articulated by Max Weber.

The student should note the similarities and differences between the structure of the federal government and the government of Georgia. The State of Georgia has a plural executive, not a unitary one. The powers of the Chief Executive must be shared with a number of other elected and appointed executive officers working in a number of agencies and departments.

In Georgia, the relationship between these officials is complex, requiring skill in intergovernmental relations. The Governor must be a lion and a fox, able and willing to assume a variety of roles with facility. With such an able Governor in charge, state government can be as sweet as an apple pie, or in this case, as sweet as a *peach cobbler*. In Georgia, under an effective leadership the various units of government can work together harmoniously, with joint policy making and mutual accommodation.

While the Constitution of the State of Georgia specifies that the chief executive powers shall be vested in the Governor, sometimes the administrative agencies function as a separate branch of government. This is especially true in Georgia, where the enactment of Article IV of the Constitution created an emphasis on independent administrative government. The primary thrust of this bureaucratic approach is due to a growing recognition of the need for expertise in governing and coordinating today's complex society. This tendency is reflected not only by the features of the plural executive described in the last chapter, but also by a wide variety of autonomous and independent departments, regulatory agencies, commissions, and authorities, described below.

TABLE 6.1
Administrative Subdivisions

Executive Departments	33
Executive Agencies	48
Statutory Advisory Boards	37
Decreed Advisory Boards	20
Authorities & Corporations	30
Interstate Agencies	8
Judicial Agencies	24
Legislative Agencies	12
Inactive Agencies	_12_
Total:	224

Source: After Jackson and Stakes, Handbook of Georgia State Agencies, Univ. of Georgia. (Note: This is not an exhaustive list.)

Administrative Leaders

The Attorney General is probably, except for the Governor in the executive branch, and possibly the Lt. Governor and the Speaker in the legislative branch, the single most powerful individual official in Georgia's State Government. As the state's chief lawyer, the Attorney General issues opinions on state law which serve to guide much of the state's and local governments' administrative apparatus. By exercising this power, the Attorney General can (1) interpret vaguely worded laws and regulations, (2) influence enforcement of laws and regulations, (3) advise legislators on probable constitutionality of pending bills, (4) determine the scope of agency jurisdiction, and thus (5) can significantly determine public policy across the entire state. The Attorney General is also the state's chief administrative link with the courts and the legal profession.

The Secretary of State is another extremely important constitutionally elected official. The Secretary of State, along with the Board of Elections, oversees the elections process, and tracks electoral changes in the State Constitution. Other duties include (1) recording financial statements from politicians, (2) granting charters to corporate entities, (3) issuing permits to do business, (4) maintaining registers of public officials and (5) oversight of a myriad of occupational boards.

Workers in many trades and professions must be licensed before they can practice in the State of Georgia. Dozens of commissions and boards administer occupation admission standards and licensing procedures, regulate their particular areas of employment, and deal with complaints by consumers. Except for attorneys, oversight of these examining, certification and regulatory boards and commissions is the responsibility of the Secretary of State, acting through the Office of the Joint-Secretary of the State Examining Boards. Some of the Examining Boards are listed below. The first table shows the major health professional boards, the second depicts a variety of other occupational groups that are closely regulated.

Executive Commissions

Article IV of the Georgia Constitution creates several powerful executive Boards and Commissions. These boards and commissions include the Public Service Commission; the State Board of Pardons and Paroles; the State Personnel Board; the State Transportation Board; the Veterans Service Board; and the Board of Natural Resources. In each case, the qualifications, salaries, powers and duties of their members are controlled by the Constitution and not by the Governor. The presiding chairmen of these boards are selected by a variety of complicated two step processes, some of which are described.

TABLE 6.2
Examining and Licensing Boards

Selected Health Professions
Composite State Board of Medical Examiners
Georgia Boards of Dentistry
Georgia Board of Nursing
Board of Examiners of Licensed Practical Nurses
Georgia State Board of Nursing Home Administrators
Georgia State Board of Pharmacy
State Board of Dispensing Opticians
State Board of Examiners in Optometry
Board of Examiners for Speech Pathology and Audiology
Board of Hearing Aid Dealers and Dispensers
Georgia State Board of Physical Therapy
State Board of Podiatry Examiners
State Board of Examiners of Psychologists
Georgia Board of Chiropractic Examiners
Georgia Board of Occupational Therapy
State Board of Examiners for Certified Waters and Wastewater Treatment Plant Operators and Laboratory Analysts
Water Well Standards Advisory Council
Board of Veterinary Medicine
State Board of Examiners for Registered Professional Sanitarians

Source: Compiled by authors from materials in Jackson and Stakes, Handbook of Georgia State Agencies, Univ. of Georgia.

The Public Service Commission

The Public Service Commission is created for the purpose of regulating utilities such as electrical power. It is composed of five members who are elected directly by the people for six year terms. The chairman is selected by the members of the commission from among themselves. The exact jurisdiction, powers, and duties of the Commission are provided for by statutes enacted by the legislature and by regulations promulgated by the Commission.

The members of the Public Service Commission regulate the railroads, issue licenses and set rates for power companies, telephone companies and other public utilities. There is a great deal of controversy over the scope of

TABLE 6.3
Other Examining Boards

Office of the Joint-Secretary of State Examining Boards
Asbestos Licensing Board
State Board of Accountancy
State Board for Certification of Librarians
Georgia Real Estate Commission
State Board of Georgia Architects
Georgia State Board of Landscape Architects
State Board of Registration for Professional Engineers and Land Surveyors
State Board of Registration for Professional Geologists
State Board of Registration for Foresters
Georgia Construction Industry Licensing Board
State Structural Pest Control Commission
State Board of Barbers
Georgia State Boards of Cosmetology
Board of Recreation Examiners
Georgia Board of Athletic Trainers
Board of Polygraph Examiners
Georgia Board of Private Detectives and Private Security Agencies
State Board of Registration of Used Car Dealers
Georgia Auctioneers Commission
Georgia Athletic Agent Regulatory Commission
Georgia State Board of Funeral Service

Source: Compiled by authors from materials in Jackson and Stakes, Handbook of Georgia State Agencies, Univ. of Georgia.

powers of the Public Service Commission. As Georgia becomes increasingly urbanized and modernized, there are cries for an increase in regulatory efforts and for reform. Some of the areas of concern involve consumer complaints over the cost of electrical power; manufacturing interest in the adequacy of the transportation systems; general distress over the quality of water: and preservation of the state's unique environmental resources.

The State Transportation Board

In contrast, the members of the State Transportation Board, who serve five year terms, are chosen by designated members of the General Assembly. There are as many members of this Board as there are congressional districts in the state. The member of the board from each congressional district is elected by a special caucus meeting of members of both houses whose respective districts are embraced or partly embraced within each congressional district. A majority vote of these legislators chooses the members of the board, who in turn pick their chief executive officer from among their ranks. This commission is responsible for building and maintaining the roads and highways of the state of Georgia, and such other duties as provided by the legislature.

The patronage and politics involved in this area can be very considerable. For example, one businessman who had tried unsuccessfully for years to persuade the State Department of Transportation (DOT) to pave the road to his sod farm finally gave up and tried an alternative approach. He began donating money to political candidates. He was impartial, giving money to candidates of both parties. Soon, he was appointed to a special commission to ferret out waste in state government. As a result, the next time the businessman called DOT about his road he received prompt and friendly service (AJAC, 2–21–92). Not all citizens end up as happy as this individual.

The State Board of Pardons and Paroles

Historically, the British King had power to intervene in criminal cases to provide justice or to settle political and military disputes by exercising the pardon power. Although Presidents and Governors usually have similar powers, in Georgia the fear of abuse, corruption and a desire to avoid hassle led to a delegation of that power to a five person commission. The members of the State Board of Pardons and Paroles are appointed by the Governor, subject to confirmation by the Senate. The Chairman of the Board of Pardons and Paroles, or any member designated by the board, may suspend the execution of a sentence of death; until the full board has an opportunity to hear the application of the convicted person for relief. The State Board of Pardons and Paroles also has the authority to pardon any person convicted of a crime who is later found to be innocent of that crime.

Thus the board, and not the Governor, is vested with the power of executive clemency, including the powers to grant reprieves, pardons, and paroles; to commute penalties; to remove disabilities imposed by law; and to remit any part of a sentence for any offense against the state after conviction. However, the Constitution does not give the Board a completely free hand. In a further division of power, the General Assembly of Georgia has a lot of direct control over pardons and paroles under the Constitution. Under some circumstances the legislature may prohibit the board from granting a pardon or parole to habitual felons or notorious criminals, and may even prescribe the terms and conditions for the board's granting of a pardon or parole to such persons. These conditions pertain to any person incarcerated for a second time for any offense for which he or she could have been sentenced to life imprisonment; and to any person who has received consecutive life sentences as the result of multiple offenses occurring during the same series of acts.

And the ever-popular anti-crime movement has resulted in some recent amendments to the constitution which allow the General Assembly to set mandatory sentencing guidelines, and in addition a 'two-strikes' amendment means that a two time loser is likely to face living in prison for a life term! When a sentence of death is commuted to life imprisonment, the board does not have the authority to grant a pardon to the convicted person until the person has served at least 25 years in the penitentiary. Georgia is not a good place for anyone to commit a crime and get caught.

The State Personnel Board

A strong governor usually has the power to directly hire and fire members of the administrative apparatus of the state, and thus to control the bureaucracy. With a weak executive, employees are more likely to respond to their immediate superiors instead of to the Governor. In Georgia, power over state employees is given to a State Personnel Board, consisting of five members nominated by the Governor and appointed after confirmation by the Senate. Their terms of office are five years, and they select their own chairman. This board sets policy for the State Merit System of Personnel Administration, and is further vested with such additional responsibilities and powers as provided by law. One critique may be in order here. While merit systems may indeed increase competency, it is sometimes at the cost of loyalty and adherence to executive policy. To further complicate matters, much of the sphere of authority of this Board overlaps with another one: the Board of Veterans Service, which is described below.

The Veterans Service Board

Article IV of the State Constitution creates a State Department of Veterans Service and its oversight body, the Veterans Service Board which consists of seven members appointed by the Governor, subject to confirmation by the Senate. The terms of its members are for seven years, and the members themselves appoint a commissioner who becomes the executive officer of the department. All members of the board and the department must be veterans of some war or armed conflict in which the United States has engaged. Exact duties and responsibilities of the board are described in statutes enacted by the General Assembly.

Any armed forces veteran who has been honorably discharged is given veterans preference in any civil service program established in state government. Wounded or disabled veterans are provided at least ten points if they have a 10 percent service connected disability, and all other veterans are entitled to at least five points. For, example if a passing grade on a test is required to get a job, the preference points are added to their scores. If tests are so easy that everyone gets high marks, veterans will get the jobs.

Commissioner of Insurance

Insurance regulation is required by Article III, Section VIII of the State Constitution. That provision calls for the General Assembly to provide for statutory regulation of the insurance business, under the direction of a Commissioner of Insurance. The Commissioner of Insurance regulates the state's multimillion dollar insurance industry. The Commissioner sets criteria for licensing, sets standards for performance, and within the framework of the law, sets rates for insurance policies for automobile drivers and homeowners and for fire, theft and casualty losses.

The Board of Natural Resources

The State of Georgia has traditionally relied heavily on its natural resources for trade and commerce. As environmental problems have developed, Georgia has acted to protect its fragile ecosystems by creating a Board of Natural Resources. Like the State Transportation Board, the size of the Board of Natural Resources is determined by according a member for each congressional district, with an additional five members to represent the state at large. And because of the geographical distribution of resources, at least one of the members must be from one of several counties specifically named in the Constitution. And the members of the board are supposed to be representative of all areas and functions encompassed within the Department of Natural Resources. All members are appointed by the Governor for seven years, subject to confirmation by the Senate. As usual, more powers and duties can be provided by legislative statute.

Intergovernmental Interactions

How do all of these agencies interact? The Legislature acts by committees. The executive branch *per se* operates by fiat and decree through the bureaucratic hierarchy. The judicial are trained in legal reasoning and hierarchy. How do the various agencies, representing a wide variety of perspectives and responsive to different interests, interact with each other to accomplish anything? Actually, there are four common patterns of agency interaction.

Usually, agencies are rational actors capable of identifying common interests and acting jointly to make and implement public policy. Sometimes one agency, perhaps enjoying sufficient funding levels, will take the initiative on a problem and other agencies will help out. This is called mutual accommodation. Sometimes, rival agencies will engage in friendly competition to see which can accomplish its goals first. This is called constructive rivalry. But unfortunately, there is yet another pattern. On rare occasions, two agencies will be controlled by opposing special interest groups, or will succumb to professional jealousy, and the result adversely affects the agencies and the public good. This pattern is called destructive conflict. Joint policy making and mutual accommodation, formalized in contracts and memoranda of agreements, are the most routine patterns of bureaucratic interaction.

Federalism is a type of political system in which many disparate units and levels of government are coordinated by a central unit. In this *apple pie* mixture, the government of Georgia is part of the larger federal system. But that is not all, Georgia belongs to a variety of other coordinating units, such as the National Governor's Association. In addition, several interstate agencies exist, sometimes operating under binding compacts, such as the Southeastern Interstate Forest Fire Protection Compact Advisory Committee; other examples include the Southern States Energy Board and the Southern Growth Policies Board (Jackson, 341). The Fisheries Commission, the Radioactive Waste Management Commission and the Historic Chattahoochee Commission are other examples. Of course, most of the daily grind of bureaucratic activity is determined by functional problems, such as conservation.

Conservation of the Environment

The conservation of environmental standards and resources is a problem of increasing significance. Georgia's farmers have long understood the necessity to replenish the land to support their agricultural crops. Taking care of topsoil, planting the right crops, and fertilizing the back-forty is second nature to good farmers. For many citizens of the state it is a simple step from soil conservation to environmental preservation. But for other Georgians, concerned perhaps with post-war modernization, or focused on short-term self-interest, or simply unmindful of the necessities of long range planning, environmental preservation has been a low priority. However, with our water tables polluted by industrial and agricultural waste and pesticides, with the virgin timber almost gone, and many wildlife species already extinct, the consequences of reckless destruction today commands our attention.

Georgia ranks near the bottom of the list of states in terms of state owned park and wilderness land. The Board of Natural Resources is charged with increasing land holdings and protection of the environment. The duties of the department include maintenance and acquisition of land, regulation and conservation of fish and game, management of fisheries, and the enforcement of state hunting and fishing laws. Unfortunately, some of the goals of the board, as in the society at large, are often contradictory and irreconcilable.

Other Regulatory Areas

The promotion of economic development and trade and commerce is a major concern of Georgia State Government. As the traditional local forestry and agricultural economy of Georgia yields to manufacturing, commerce and recreation, several agencies have been created to coordinate the efforts of private companies and public agencies to foster economic and industrial growth. In today's global marketplace, the attraction, location and encouragement of business enterprises and economic opportunities are legitimate, indeed essential, concerns of state government.

Special Authorities

There are some economic and functional policy areas that require narrow expertise, technical administrative competency and unique management skills. Sometimes these policy areas involve geographical considerations that cannot be easily handled by local government, or dealt with in a cost-effective fashion by generic state laws or state agencies. Two obvious examples are the metropolitan airport in Atlanta, and the international seaport in Savannah, but there are many more. In fact, there are 391 different special districts in the State of Georgia, some of the 1,271 different governmental entities in the state.

Their interactions often depend upon the functional issues but may center on the resolution of intergovernmental conflicts; the need to facilitate development, or to provide flexibility for quasi-commercial enterprises. Often the driving force behind the creation of a special authority is the desire to finance an enterprise without exceeding the debt limitations of a parent governmental entity; or to quiet a taxpayer revolt by financing operations with specific user fees instead of with general revenues or property taxes.

However, the proliferation of special authorities has led to increasing concerns about waste and mismanagement. In 1972 the General Assembly enacted a reorganization plan designed to deal with the problem. This plan created a centralized State Financing and Investment Commission. The State Financing and Investment Commission might be called a *super commission*. It is composed of the major state political leadership: the Governor, the Lt. Governor, the Speaker of the House of Representatives, the Attorney General, the Commissioner of Agriculture, the State Auditor, and the Director of the Fiscal Division. Together, this collective body of political power can coordinate a powerful response to any problem. The goal is to ensure that Special Authorities contribute to efficient government.

TABLE 6.4
Types of Authorities

Agricultural Authorities
Building Authorities
Development Authorities
Educational Authorities
Foundations
Highway Authorities
Municipal Authorities
Park Authorities
Port Authorities
Power Authorities
Residential Finance Authorities
State Tollway Authority
Stone Mountain Memorial Association
World Congress Center Authority

Source: Compiled by authors.

In 1996, Article IX, Section IV was amended to allow the creation of "regional facilities" These regional facilities mean industrial parks, business parks, conference centers, convention centers, airports, athletic facilities, recreation facilities, jails or correctional facilities, or other similar or related economic development facilities. Counties and municipalities are authorized to enter into contracts with contiguous counties for the purpose of allocating the proceeds of ad valorem taxes assessed and collected on real property for development purposes, and unless otherwise provided by law, the regional facilities can qualify for any income tax credits, regardless of where the business is located. Many people don't like bureaucracy. Although the pressures of modern society require the modification of government towards increasingly bureaucratic models, the creeping snails' pace and heartless impersonal nature of bureaucracy engenders hostility and anger. Nevertheless, the growth of bureaucracy is inevitable. One ironic effect is that the oversight powers of the legislature and the Governor have dwindled as the size and scope of bureaucracy has grown.

Conclusion

The administrative machinery grinds slowly, but it usually grinds well. The charges against the lady tourist arrested on the bus were dropped and she initiated a lawsuit against the bus company. The senior citizens who couldn't play bingo have received a sympathetic ear from their state representative who initiated a provision to exempt their organization from criminal categorization. And now of course non-profit organizations run all sorts of raffles. And the county commission chairman who decided that a professionally trained manager was necessary is simply falling in line with the trends, based on the requirements of the citizens of the State of Georgia.

The present Constitution of the State of Georgia, reflecting these pressures, has created the most administratively oriented government in the history of the state. Unfortunately, once created, bureaucratic organizations soon learn how to protect their funds, their resources and personnel staffing levels, and even their autonomy. It is the task of the other branches of government to ensure that the bureaucracy remains responsive to the general public, and not just to their particular special interests.

FIGURE 7.1. Local Courthouse

7

The Georgia State Judiciary

The Vested Judicial Power

Georgia's State Motto: "Wisdom, Justice and Moderation", not only reflects our traditional and individualistic cultural values, but also the rich heritage of the judiciary. The power of the courts is the power of the pen (reasonable explanations of decisions). Like the executive power, the judicial power is decentralized, but not as decentralized, because the judiciary is based on definite principles and has clear lines of authority running to a pinnacle of power, the state (and ultimately the national) Supreme Court. The judicial power of the state is vested "exclusively" in seven classes of constitutional courts. Article Five, Paragraph II provides that all courts of the state shall comprise a unified judicial system.

Generally, the judicial branch of government enjoys a higher respect in the minds of the public than that of the other branches. As a result, the courts often resolve disputes between the other branches. For example, during the sorry political jockeying of the so-called three-Governors fiasco, arising from the premature death of Governor-elect Eugene Talmadge on December 21, 1946, the State Supreme Court had to resolve a bitter controversy. Three people claimed the Governorship: Ellis Arnall, the sitting Governor attempted to stay on; political boss Herman Talmadge was elected by the legislature; and the newly elected Lt. Governor, M.E. Thompson claimed to be acting Governor (Wolfe). The Supreme Court decided in favor of Thompson and the issue was resolved.

The Georgia Supreme Court stands at the top of the legal ladder in the state. Starting at the bottom, in ascending hierarchal order, the seven constitutional courts are: magistrate courts, probate courts, juvenile courts, state courts, superior courts, the Court of Appeals, and the Supreme Court. The last three courts, the superior courts, the Court of Appeals, and the Supreme Court, have high status because they are courts of unlimited jurisdiction which can and do handle all types of legal cases, civil and criminal. In contrast the four lower courts, magistrate, probate, juvenile and the state courts are courts of limited jurisdiction.

Actually, there are many types of courts of limited jurisdiction. Some of these are created by the state constitution and some are created by the statutes (laws made by the legislature), but all are alike in that their scope is limited to rather specialized types of cases. The juvenile courts can handle only cases involving minors, and the probate courts only deal with inheritance, wills and related matters. The magistrate courts deal with minor disputes, such as between merchants and customers, or with landlord and tenant problems, and the state courts serve to handle minor criminal and civil cases in the larger urban counties; they serve to 'back up' the Superior Courts.

In addition, the general assembly may establish or authorize the establishment of municipal courts and allow some administrative agencies to exercise quasi-judicial powers. When municipal courts are created, they have jurisdiction over violations of city laws, or ordinances, and such other jurisdiction as provided by law. The City Court of Atlanta has unique status in the system, and blends municipal court powers, magistrate court powers, and civil court powers.

Also, there are special units within some agencies that look like courts and function like courts, but are not really judicial courts at all. These are "quasi-judicial" units created to hold hearings into alleged violations of administrative laws (rules and regulations made by bureaucracies) These units usually have an officer called an administrative law judge (ALJ) who specializes in administrative law; functioning independently of the unified legal system, except of course for appellate courts' judicial review. As the trend towards an administrative state continues, such functional quasi-judicial units will become more common.

Under a constitutional amendment enacted in 1996, the General Assembly may now enact legislation, if approved by two-thirds of the members in each branch, that provides for the imposition of sentences of life without parole both for persons convicted of murder, and for convicted for a second offense involving murder, armed robbery, kidnapping, rape, aggravated child molestation, aggravated sodomy, or aggravated sexual battery. Such mandatory sentencing guidelines erode the powers of juries, judges and courts.

Another recent amendment provides authorization for the creation of special pilot projects for courts. The General Assembly may enact legislation providing for, as pilot programs of limited duration, courts which are not uniform within their classes in jurisdiction, powers, rules of practice and procedure. Similarly the standards for selection, qualifications, terms, and discipline of judges for such pilot courts and other matters can now be enacted by the general Assembly. Although the amendment specifies that the new pilot courts shall not deny equal protection of the laws to any person in violation of the law or the constitution, any kind of special treatment of particular kinds of accused persons should always be subjected to careful scrutiny.

Historically, a wide variety of other courts have existed under prior constitutions. These include Justice of the Peace Courts, Small Claims Courts, county recorder's courts, and civil courts; but these generally ceased to exist on June 30, 1983, unless they were incorporated into the present system. While the pre-

FIGURE 7.2. We Have the Final Decision.

siding officers of these courts have a variety of titles, the old and honorable title of "judge" is used to include magistrates, judges, senior judges, and even Justices of the Supreme Court. It is usually a good idea to address them as "Your Honor", and to address Supreme Court members as "Justice".

The power of judges is strictly limited by the Constitution. Judges can only react to existing cases properly brought before them. However, judges are mobile within the court system, and often substitute in another court, if they are requested to do so, and if they have permission from the judges of their own court. In general, each court may exercise those powers necessary for it to do its constitutional or statutory duty; but only the superior and appellate courts have the power to issue process in the nature of mandamus, prohibition, specific performance, quo warranto, and injunction. Writs of mandamus positively order other state officials to do their duty; specific performance enforces private contracts; and prohibitions and injunctions negatively prevent specified actions from being committed. Each superior court, state court, and other courts of record may grant new trials on legal ground.

The Unified Judicial System

The judicial power of the state is vested exclusively in the court system. All courts of the state comprise a unified judicial system. Except as otherwise provided in the recently amended Constitution, the courts of each class must have uniform jurisdiction, powers, rules of practice and procedure, and selection, qualifications, terms, and discipline of judges. However, probate courts are not required to adhere to uniform organizational or procedural standards

The state is geographically divided into judicial circuits, each of which must represent at least one county. Each county shall have at least one superior court, magistrate court, a probate court, and, where needed, a state court and a juvenile court. In rural areas with small case loads, the General Assembly may allow the judge of the probate court to serve as the judge of the magistrate court, but in the absence of a state court or a juvenile court, the superior court will exercise all of these jurisdictions. Superior courts have jurisdiction over title to land.

The Lower Court Jurisdiction

Centuries of experience have shown that cases should be handled locally where the issues and persons are well known. Forum shopping for judges who favor a particular point of view is generally prohibited. On some occasions however, when a case is brought to the wrong court, that court will transfer it to the appropriate court in the state having proper jurisdiction or venue.

Divorce cases are usually tried in the county where the defendant resides, but if the defendant is not a resident of the state, then it will usually be tried in the county in which the plaintiff resides. Special rules provide for military personnel or their dependents residing on any United States army post or military reservation. They can sue for divorce in any adjacent county.

Have you ever signed a loan for a car, or cashed a check written by a bank? If you have, and a legal problem develops, where can you be sued? Suits against the makers and endorser of promissory notes, or the drawers and acceptors of bills of exchange or like instruments, will be tried in the county where the maker or acceptor resides. Special problems develop when there are multiple parties on one side of a law suit. Determining the proper venue (court with jurisdiction) is often a problem in multiple party cases.

Multiple parties may be joint obligers (owing child support), joint tortfeasors (two fraternity brothers hazing freshmen), joint co-signers or co-partners. Multiple party defendants may be tried either in their county of residence or in the county where the alleged offense occurred. All other civil cases, except juvenile court cases, are tried in the county where the defendant resides. Equity cases, such as injunctions in domestic disputes, are tried in the county where the defendant resides.

All criminal cases are tried where the crime was committed, except cases in the superior court where the judge is satisfied that an impartial jury cannot be obtained in that county. The superior courts have very broad jurisdiction. They have exclusive jurisdiction over trials in all felony cases, except juvenile; in all cases respecting title to land; in divorce cases; and in equity cases. In addition, the superior courts have appellate jurisdiction from municipal, magistrate, and probate courts.

Every week in Georgia, many hundreds of people are sent to prison. They are convicted of serious felonies such as murder, kidnapping, assault, robbery, and auto theft. A major reason for Governor Miller's emphasis on increasing the number of prison beds is that with nearly 37,000 inmates currently in the state prison system, there are numerous others sitting in county jails waiting to be transferred (www.ganet.org/corrections/population.html).

Prison Overcrowding

A popular approach throughout the nation to address the perception of crime out of control is the so-called "three strikes and you're out" proposal championed by President Clinton. Under a three strikes plan, an offender sentenced for a third felony, regardless of the gravity of that felony, automatically receives a life sentence. Georgia has gone this plan one better; it has a "two strikes and you're out" policy. The result has been to significantly increase the size of the prison population in Georgia, already one of the highest in the nation. More prisoners need more prison beds, which leads to much more prison construction. But the state can hardly keep up. Despite a decrease in the crime rate in Georgia and elsewhere in the country, Georgia keeps sending more and more people to prison. The Georgia Department of Corrections currently operates 39 prisons, 24 county work camps, transitional centers, prisoner boot camps, or pre-transitional centers, 17 diversion centers, 13 detention centers, and two probation boot camps. In the past ten years, the inmate population in Georgia has doubled, giving the state the dubious distinction of having the country's eighth largest number of adults residing in prison.

Critics of this approach argue that "locking up" more people when the rate of crime is actually declining is certainly punitive but has little or no effect on the overall rate of crime. Moreover, it is quite costly for the following reasons: 1) prison beds are expensive and must come at the expense of something else, probably higher education, if the experience of California is instructive; 2) prisoners who are not released early grow old in prison, and while in their middle and late age they pose little threat to society, they are likely to be in poor health and in need of expensive medical treatment, and; 3) prisoners with no hope for parole require much more scrutiny and control by prison personnel and tend to be more violent than prisoners who know that "good behavior" may get them released.

Discretionary Venue

People are not the only civil and criminal defendants. Legally, corporations can be classified as persons, and can be regulated, sued, and punished for violations. Where should a case involving a large company be tried? Where it has its multi-million dollar headquarters or where its truck, for example, ran over a pedestrian on a rural road? In Georgia, the Constitution provides that venue will be determined by the state legislature by statute. Nevertheless, the power to change the venue in civil and criminal cases is vested in superior courts, largely at the expert discretion of the presiding judge, as provided by law.

The Higher Courts

The Court of Appeals consists of not less than nine judges who, like many of the administrative commissions discussed in the previous chapter, elect from among themselves a presiding officer, here called the Chief Judge. Members of the Court of Appeals may sit in panels of not less than three Judges as prescribed by law or and by its rules.

The Court of Appeals is a court of review and exercises appellate and certiorari jurisdiction (unlike appeals as a matter of right, certiorari is a discretionary review) in all cases not reserved to the Supreme Court or conferred on other courts by law. The decisions of the Court of Appeals bind all courts except the Supreme Court as precedents. In Georgia, the Court of Appeals may certify a question to the Supreme Court for instruction, to which it will then be bound. In the event of an equal division of the Judges when sitting as a body, the case will be immediately transmitted to the Supreme Court.

The Supreme Court is composed of seven Justices, who elect their own Chief Justice. The Chief Justice of the Supreme Court acts as the chief presiding and administrative officer of the court. In other words the chief Justice has approximately the same role with regard to the court system that the Governor has with the bureaucracy. The Justices also elect a Presiding Justice to serve if the Chief Justice is absent or is disqualified. A majority vote is necessary to hear and determine cases. If a Justice is disqualified in any case, a substitute judge may be designated by the remaining Justices to serve. The Georgia Supreme Court is primarily a court of review, but as to other state courts, it exercises exclusive jurisdiction in the following cases:

TABLE 7.1
Exclusive Jurisdiction

(1) In the construction of a state treaty,

(2) the construction of the State Constitution,

(3) In construction of the United States Constitution,

(4) Determining the constitutionality of a law,

(5) the constitutionality of an ordinance,

(6) Interpretation of a constitutional provision,

(7) all cases of election contest, and

(8) answer questions of law from other jurisdictions

Source: Compiled by the authors.

Unless otherwise provided by law, the Supreme Court has appellate jurisdiction of the following classes of cases:

TABLE 7.2
Appellate Jurisdiction

(1) Cases involving title to land;
(2) In all equity cases;
(3) All cases involving wills;
(4) Any habeas corpus cases;
(5) Cases involving extraordinary remedies;
(6) All divorce and alimony cases;
(7) Cases certified by the Court of Appeals; and
(8) Cases in which a sentence of death was imposed or could be imposed.

Source: Compiled by the authors.

In addition to the jurisdictions described above, the Supreme Court of Georgia may review by certiorari cases in the Court of Appeals which are of gravity or great public importance. The decisions of the Supreme Court bind all other courts as precedents. The Supreme Court is required, with the advice and consent of the council of the affected class or classes of trial courts, to issue orders adopting and publishing uniform court rules and record-keeping rules which shall provide for the speedy, efficient and inexpensive resolution of disputes and prosecutions. Each council shall be comprised of all of the judges of the courts of that class. The Supreme Court and the Court of Appeals must dispose of every case at the term for which it is entered on the court's docket for hearing or at the next term.

There are also many judicial bureaucratic agencies, most of which operate under the oversight of the Supreme Court's administrative function. They supervise the state's practicing attorneys, create Administrative District Councils, issue rules of court, and set standards in a wide variety of contexts. Twenty-four agencies are listed in *The Handbook of Georgia State Agencies*. Excluding the court entities already discussed above, these are listed on Table 7.3.

Controlling Judicial Personnel

Because of the neutral non-partisan orientation of the courts, and the special training of judicial personnel, the selection, terms of office, compensation and discipline of Judges creates special problems. Superior court and state court judges are elected on a nonpartisan basis for a term of four years. The Judges of the Court of Appeals and the Justices of the Supreme Court are

TABLE 7.3
Georgia Judicial Agencies

State Bar of Georgia
Board of Bar Examiners
District Attorney's Offices
Judicial Administrative District Councils
Judicial Council and Administrative Office of the Courts

Judicial Qualifications Commission
Judicial Nominating Commission for the State of Georgia
Council of Juvenile Court Judges
Council of Magistrate Court Judges
The Council of Probate Court Judges of Georgia
Executive Probate Judges Council of Georgia
Advisory Council for Probation
Prosecuting Attorneys' Council of the State of Georgia
The Council of State Court Judges of Georgia
Superior Court Clerks Training Council
The Council of Superior Court Judges of Georgia
Superior Courts Sentence Review Panel

The Institute of Continuing Judicial Education of Georgia
Board of Court Reporting of the Judicial Council
Georgia Indigent Defense Council

Source: After Jackson, E.L., *The Handbook of Georgia State Agencies.* (Athens, Georgia: Institute of Government, Univ. of Georgia, 1975).

elected on a nonpartisan basis for a term of six years. In addition to age and residency requirements set by the state legislature, appellate and superior court judges must have been admitted to practice law for seven years. Lesser experience is required for state and juvenile court judges who only need to have practiced law for five years. The level of experience for Probate and Magistrate judges is not set in the constitution, but rather by the General Assembly. Probate and Magistrate Judges are not required to have formal legal training. In fact, it is not uncommon in rural areas for these judges to lack any formal education beyond high school.

In the higher courts, legal training, a license to practice law and extensive experience in the courts is expected. When Justice George T. Smith lost his legal challenge to the mandatory retirement age, Governor Miller appointed

FIGURE 7.3. Beneath the Robes.

an experienced replacement. The newest Georgia Supreme Court Justice was a 36 year old black woman whose appointment was "a dream come true" (Ass. Press, 1-18-92, A3). Judge Leah Sears-Collins, a trial court Judge in Atlanta thus became the first woman on the Georgia Supreme Court. She is a graduate of Emory University's law school who was elected to the Atlanta Superior Court in 1988. Justice Charles Weltner of the Georgia Supreme Court, a nationally recognized jurist, said the new appointee "is known to be a careful and a thoughtful and a patient judge" (Ibid). The unique training required to qualify as a judge sometimes makes it difficult to select candidates who are representative of the varied interest groups in the State of Georgia.

The one hundred and forty-three Superior Court and appellate court judges receive compensation and allowances as provided by law, and may also receive county supplements. County governing authorities have authority to supplement salaries under the current constitution. Over eight hundred judges who serve in the lower courts are paid by their respective entities. An incumbent's salary, allowance or supplement cannot be decreased during the incumbent's term of office. All judges must retire by age 75 and must reside in the geographical area in which they are selected to serve. The Georgia judicial structure is depicted in Figure 7.5.

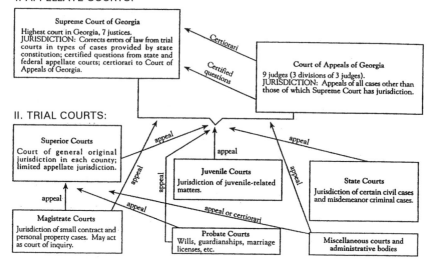

FIGURE 7.4. State Court System in Georgia
Source: Supreme Court of Georgia, a publication of the Supreme Court (Atlanta, Georgia 1998).

Judicial Vacancies and Removal

Article VI, Section VIII of the Constitution specifies that routine judicial vacancies will be filled by appointment by the Governor, (except as otherwise provided by law). Generally, an appointee to an elective office serves until a successor is duly selected and qualified, following the next general election which is more than six months after such person's appointment. In Georgia, the Governor does not have the power to suspend or remove a judge for misconduct. Instead, the power to discipline, remove, and cause involuntary retirement of judges is vested in the Judicial Qualifications Commission.

The Judicial Qualifications Commission consists of seven members. Two are judges selected by the Supreme Court; three are members of the State Bar elected by the Board of Governors of the State Bar; and two are non-lawyer citizens appointed by the Governor. Any judge may be removed, suspended, or otherwise disciplined for willful misconduct in office, or for willful and persistent failure to perform the duties of office, or for habitual intemperance, or for conviction of a crime involving moral turpitude, or for conduct prejudicial to the administration of justice which brings the judicial office into disrepute.

When a judge is indicted for a felony by a grand jury of the state or of the United States, the Attorney General or district attorney will inform the Judicial Qualification Commission. The commission then reviews the indictment, and determines whether the indictment adversely affects the administration of the office or the rights and interests of the public. If so, the commission will suspend the judge immediately, pending the final disposition of the case or until the expiration of the judge's term of office, whichever occurs first.

It should be noted that indictments are not convictions, and sometimes are motivated by political considerations. If an indicted judge who is suspended from office is not immediately tried at the next regular or special court term, the suspension will be terminated and the judge will be reinstated to office. If the indictment is not prosecuted, or if the judge is acquitted, or if the conviction is later directly overturned, the judge shall be immediately reinstated to the office. When a judge is suspended, he or she will continue to receive a salary. Furthermore, the commission does not review the indictment for a period of 14 days from the day the indictment is received. During this period of time, the indictment may be quashed, or the judge may resign or authorize the commission to suspend him from office. Any such voluntary suspension is subject to the same conditions for reinstatement, or declaration of vacancy as for a nonvoluntary suspension. After any suspension is imposed, the suspended judge may petition the commission for a review. If then the commission determines that the judge should no longer be suspended, it may reinstate the office.

Of course, immediately upon initial conviction for any felony, the constitution requires that the judicial official must be immediately suspended from office, and may not receive any more salary, allowance or compensation. But if the conviction is later overturned and the judge is reinstated to the office, then he is entitled to receive any backpay. For the duration of any suspension, the governor will appoint a replacement judge. And upon a final conviction with no appeal or review pending, the office shall be declared vacant and a successor to that office will be appointed by the governor as described.

It is interesting to note that the sunshine law does not apply to the Judicial Qualifications Commission. The findings and records of the commission, and even whether the judge has or has not been suspended, is not open to the public; nor is it admissible in evidence in any court for any purpose. No action shall be taken against a judge except after hearing and in accordance with due process of law. No removal or involuntary retirement shall occur except upon order of the Supreme Court after review. Any judge may be retired for disability which constitutes a serious and likely permanent interference with the performance of the duties of office.

District Attorneys

Another significant official in the legal system is the district attorney. A district attorney for each judicial circuit is elected for a term of four years. Vacancies are filled by appointment of the governor. The qualifications include having been an active-status member of the State Bar of Georgia for three years immediately preceding such person's election. The district attorneys receive such compensation and allowances as provided by law and like some judges may receive local supplements to their compensation and allowances.

It is the duty of the district attorney to represent the state in all criminal cases in their superior court and in all cases appealed from the superior court or the juvenile courts, and to perform such other duties as shall be required by law. District attorneys enjoy immunity from private suit for actions arising from the performance of their duties. Any district attorney may be disciplined, removed or involuntarily retired as provided by general law.

Transitional Notes

The City Court of Atlanta survived the constitutional revisions. Such municipal courts, county recorder's courts, and Civil Courts of Richmond and Bibb counties, and administrative agencies having quasi-judicial powers continued with the same jurisdiction as these courts and agencies had when the 1983 Constitution went into effect. Justice of the peace courts, small claims courts, and magistrate courts operating on the effective date of the new Constitution and the County Court of Echols County became magistrate courts. The County Court of Baldwin County and the County Court of Putnam County became state courts, with the same jurisdiction and powers as other state courts.

Conclusion

The structure and functioning of the state judiciary is unique. It is perhaps the most traditionalistic of the branches of government. The members of the legal profession are immersed in centuries of legal lore and tradition. To a great extent, the profession attempts to embody what Daniel Elazar calls the basic traditionalistic ethic: a political actor attempting to carry out a positive role in the community, but limited to securing the continued maintenance of the existing order. However, the members of the judiciary are not expected to benefit personally from their activity.

In time, the professional members of the public service, the career bureaucrats, can be expected to develop a similar high level of status and acceptance. However, the British judiciary existed for hundreds of years in a dependent relation with the British crown, before judges achieved constitutional independence in the Americas. If a similar amount of time is necessary for the public administrators to achieve equal status in their own fields, it is no wonder that bureaucrats have a long way to go to match the esteem given to the judicial branch of government in the State of Georgia.

FIGURE 8.1. Georgia Department of Revenue

8

Budgeting and Finance

Introduction

What does budgeting and economics have to do with state government? Isn't it true that government doesn't have to budget because it has unlimited income mainly from tax dollars? Actually, this myth about government could not be more wrong.

Every state government, including Georgia's, has a constitutional requirement to carefully budget its money. In fact, arguments over how to obtain budget money and how to spend it constitute the bulk of all political conflict. Politics can be defined as the struggle over who gets what, when and how (Lasswell), but most political battles take place over who pays what, where, how, why and when. The state's fiscal (budget) year runs from July 1 to June 30, and every day sees conflict over finances. This section begins with taxes.

State Taxes and Revenues

Like all the rest of us, states have to pay their bills. Unlike the United States Government, which does not separate operational budgets and capital budgets, all states, except Vermont, have to balance their operational budgets. An operational budget includes the expenses for ongoing routine operations. In contrast, a capital budget is used for expensive long-term building projects such as highway and bridge construction. While it is recognized that building projects may have to be funded by bonds and other debt creating instruments, state constitutions usually require that operational budgets must be paid for on an ongoing basis. That is, states can not spend more than they take in as revenue. Thus, they must have revenue sources that provide enough income for them to meet their needs and responsibilities each year. Because Georgia sells bonds to borrow money for capital projects, the state is in debt, like the other states, like the federal government, like most home owners; indeed, like most people. The total indebtedness of the State of Georgia in the fiscal year 1994 was over five billion dollars (W. Almanac 1997, 135). In fact, every Georgian owed over seven hundred dollars when per capita debt was taken into account. Some comparative fiscal statistics are presented in tables 8.1 and 8.2.

TABLE 8.1
Georgia 1994 Fiscal Statistics

Per capita debt:	$733
Per capita taxes	$1245
All Revenues:	$18,265,000,000
Expenditures:	$16,823,000,000
Indebtedness:	$ 5,174,000,000

Source: World Almanac, 1997.

TABLE 8.2
All States 1994 Fiscal Statistics

Per capita debt:	$1,582
Per capita taxes	$1,439
All Revenues:	$845,887,000,000
Expenditures:	$779,459,000,000
Indebtedness:	$410,998,000,000

Source: World Almanac, 1997.

Table 8.1 displays the sum totals of capital and operational budgets for the State of Georgia. In fiscal year 1994 the total revenues slightly exceeded expenditures, but most of the surplus was recycled into debt retirement and new capital projects. It should be noted that the entire debt is about one-third of annual revenues. The residents of Georgia have less than half of the debt burden of the average state, and only half of the per capita debt burden. The State of Georgia has low taxes and a sound fiscal structure.

The tax powers of the state are too valuable to be left only to the fads and fancies that buffet our politicians. Article VII of the Georgia Constitution deals with taxation and finance. It places the power to tax with the General Assembly, although that power may be delegated in part to local governments. Currently, the bulk of Georgia's revenue comes from three sources: ad valorem taxes, income taxes, and sales taxes.

Ad valorem is a latin term meaning "according to the worth." An ad valorem tax is a tax determined by the value of that which is taxed. Those of you who own cars know that you have to buy license tags for your car each year. In addition to a small license tag fee, which varies from county to county in

Georgia, you may be required to pay an ad valorem tax on the value of the automobile. If your car is an old 'junker', there may be no ad valorem tax assessed. If, on the other hand, it is a new or relatively new car, you may have to pay hundreds of dollars according to the value of your vehicle. Because of variations in local government tax levels, the amount that you pay can vary markedly from county to county. Ad valorem taxes on automobiles are among the most popularly detested levies in the nation. When the Republican candidate for Governor of Virginia came up with the idea of eliminating the ad valorem tax on automobiles in the Commonwealth, his candidacy took off, and he won the 1997 race going away. By 1998, a number of gubernatorial candidates in several states were proposing to follow Virginia Governor Gilmore's lead in running against this tax.

The county, acting as a subdivision of the state, also collects ad valorem taxes on tangible personal property and tangible real property. Tangible personal property includes all manner of possessions—jewelry, furs, boats, and even money itself. Tangible real property is real estate—land. Since land can not be moved or hidden, it is a stable source of revenue for the government. Over time, states have allowed local governments to assess the property tax and to keep the proceeds to defray their own expenses. Because land is used for a variety of purposes, and the purposes often determine its value, differently used property is taxed differently. For example, agricultural land is taxed at seventy-five percent (75%) of the value of other land, and the land on which you live is entitled to a homestead exemption, a reduction of the taxes you would otherwise pay.

Only nine states lack a state individual income tax. Georgia is not one of them. In Georgia the personal income tax is a very important source of revenue for the state. Based, at least in theory, on the ability to pay, the income tax is progressive, meaning that the more income you earn, the more tax you pay. If a tax is designed so that people with small incomes pay a smaller percentage, it is called a progressive tax. However, the progressive scale is somewhat flat, so that income exceeding $7,000 is taxed at a maximum rate of only 6.0%. Thus, a person earning over one million dollars a year would pay at the same rate as a person earning only $7,001.

Moreover, the Georgia state income tax system is linked to the federal government's Internal Revenue Code. In 1986, the federal government reduced the number of tax brackets to three: fifteen (15), twenty-eight (28), and thirty-three (33) percent.[1] But in 1993, Congress changed the 33% bracket to 31%, and added new brackets at 36% and 39.6%. Georgia has not yet revised its code, so that the linkage to the federal revenue code is somewhat confused and probably results in a loss of revenue for the state. Like the ad valorem tax, the income tax is also unpopular. Republicans in the 1998 Session of the General Assembly promised to try to repeal the income tax over a period of several years. However, they could not muster the necessary votes, partly because they couldn't figure out how to replace all that lost revenue. In addition to the individual income tax, Georgia, like forty-six other states, levies an additional income tax on corporate profits.

Similarly, like forty-five other states, Georgia has a sales tax. Although it is officially set at four percent, counties may add an extra one percent local option sales tax and an additional one percent special local option sales tax providing the latter is approved by the local citizens in a voting referendum. In 1996, voters approved an amendment to the Georgia Constitution permitting school districts to add another Special Local Option Sales Tax (SPLOST) if they could get a majority of the voters to agree to it. Agreement would allow one more penny to be added to the overall sales tax. Usage of the basic four percent sales tax and the one percent optional tax is fairly standard throughout the state; but the additional special one percent tax is earmarked for use only for special capital building projects—such as new courthouse, a new jail, road construction—and has an automatic "sunset" provision which acts to terminate the tax within five years or less of its approval. The same provisions apply to the school district SPLOST. With all these "piggy-back" sales taxes, many people in Georgia pay sales tax of seven percent.

It is common for progressive states to try to exempt from sales taxes certain necessities such as food, medicine and clothing so that sales taxes will be less burdensome on poor people. Although Governor Zell Miller recommended in 1990 that certain food items be exempted from the tax, and the Georgia legislature then passed laws to that effect, the wording of the law was subsequently challenged in court and the State Supreme Court invalidated the food exemption because the language was unclear and confusing. When the Governor and the General Assembly pass a tax or a revenue bill, the Supreme Court gets a shot at it, and of course eventually it can go full circle back to the legislature.

In 1996, the General Assembly again passed a law which exempted food from the sales tax and which would be fully effective by 1998. Thus food joins some 60 other sales tax exemptions in Georgia, including Bibles and the fuel used to heat chicken houses. In the 1998 Session of the General Assembly, bills were introduced to exempt from sales taxes Boy Scout popcorn, wheelchairs, children's caskets, cropdusting planes, grass sod, and about a dozen other things (Valdosta Daily Times, February 12, 1998, p. 3-A). Although its sponsor argued that the Boy Scout popcorn provision would only result in a loss of about $11,000 a year in revenue, and besides it was only fair since Girl Scout Cookies are exempt, all of these tax exemptions add up to a sizable amount. The exemption on food alone is estimated to cost the state treasury about half a billion dollars.

In addition to the major forms of taxes described above, Georgia also collects revenue from a variety of other types of taxes. These include the so-called 'sin' taxes on alcohol and tobacco products; severance taxes on lumber products taken from state owned lands; and motor fuels taxes on every gallon of gasoline sold in the state. The motor fuels tax revenues are then earmarked for building and maintaining the state's fine system of roads and highways.

Budgeting and Finance 107

FIGURE 8.2. Juggling the Budget.

In the 1980s many states joined a growing movement to derive some revenue from legalized gambling, but Georgia lawmakers at first resisted the temptation to establish a lottery or parimutuel betting on horse racing. The success of the lotteries in other states, however, put great pressure on Georgia legislators and in 1991 the General Assembly passed a bill placing a constitutional amendment for a state lottery on the November 1992 ballot, to allow the citizens to make their voices known on the issue. The voters spoke, and approved the budget amendment. In the first state budgetary period of operation, the proceeds from the lottery were over $879 million, including a surplus of income over expenditures of approximately $28 million in additional revenue for the state (Leg.Budg.Off.). This was a substantial vindication of the governor's plan. However, financial experts caution us not to rely too heavily on these funds, because as the novelty of the new lottery wears off, sales might decline, so that future income from this source may be less than hoped for. In fact, by 1998 there were signs that interest in the Georgia Lottery was indeed tapering off. However, by that time over 550 million dollars a year were going to education in Georgia.

Are Georgians overtaxed or undertaxed? That may sound like a silly question, for who ever feels that he or she is *under*taxed? Objectively, however, when Georgia is compared to other states, how does Georgia fare? In a recent year, per capita state and local tax revenue in Georgia was around $1,800, which placed Georgia 32nd among the states. And, when this per capita state and local revenue is examined as a percentage of personal income, Georgia ranked 37th. In other words, Georgia ranks below the median both in terms of the amount of taxes collected from the average person and according to the amount that each person could afford to pay (Dye, 508). Tax-paying Georgia citizens can be thankful that, comparatively, Georgia ranks as a rather low-tax state. By signing into law the $100 million dollar tax cut in 1994 and a $205 million dollar reduction in 1998, Governor Miller reduced the tax burden even further.

How about the distribution of the tax burden? Are Georgians fairly taxed according to income levels? Again, that might sound like a silly question, because no one ever thinks his or her own tax burden is fair. And the fact is that Georgia ranks twenty-seventh in the nation in terms of tax progressivity (Gray, 314–315). That means that Georgia is slightly less fair than the average in assessing taxes in proportion to ability to pay.

Does Georgia need tax reform? Many economists and political scientists argue that it does. Although a study of state tax systems in 1990 showed that Georgia's system is particularly elastic and therefore likely to be able to withstand fiscal crises, by the time the study was published Georgia, like the rest of the nation, was in fact beginning to experience growing fiscal crisis (Gold, 31–33). Owing to the increasing severity of the recession of the 1990s, personal income in Georgia was down, while personal misery was on the rise. With a decline in federal grants in aid to the states, a decline in state revenue collections, and an increase in necessary operating expenditures, Georgia, like the rest of the states, was in serious fiscal trouble. To be sure, other states were suffering worse, but the knowledge of that did not ease our pain very much. Editorials in major newspapers like the *Atlanta Journal/Constitution* and other influential voices around the Peach State raised the cry for meaningful fiscal and tax reform.

Another suggestion for reforming Georgia's tax system is to tax services along with the sale of commodities. In an economy more and more dependent on services, it makes sense to tax car washing, dry cleaning, haircuts, lawyer's fees, dentist's fees, etc. Moreover, since those with higher incomes tend to spend more of their money on services than those with lower incomes, a tax on services would be more progressive than sales taxes on commodities. Whether the general Assembly will seriously consider tax revision, especially if it entails new taxes, depends largely on whether the state experiences another fiscal crisis.

As noted above, in 1994 and 1998 the General Assembly, at the urging of Governor Miller, "gave back", respectively, $100 million and $205 million dollars to Georgians in the form of tax relief. Georgia could do this because the state's revenues were surging, partly as a result of significant economic recovery and partly as a result of the success of the lottery. In introducing the 1994 tax cut Miller announced:

In the old days, under the old ways, an increase in state revenues would have been treated as feeding time on the hog farm. I am giving this money back to the hard working families and senior citizens of Georgia (Miller, Feb.24, 1994).

One "solution" that the state has to fall back on when confronted with budgetary shortfalls is raising user fees or by borrowing. The instrument by which debt is incurred is called a bond. When the state sells bonds, with a promise to buy them back with interest, it borrows money. Bonds may be either general obligation bonds or revenue bonds. A general obligation bond in a sense creates a lien on all the taxpayers of the state, since the guarantee of repayment to the buyers is placed on the "full faith and credit" of the state. This means that future tax revenues will be used to retire the bonds when they come due. A revenue bond, on the other hand, is retired with the revenues from particular money-making enterprises: e.g. tolls from bridges, fees from water and sewer systems, profits from education loans. Should those revenues fall short, however, the investors would be in danger of diminished or no returns, or even losing their investment entirely. For that reason, revenue bonds are riskier than general obligation bonds and must offer higher interest rates to capture investment capital. Allowable reasons for state debt are depicted in Table 8.3.

TABLE 8.3
Allowable State Indebtedness

1. Public debt without limit to repel invasion, suppress insurrection, and defend the state in time of war.
2. Public debt to cover for a temporary deficit in the state treasury in any fiscal year created by a delay in collecting the taxes of that year.
3. General obligation debt for:
    a) capital budgets to acquire and develop land, waters, highways, buildings, or facilities of the state and its agencies and authorities.
    b) educational facilities for school systems and public libraries.
    c) loans to political subdivisions, and local authorities, for water or sewerage facilities.
4. Guaranteed revenue debt obligations issued by an instrumentality of the state for:
    a) toll bridges or toll roads,
    b) land public transportation facilities,
    c) water facilities or systems,
    d) sewage facilities or systems,
    e) loan programs for citizens for education

Source: Compiled by authors.

Article VII, Section IV of the Georgia Constitution addresses the matter of state debt. Paragraph I of that section contains a list of six purposes for which the state may incur debt. The purposes include crisis events, like debt to repel invasion, for suppression of insurrection; and more routine problems such as temporary cash flow shortages or problems financing local governments or special projects.

The ability of a state to sell bonds to investors depends largely on a state's bond rating. The higher a state's rating, the more attractive its bonds are on the bond market. The two principal bond rating agencies are Moody's and Standard and Poor's. Moody's gives Georgia its highest rating (Aaa), while Standard and Poor's put Georgia in its second highest rating category (AA+) (AJ/AC, Jan.13,1994).

Georgia State Budget

In 1998, the General Assembly responded to Governor Miller's continuing state development plans (originally labeled *Georgia Rebound*) and passed a twelve and a half billion dollar budget. In actual numbers, the budget passed by the General Assembly added up to $12,528,603,880 (HB 1250). This budget included over $530 million dollars in revenue from the lottery, dedicated to education, and this level of lottery income will, one hopes, be a constant revenue source for the foreseeable future.

By far the largest single expenditure goes to school districts for general secondary education, almost five billion dollars. About three billion dollars each is also spent for basic human resources and for health care which is becoming more expensive each year. Two billion dollars was appropriated for higher education: universities, colleges, technical training and adult education. And despite a slight reduction in crime levels, public safety and protection costs well over a billion dollars also. Roughly half a billion dollars is spent for capital construction projects, and for transportation construction and repairs. The remaining monies are spent for a wide variety of miscellaneous activities, like economic development, agricultural programs, and for purchasing land to preserve environmental resources. The following tables display a breakdown of the state budget that was passed by the 1998 session of the Georgia General Assembly.

Arguing over the distribution of government revenues in Georgia is as American as apple pie. Public school education gets the biggest slice of the pie in Georgia, well over one-third. Large pieces go to health care, human resources and to higher education. Smaller pieces go to prisons and to roadway and other heavy construction projects. A large portion of the budget goes to miscellaneous projects within departmental agencies. These slices of pie are shown on the following figure.

TABLE 8.4
1998 Legislative Appropriations

Program Areas	Appropriations	Percentages
Education*	$ 4,969,052,637	39.6%
Human Development	2,868,598,744	22.9
Higher Education	1,876,483,516	14.9
Public Protection	1,171,942,690	9.4
Transportation	564,751,771	4.5
Debt Service	412,050,710	3.3
General Administration	397,868,992	3.2
Natural Resources	135,240,259	1.1
Economic Development	132,614,561	1.1
Sub-totals	$12,528,603,880	100.0%

*Figures include money from lottery revenues.

Source: *Comparative Summary of H.B.1250,* 1998.

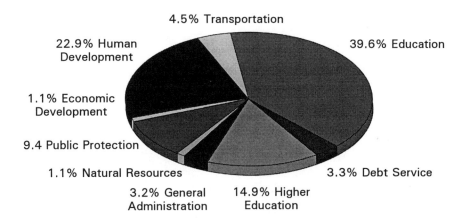

FIGURE 8.3. Dividing the 1998 State Budget Pie
Source: Courtesy of State Budget Office, *Comparative Summary of H.B. 1250,* 1998.

Educational Expenditures

The principal responsibility of most state governments is public education, and Georgia is no exception. In fact, Georgia devotes more than half of its entire budget each year to primary, secondary, and higher education. This educational turf is divided between two major bureaucracies: the State Board of Education and the State Board of Regents. The great bulk of the state appropriations is allotted to the secondary and grade school institutions, almost four billion dollars ($3,819,767,157), most of which is supervised primarily by the State Board of Education. Overall responsibility for administering Georgia's system of primary and secondary education rests with the State Board of Education. It makes policy for the state education systems, sets standards for teacher education programs, certifies teachers, establishes minimal salary levels, imposes graduation requirements, etc. Its members represent each of the congressional districts and are appointed by the governor and confirmed by the state senate. Members of the State Board of Education serve for seven year terms. As discussed in chapter three, the State School Superintendent is the chief executive officer of the State Board of Education, but local school district Superintendents actually control the schools' operations and budgets.

Local Government Expenditures

In 1996 the City of Atlanta played host to the International Olympic Games. The construction projects involved, but more importantly the increased global image of Atlanta (and Georgia) as an international economic player, were worth billions of dollars in trade and tourism in the future. To help the economy, the State of Georgia granted a charter to a special purpose entity named the Metropolitan Atlanta Olympic Games Authority, (MAOGA). Following the lead of Los Angeles, MAOGA was determined to support the Games by private financing and donations, without direct substantial governmental subsidies. The bulk of revenues will come from selling television rights, corporate sponsorships, ticket sales and merchandise proceeds; but of course some governmental support was necessary, even if it was only utility hook-ups and public safety protection.

Such governmental support was offered by county and city entities. For example, the Atlantic City Council elects a number of its members as board members of special purpose government authorities, and MAOGA is no exception to the rule. The city also worked closely with the Atlanta Committee for the Olympic Games (ACOG), a private sponsor. One measure of city participation in the Olympic effort was its support of negotiations between ACOG and the Atlanta Braves organization. The ACOG proposed to build a new stadium in downtown Atlanta, and then to lease it to the Braves for 20 years; but the

Braves demanded that the city agree to maintain the facility for the duration of the contract. Faced with a threat to move the team from the downtown area if the new stadium deal was not approved, the city agreed, but only after the Braves' organization agreed to sweeten the pot with annual maintenance payments totaling about four million dollars during the course of the contract (Blackmon, H4). After this effort, similar talks began with the Fulton County Commission, another player in this complex issue.

Although city governments are mere creatures of the state, and are almost certain to lose in any power contests with the state or federal governments, they can at least take symbolic actions against what they perceive to be unfair laws or practices. For example, Atlanta's city council passed a resolution declaring October 27th to be *"Unfunded Mandates Day"* (Banks, 7) as part of a highly visible effort to complain about the state and federal governments' tendency to enact laws requiring cities to provide services without providing financial resources to compensate the city for the new strains on its budget. State and local government budgets, like their policy areas, are closely intertwined and interdependent.

TABLE 8.5
Atlanta General Fund Budget: 1993

Department	Amount	Percent
Police	$88,228,670	23.7%
Fire	43,851,302	11.7
Public Works	55,161,707	14.8
Administration	41,484,008	11.7
Parks & Recreation	20,441,395	5.5
Education Support	15,518,927	4.2
Non-Departmental	75,490,374	20.3
Other Public Safety	26,979,636	7.2
Council Management	3,193,968	0.9
Totals:	375,760,947	100.0

Source: Atlanta City Council, *1992 Annual Report* page 9.

As we saw in an earlier chapter, while the entire budget of the city of Atlanta was about a billion and a half dollars back in 1992, the basic general revenues of the city were about three hundred and thirty million dollars ($331,246,387), and the basic general operating budget in 1993 cost about $375,760,947; not counting major capital projects and airport budgets. The city revenues are not as extensive as they would like, and certainly not as large as the state government's revenues.

State Income Sources

Investigation of any subject, issue, or concern in government almost always leads discussants to the subject of money; how much is needed against how much is available. Georgia is no exception to this generalization. It should not be forgotten that there are over 1320 local governments in Georgia. As explained in the next chapter, each of these local governments operative in Georgia is a taxing entity, funding and serving the variety of needs of the state's socio-economically diversified citizenry. Some of their money is locally raised and spent, but much of it comes from Georgia State Revenues.

State Income Sources and Budget

Income in the State of Georgia, known as revenue, is derived from a variety of sources. Included in income sources are the two largest: income taxes and sales taxes. Actual revenues for the year 1997 totaled $10,543,106,460 (Leg.Bud.Off.). Personal income tax receipts accounted for the singularly largest source of income, about $4,754,777,319; and sales taxes for that same year generated revenues of $4,067,195,405. Of the other revenue sources the corporate income tax brought in $706,912,315; motor fuels tax brought in $416,895,526 and various fees and sales brought in the remainder of the revenues. These included such taxes as motor vehicle licenses, the so-called "sin taxes" on alcoholic beverages and tobacco, and property taxes.

The lottery, passed by the voters as a constitutional amendment, has proven to be a phenomenal success, although it appears to be losing a bit of its luster. Nonetheless, it will be generating expected revenues, for 1998, from the Georgia Lottery Corporation of about $530,000,000 dollars (HB 1250). Faced with such figures, even the most diehard opponents of the lottery plan are throwing in the towel. One writer said: *"accept it for what it is, . . . a voluntary, flat rate tax of 37% on every dollar spent on the lottery"* (Wooten, F7). That is pretty good for a "sin tax", in fact it is a heavier tax than state governments impose on any other "bad habit". This is a also big economic boom for the state treasury, and is likely to remain so, at least until all the other states adopt a similar lottery. While Georgia generally commits the money to educational purposes, some experts believe it would be wiser to shift the money into the general fund, or for special one-time projects (Wooten, F7). But however you cut the pie, it looks as though it is here to stay.

When the sales tax was enacted in Georgia, a very small tax was applied to most purchased goods, initially excluding services. Today, the early low sales tax has risen to more than four percent, and as a result the state's lowest and middle income citizens pay higher percents of their income into the state's coffers. This **"regressive tax"** (harder on poor people) has, however, become so critical to Georgia's budget that it is not anticipated that any substantial change will take place in the near future.

Income to the state from federal sources is substantial in Georgia, but because of the traditional reluctance of our citizens to accept the strings attached to federal money, (and the penalty of increased federal control of state interests), the income from such sources is not as much as it might be. In fact, the State of Georgia receives among the lowest per capita (37th) for federal funding from grants in the entire United States.

TABLE 8.6
Georgia—1997 Budget Revenues

General Tax Revenues	
Income Tax (Individual)	4,754,777,319
Sales Tax—(Gen.) — —	4,067,195,404
Income Tax (Corporation)	706,912,315
Motor Fuel Tax — — —	416,895,526
Motor Vehicle Fees — —	203,187,693
Alcohol (all) — — —	127,253,059
Property & Estate — —	98,453,599
Tobacco Revenues — — —	84,737,805
Misc — — — — — — — —	83,694,738
Total Revenue Budget:	10,543,106,460

Source: Courtesy of State Revenue Department, *Statistical Report: FY 1999* (Atlanta, 1997)

The means of management of the State's budget is established in the State's constitution which prohibits borrowing money for each year's current operating budget. All state operations are, therefore, on a pay-as-you-go system.

Although the State does meet its constitutional limits in spending, each biennial session of the legislature, as well as the increasingly frequent special sessions, must engage in constant juggling of funds to balance the budget. The pie chart presented shows the origin of state revenues.

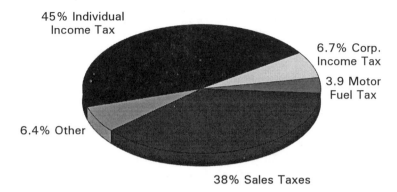

FIGURE 8.4. Origin of States Revenues
Source: Courtesy of State Budget Office, *Budget Report: Fiscal Year 1995.*

One reform often suggested to control over-inflated budgets is the exercise of the Governor's line item veto power. Governor Miller has used this power on several celebrated occasions, against the secret legislative educational slush fund (Lauth & Reese, 15-16) and as well as an indigent legal services fund and a provision involving excess federal funds (Ibid, 16). But a recent study has shown that this may be an over-rated power. As the researchers indicated:

> The line-item veto is used in Georgia as an instrument for resolving inter-branch difference on appropriations bills, but it is not a[n] instrument of partisanship, and it is not primarily an instrument of fiscal restraint (Lauth & Reese, 21).

Budgetary Increases

The sources of state revenues change over time, and so do the expenditures. Within the last 10 years, new challenges and demands for increased expenditures on various functions have occurred frequently. Particularly, the issue of expenditures on education have created political, as well as economic and legal, havoc within the State. On the other hand, as primary expenditures of the state's budget has been on education, other functions of the state's government have been the recipients of too few expenditures, also creating very real immediate problems—prison and correctional facilities shortages—and in the near future there is sure to be increased need for expanded expenditures on health concerns—particularly with increasing attention and demand for service to AIDS victims. But in general, the State of Georgia has low taxes and a sound fiscal structure.

Conclusion

Each year, billions of dollars are spent by the Georgia State Government and its agencies for general secondary education, and additional billions spent for human resources, health care programs and for higher education. Law enforcement, corrections, capital construction projects, and transportation programs cost hundreds of thousands of dollars, and more money is spent for a wide variety of miscellaneous activities like purchasing land and for preserving environmental resources.

Budgetary politics is often a fierce struggle over who gets what, and who pays. But in general the people of Georgia have enacted a Constitution that creates a complex array of checks and balances to ensure that the powers of the state are used effectively to benefit the health and well-being of all the citizens.

FIGURE 9.1. Children at Play

9

State Education Policy

As we shall see in the next chapter, local government has a lot in common with educational institutions in the State of Georgia. The local school and college institutions have the power to tax and levy fees for services, to hire personnel, to make regulations and rules, to maintain public safety, and they all have the power to compel obedience. But it is common to think that they also have a higher mission, an idealistic duty to educate our children and to help society to continue to improve over time. And of course education and local government have another thing in common: both are arenas of political conflict. In this chapter we will review the major educational institutions, their structures, their goals and policies, and their finances.

State Educational Structure

Public education is a principal responsibility of most state governments, and Georgia is no exception to the rule. In fact, Georgia devotes more than half of its entire budget each year to primary, secondary, and higher education. In 1998 the Georgia General Assembly took this responsibility seriously enough to budget over six and a half billion dollars ($ 6,500,000,000) to funding all levels of education in the state. Traditionally, a distinction is made between the public schools offering of kindergarten through twelfth grade, and the higher educational, or college institutions. This division is reflected in two major bureaucracies: the State Board of Education and the State Board of Regents. The increasing high levels of state appropriations to these two types of institutions reflects a commitment to providing a sound educational system for Georgia's students.

Overall responsibility for administering Georgia's system of primary and secondary education rests with the State Board of Education. It makes policy for the state education systems, sets standards for teacher education programs, certifies teachers, establishes minimal salary levels, imposes graduation requirements, etc. Its members represent each of the congressional districts and are appointed by the governor and confirmed by the state senate. Members of the State Board of Education serve for seven year terms. As discussed in chapter five, the State School Superintendent is the chief executive officer of the State

Board of Education, but local school district Superintendents actually control the schools' operations.

In addition to the basic educational system, Georgia has over a hundred college and university campuses. A large number of college students attend the extensive system of public colleges and universities. There are 34 public institutions of higher learning in the state, divided into four tiers: research universities, regional universities, four-year colleges, and two-year colleges. Governance of the University System of Georgia is the responsibility of the State's Board of Regents.

Local School Districts

Each of Georgia's 159 counties maintains a separate school system, and 28 of the larger cities have independent school systems. The Georgia Constitution provides for separate Boards of Education to manage and control each of these many school systems and allows them to be either elected or appointed, as a local option. Most of the Boards of Education in Georgia are elected. Administration of school policy in each district is the responsibility of the state's Department of Education, the local School Boards, and their local school superintendent, who may be elected by voters in the district or appointed by the local Board. Primary education is big business in Georgia, absorbing almost five billion dollars in state funds and perhaps as much more in local funds.

In the early 1980s, the national government's publication of *A Nation at Risk—The Imperative for Educational Reform,* brought to light problems with proliferation of school districts, the amount and quality of their control and direction of the educational process, finally resulting in extensive reform of States' educational systems. By the late 1980s, challenges to funding reforms became the focus, particularly when it became apparent that the almost decade old reforms of educational quality associated with teachers and students had produced little success—testing of students revealed that many students were still performing well below the national average.

School districts are the single most common type of special purpose district government in Georgia. School Districts, both county based and independent, or special combinations of the two, don't have to seek special permission from the state for every little thing they do, but they are constrained by their mission requirements and responsibilities, by the state constitution, state statutes and the state Department of Education. Some of these responsibilities are outlined on Table 9.1.

TABLE 9.1
School Responsibilities

1. Prepare children to join society.
2. Teach them the basic skills, the three r's.
3. Acquaint them with their historical heritage.
4. Strengthen their sense of morality.
5. Strengthen their interpersonal skills.
6. Ensure that they have a sense of self worth.
7. Promote a sense of national patriotism.
8. Prepare them for a job or a career.
9. Give them guidance and counseling.
10. Strengthen their bodies as well as their minds.
11. Libraries, and arts and sciences facilities.
12. Provide trained and dedicated teachers.
13. Train them to meet the new global challenges.
14. Prepare them for a changing future.

Source: Compiled by authors.

Funding for these basic elementary services is primarily derived from state formula funds, local option property taxes on residents' habitations and other privately owned lands and on businesses and from sales taxes and bond revenues. Generally, it is the locally elected School Boards and their professional staffs who are responsible for overseeing daily operations of local school budgets, and the Boards set appropriate tax rates for property in the district (within state constitutional limits).

Though parents and voters may not be familiar with every narrow aspect of the children's education, they are always aware of the level of taxation in the community, quick to fault any doubtful expenditures, and generally familiar with where responsibility rests; in the hands of the Board of Education. And at the local school district level, both blame and credit is quickly assessed and acted upon in the voting booth. Community satisfaction with budgetary and teaching policy is reflected in re-election; while failure in either area is usually reflected in community unrest and by voter election of a new school board at the first opportunity.

Of course, in Georgia, school districts are also closely accountable to state agencies. Like other local governments and special districts, school districts have no independent sovereignty, no right to exist independent of the authority and approval of the state government. In Georgia, the state Department of Education reviews local school districts to make sure that they comply with the requirements of the state constitution.

A century ago many school districts were run directly by city officials, but sometimes politics got in the way of education. For example, in the City of Chicago, with a strong mayor system of government, the mayor directly appointed the school teachers. Unfortunately, usually political supporters got the jobs because of their loyalty to political parties, and not because of their skills. In short patronage, and not merit or ability, determined who was hired as teachers. And in Chicago, with a large ethnic immigrant population, this often meant that the teachers often could not readily read or write English, it even meant that they sometimes could barely even speak the language, let alone teach it effectively to the students.

The average local school board meets once or twice a month. Citizens and parents are invited to attend the sessions and to bring complaints and issues to the board meetings. Board members often work on committees, such as textbooks, curriculum, facilities, personnel and budgeting. They review proposals and recommend policy to the board. But always the local citizens, and particularly the parents of the school children, are keenly sensitive to the costs of education and are anxious to make sure that they retain control over their schools, the teachers that are hired, and the skills, lessons and attitudes that are inculcated. And since every community has differences of opinion over what should be taught, and how it should be taught and by whom, it is not uncommon to find people filing law suits to get their way if they find themselves outvoted at the local level. With billions of dollars at stake, and their children's future at risk, it is little wonder that passions over educational policies sometimes boil over into the political arena.

Much of the state funding for the primary and secondary levels of education is appropriated in the form of Quality Basic Education (QBE) funds. In 1998 the General Assembly approved 1.17 billion dollars to the Kindergarten through third grade levels; another 987 millions dollars to grades four through eight; and about 410 million dollars to grades nine through twelve. It is basically the job of the local community to raise more money to supplement the state funding, which may require taxation for operational costs and bond issues for capital expenditures (new classrooms). For society as a whole, and certainly for the parents of school age youngsters, this system of free public education is a good deal; but there are also some who feel as though they are being taxed too heavily, and who may try to challenge the policy.

Usually school districts in Georgia try to downplay the politics as much as possible and try to focus on providing good educations for the children. Usually this is done by hiring a highly trained professional education manager, the Superintendent. In this type of system, the organization chart is very similar to the Council/manager form of local government, but the influence of the professional manager, the Superintendent of Schools, is very closely related to the strength of their educational credentials, and usually a doctorate in educational

FIGURE 9.2. Educational Burden

administration is required. While an outstanding superintendent might seek to influence the board with their personal charisma, it is more likely to be their expertise in education, personnel management and budgeting powers that determine their degree of success on the job. However, the superintendent does not make basic educational policy but only implements policies adopted by the board members.

Educational systems, like all bureaucracies, have a hierarchical structure. All hierarchies are identifiable from top to bottom, with decreasing control evident at the bottom of the chart. For instance, if one reviews a power chart of the school system in the following graph, it is apparent that assigned power exists at the top of the hierarchy, while the least power in the system is associated with those at the bottom, the teaching faculty and the students.

The hierarchical **"flow chart"** of the educational bureaucracy reveals that there are many levels of bureaucracies, but the main ones are the state level officials, particularly the eleven member State Board of Education and its independently elected State School Superintendent, and the almost two hundred locally elected School Boards. Each of these has thousands of career specialists who function as administrative, technical or line level bureaucrats.

Candidates for local school district boards are presumed to have appropriate abilities, skills and interests to convince the voters that they will represent their interests. Of course, professionally trained Superintendents often have major impact on who will run for the positions on school boards. In theory, the voters constitute the clientele of the educational bureaucracy. Although displayed on the chart as a unitary entity, the voters are of course really a disparate collection of pressure groups, all with independent and often contradictory goals.

124 Chapter Nine

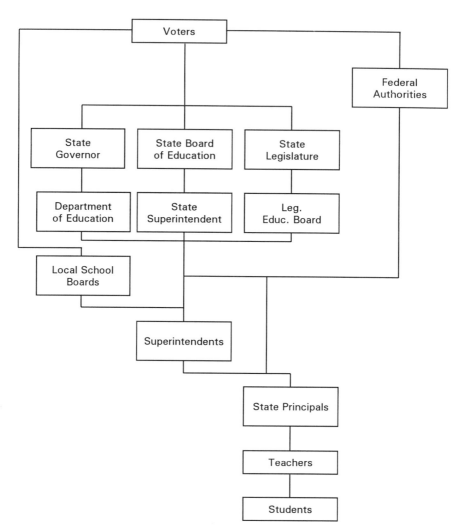

FIGURE 9.3. Educational Bureaucracies

Sources of Funds for School Districts

The vast majority of educational funds in Georgia are received from taxes, local property and sales taxes, local bonds and state general revenue taxes. The State of Georgia limits the amount of property taxes the city can adopt. Sometimes, parents may support increased requests for federal funding in the form of "grants." However, other participants in the school's governance may be reluctant to do so, because the federal money may have strings attached to them that do not fit the goals and values of the local community. Grants for such things as demonstration projects in sex education are a prime example. School districts are less likely to object to state grants, however, because there is usually more compatibility of values at the local and state levels. Georgia's use of lottery funds to put computers in classrooms, for example, is a popular program at the local level. Unfortunately, there are often funding disparities between and within school districts, so that some schools have more money than others. When this is because parents donate money to their children schools comparatively little attention is paid; but when public sector funds are not fairly distributed you can be sure that it will become a major political dispute.

Inner-city schools, especially in the Atlanta metropolitan area, are often the subject of discussion, research, and special funding requests. Though often receiving special attention and funds, these inner-city schools tend to deteriorate rapidly, because of the large numbers of pupils they try to serve. And since sometimes poverty stricken families reside there, and as more and more wealthy people move to the suburbs, this weakens the revenue bases of the schools. In 1998, the state attempted to balance out the differences with additional funds, such as $800 million under the Fair Share program; another $204 million under the basic Equalization Formula; and $210 million for pre-kindergarten programs.

Higher Education in Georgia

The State of Georgia devotes more than half of its entire state budget each year to educational programs, including primary, secondary, and higher educational efforts. In the last legislative session, the Georgia General Assembly voted to appropriate almost two billion dollars for post-secondary education, or higher education, in the state. Traditionally, a distinction is made between the colleges and universities, and the technical colleges and adult education training facilities. The higher levels of education are administered by the State Board of Regents, and there is little formal local community control, or local funding from the area. Instead of a local board, there is usually an institutional college President, often assisted by a faculty senate on campus. Political administration of

Georgia's system of higher education rests with the State Board of Regents, and by the system Chancellor, hired by the Regents. The Regents make policy for the state's academic institutions, set standards for faculty, establish salary levels, impose graduation requirements, etc. Its members are appointed by the governor and confirmed by the state senate.

The Regents, in turn, select the Chancellor of the System, usually conducting a nationwide search to find a good professional educator. An effective administrator is needed, because Georgia has over a hundred college and university campuses. Hundreds of thousands of students attend the extensive system of public colleges and universities, studying a wide variety of subjects and academic disciplines. There are 34 public institutions of higher learning in the state, divided into four basic tiers: research universities, regional universities, four-year institutions, and two-year colleges. Georgia has a unified system of higher education, with a common core curriculum, a well designed college system will have specialized programs on each campus.

Colleges and Universities are vital to healthy economic growth, particularly in these times of global competition. Georgia has been putting large sums of money into higher education in the last decade. Under the guidance of Chancellor Stephen R. Portch, and with funding made available because of the Georgia lottery, the state legislature has provided not only adequate operations funding, but also supported a multi-million dollar expansion and renovation campaign. In addition the state has adopted Governor Miller's Hope Scholarship Program, which basically pays the college tuition of any Georgia student who maintains a "B" or better grade point average. This program, linked to his original Georgia Rebound initiative, has allowed the state to also create a solid educational grant and loan program, expected to expand as lottery revenues increase, which ensures that every student can pursue their educational dreams and be able to compete in the emerging global marketplace.

Insulated from political pressures and partisan bickering, the Board of Regents acts as trustee of Georgia's 34 public colleges and universities, with a one and a half billion dollar budget and a student population of over 200,000. The system Chancellor is continuing to exhibit the kind of strong leadership Georgia enjoyed in the past, while working with a close knit Board of Regents mostly appointed by the two-term Governor, Zell Miller. Under this group, the number of institutions designated as universities has increased. However, the Governor has come under some criticism for appointing business and political elites to the board, movers and shakers (often contributors to his campaigns), and predominantly white males (Vickers, Robert J., C11). These appointments can be tricky business, for although political pressures years ago led to the creation of special insulation against political tampering with the university system, politics of course continues to play a role in educational policy and administration.

Among Georgia state agencies, the Board of Regents is unique because its budget is not presented on line-item budgets. As discussed in an earlier chapter, after the Talmadge Administration tried to manipulate the university system for partisan advantages, the Constitution was rewritten to require the General Assembly to appropriate monies to the Board of Regents in a lump sum, to be used as the Board of Regents deems proper. The subtle disciplinary characteristics and features of higher education require special insulation from partisan politics. Thus, once money is appropriated, the system of higher education is generally placed out of the budgetary reach of both the executive and the legislative branches.

Educational Policy

Educational policy in Georgia continues to evolve, while searching for a way to improve the skills and score levels of the state's students. One reform effort, the state's Quality Basic Education program (QBE) was attacked in 1994 after eight years in operation because it allegedly failed to significantly improve student achievement levels (Zanardi, 1). However, encumbered state QBE monies are still be available to local school districts for various initiatives to improve education services, billions of dollars in the 1998 budget. The Board of Education also decided to phase out the high school *'general diploma'* in favor of more rigorous programs in vocational education and college preparatory tracks. Until Georgia students educational indicators improve, such as competency ratings and higher SAT scores, educational policy will continue in flux.

Few ideas about how to improve American education have generated as much controversy and struggle as public financial aid to private and religious education. America was founded in large part by refugees from religious wars, who determined to defuse the potential for strife by separating the powers and finances of church and state. But today, as the average quality of public education falls below acceptable levels, particularly with regard to the technical skills so vital in an era of global competition, attacks on the public school system are mounting. The poor showing of students' test scores is probably attributable to several factors, such as open enrollment, grade inflation, poor discipline and the decline of the traditional family in the post-industrial era. Among the reformers, some persons would like to create an educational marketplace, in which private and religious schools would be eligible to receive public funds in the form of certificates or *"portable vouchers"* for students (Delk, F2). Religious leaders, such as Atlanta's Roman Catholic archbishop, John F. Donoghue, are urging priests to become involved in the campaign, said Glenn Delk, a supporter of the plan (FTU, 10–19–93, at B3).

Since the founding of the public school system, erosion of the so-called *"wall of separation"* between church and state has been slow and steady. While there are no public calls as yet for mandatory religious taxes, many supporters of *"school choice"* see a window of opportunity to gain publicly financed support of private institutions. Some supporters claim that test scores in private institutions are higher; but critics attribute some of that to *"creaming"* because the public schools have to admit all who apply, while private institutions can deny admission and services to persons at their discretion. The cost of supporting private institutions through vouchers would require a tax boost of between three to seven percent according to House Speaker Tom Murphy (A.Press, 11-15-93, 1); a cost of perhaps two billion dollars. A bill to do just this was introduced in the 1994 legislative session, in the form of a proposed constitutional amendment, but it failed to gain support and was not acted upon.

School boards serve to set policies such as property tax rates for their districts (under state limits); and to choose textbooks; to make capital improvement proposals; and a host of other decisions—but perhaps the most important work of the boards is the hiring of a professionally trained Superintendent who will implement the board's educational policies. Skilled professionals, focused on the technical and educational aspects of their jobs, are less likely to be imbued with outlandish ideas and political partisanship.

Educational Morality

Plato said that those in charge of a city must—see that education is not corrupted without their noticing it. If a school graduates many people with High School Diplomas who cannot read or write, then they are not doing their jobs. Who is in charge of our educational policy? State level participants include the Legislators who are members of educational oversight committees in the General Assembly, members of the Board of Regents and its staff, members of the Department of Education and its staff, the Governor's appointed officials in the Department of Education, and occasionally members of the judiciary, who hear policy disputes in their courtrooms. The Legislative Education Board and many individual committees are responsible for reviewing all aspects of educational policies and finances, including reactions to policy initiatives introduced by other participants.

At the local secondary level, influential persons associated with policy formation and implementation in the education system are primarily the various locally elected Boards of Education, the administrators hired by them and the professional faculty of the technical schools and colleges and the universities. These experts serve with the explicit responsibility for carrying out policies established by these boards and implicitly with the policy mandates of more distant representatives of the public's wishes, such as state agency personnel, the state school superintendent and the members of the general assembly. The Superintendents of the school districts, school principals, and finally the professional faculty members of the schools implement the lowest level of policy, line level interaction with the students. The professional administrative and bureaucratic levels, which are not elected, may actually hold major power over the public bodies nominally responsible for making policy, because they inform their respective elected bodies of the direction local policies should take. In addition, the faculty and teachers themselves, sometimes individually, and sometimes through their representatives, such as the Georgia Educational Association, often effect educational policy as well.

The educational establishment is the largest bureaucracy in the state, as it is in many states, and examining the successes and failures inherent to the system may clarify general understanding of bureaucracies throughout the state. Candidates for local independent school districts are also presumed to have such abilities, skills and interests as are needed for them to be selected by the voters to represent their interests. An English philosopher and legislative leader, Edmund Burke, described two fundamental types of representatives, the delegate, faithfully executing the desires of constituents; and the trustee, who uses personal wisdom on the behalf of constituents if for some reason they are unaware of their own best interests. Thus, the primary factor in the success in this hierarchical model is the voters, and one hopes their responsible selection of those who will make policy for the educational bureaucracy. When the voters are informed of the facts and sensitive to their own best interests, and act responsibly on that knowledge, this is an ideal system. All we need to do then is to allow voters to select good delegates as their representatives on local school boards, and they will provide the professional educators with local community input on value preferences. But whenever these professionals raise questions of expertise and superior judgment that runs counter to local culture, the political hackles of the school board and the general public are certain to rise.

One significant effort in schools today is increasing the awareness of the controversies surrounding alcohol and drug abuse. Community values have changed a lot over the years. While perhaps in rural pioneering days it was necessary for individuals to be able to self-administer herbal home remedies for illnesses and wounds (alcohol, opium, tobacco and herbs were used both for treatment and as pain killers), it was tolerated only because there were no professional medical facilities available; but that is certainly not true today. And when in the past these substances were abused, although it may have offended citizens to see other people losing control over their bodies and minds, no one was likely to be harmed by their foolish excesses. But today it is *not* funny to see a drunk behind the wheel of a two thousand pound automobile, especially when they begin careening over a double yellow line on a modern roadway.

Today, we all live in an interdependent society, and are extremely vulnerable to the shortcomings of our fellow travelers on life's road. Society no longer allows ordinary people to treat themselves, good quality health is usually available to use who need it. Physicians can now be trained to administer whatever medicines are necessary, and one by one the foods and substances traditionally available to us for self-treatment, pleasure and escape are being closely regulated and outlawed. Education on the problems of drug abuse and the reasons for curtailing the freedoms of the pioneering past is a vital necessity in the modern school. While additional school funding for all problems may not have kept pace with need, drug abuse programs have been well funded.

Another problem today is discipline in the classroom. Teachers have to discipline their students to sit and listen so that they can learn the subjects; otherwise youthful values and energy will prevent learning from occurring. But in too many schools student discipline is all but nonexistent. The teacher's cane is gone, students are not disciplined or respectful, instead they often assault the teachers. This is horribly wrong, and it is not too strong to call it a perversion of the educational system. Public school teachers today are not allowed to discipline students; those who try to do so are likely to be fired and blackballed from the profession.

Perhaps one of the major reasons for modern day difficulties of the educational system is the profound change in families. The developing child needs love, caring, a secure home environment and firm discipline and guidance. But as rural lifestyles have faded away, and as the population has flocked to the anonymity of the cities, traditional living patterns are disappearing. Without agriculture's need for basic manual labor pools and its close intense personal scrutiny, and with society's increasing need to fully utilize its intelligent human resources, more women are able to reject domestic roles. Almost half of modern marriages now end in divorce, and perhaps a million children every year undergo the trauma of watching their parents split up. The job demands and opportunities of the modern world have encouraged nothing less than rebellion against the traditional patriarchal culture, and individual interests and career goals have placed children in a secondary and precarious position. Marriages and commitment are seen as interfering with lifestyles of pleasure and convenience, with divorces and fatherless homes likely to be viewed as temporary and unimportant. Too often the schools are expected to take the place of the traditional family, particularly in the inculcation of values and morality.

We need stricter enforcement of child support orders, income tax credits for families with children, good affordable child care facilities, more flexible schools. But even more important is the need for parents to assume responsibility to keep marriages together, to sacrifice, if need be, such individual goals as ego-gratification, career advancement and independence for the sake of the children they choose to have. Marriage is not irrelevant to the child.

The complex system of public education in the State of Georgia functions inter-dependently. However, we cannot just look at the secondary and higher education systems themselves. The responsibility for making sure that the state's younger generations are adequately prepared for the challenges of the future rests on a wide variety of people: citizens, parents, elected officials, professional educators, and the students themselves. In our emerging climate of global economic competition, the need for strong schools has never been greater.

FIGURE 10.1. Savannah City Hall

10

Local Government

Introduction

The primary local level of government is the county, which often functions as a subdivision of the state, and is subject to the actions of the state legislature and the limitations of the state constitution. Only the states of Connecticut and Rhode Island lack county government, although in Louisiana and Alaska similar local structures exist, called, respectively, parishes and boroughs. In addition, all states have municipal corporations, although they may be variously called cities, towns or villages. Many states classify cities according to first class status, second class or third class status, specifying the types of municipal structure and degree of local autonomy they enjoy. In addition, all states have created various single purpose special districts to provide specific services to local communities. School districts are the single most common type of special purpose district, and public utilities are the second most numerous, like water and health districts.

Counties and municipalities, or permitted combinations of the two, are given home rule, meaning that they don't have to seek special permission from the state for every little thing they do. General local government entities are given the following supplementary powers by Article Nine, Section II of the Georgia Constitution.

The General Assembly may (and often does) expand these powers, and in addition may regulate, restrict, or limit them. In other words, local government in Georgia is very much state government applied locally. Currently, a lot of activity centers on special single purpose districting. Special districts have proliferated all over the country, and Georgia is no exception. While the school district is still the most common type of special district, it is also the one kind of special district that is actually declining in terms of real numbers, because of consolidation. Also called authorities, special districts have been created to provide transportation, soil conservation, libraries, water, sewage disposal, etc. In short, because they can be empowered to collect taxes and to make expenditures, these special purpose governments are in fact just as much governments as are the more common and traditional general purpose-governments, such as counties and municipalities.

TABLE 10.1
Municipal Responsibilities

1. Authority for police and fire protection.
2. Garbage and solid waste collection and disposal.
3. Public health facilities and services, including hospitals, emergency services, animal control.
4. Street and road construction and maintenance.
5. Parks and recreational programs and facilities.
6. Storm water and sewage and disposal systems.
7. Water storage, treatment, and distribution.
8. Create and maintain public housing.
9. Provide public transportation.
10. Libraries, and arts and sciences facilities.
11. Terminal and dock and parking facilities.
12. Codes for building, plumbing and electricity.
13. Air quality control.

Source: Compiled by authors.

County Government

Georgia has 159 counties, more than that of any other state except Texas. The Georgia Constitution in Article IX states that there shall not be more than 159, but within that framework counties may merge or consolidate, providing that a majority of the voters in each of the counties approve. This is an unlikely event given the attachment that Georgians have to their counties. The Constitution requires a degree of uniformity in county government. Each county must elect a clerk of the superior court, a judge of the probate court, a sheriff, and tax officials. Traditionally, the tax officials have been a tax collector and a tax receiver, but in some counties these offices have been replaced by a single tax commissioner. Of course, each county elects a set of county commissioners, and may elect a variety of other county officials.

Generally, Georgia's political sub-divisions enjoy home rule jurisdiction. The county commissioners, and any other elected officials, are subject to the home rule provisions of Article IX. The idea of home rule is that a municipal government is allowed to conduct its own affairs with a minimum amount of interference from state authorities, as long as the local options are consistent with the Georgia Constitution and the general laws enacted by the General Assembly of the State.

In general, the powers of local government in cities and counties are defined in their official state charters. The form or structure is the primary determining factor in how power is distributed and in how both personnel and budgets will be managed. If the form allows primary power with one individual (a strong mayor) the individual will be held accountable for conditions and issues associated with personnel and budget matters; the reverse is true when the form provides for responsibility divided among an entire city council or on the county commission.

Georgia County Government

In Georgia, the 159 separate counties are run by county commissioners who function as a legislative body, although they may have executive responsibilities as well. Actually, Georgia county government can take a variety of forms (Ammons and Campbell, 1993). The most common type of county government is the traditional form which is found in 93 of Georgia's counties. In the traditional form, commissioners serve as both legislators and executives, although they may entrust more of the executive authority to the chairperson, who may serve either in a part time or a full time capacity.

The second most frequently used form of county government in Georgia is the commission-administrator form. In the 34 counties that employ this system, the commissioners appoint a full time administrator to administer the day-to-day activities of the county. While the administrator may have some power over budgetary matters and may hire and fire some county employees, those powers are somewhat limited.

Limited, that is, by comparison to the powers of a county manager. The commission-manager form is the third most popular form of county government in Georgia. Employed in 20 counties, the commission appoints the manager (just as it does in a county-administrator system), but the managers' duties are somewhat more substantial than they are in the county-administrator system. The manager has the power to hire and fire all department heads, prepare and submit the budget to the commission and generally administer the county's affairs in the same manner that a city manager manages the city government.

Georgia is unique among the states in having single commissioner county governments. As of 1995, 13 Georgia counties utilized the single commissioner system (ACCG, Survey of County Governments, 1995). In such a system, found only in small rural counties, the commissioner is both the legislator and the executive. Challenged in 1994 as a violation of the 1965 Voting Rights Act, the single commissioner system in Bleckley County was upheld by the U.S. Supreme Court (Holder v. Hall, no. 91-2012, 1994). The court held that Bleckley County, which was 22 percent African American, did not dilute minority voting strength by having only one county commissioner.

DeKalb County is the sole example of the final form of county government in Georgia. It has an elected executive, much like a president or a governor or a strong mayor, who has the power to appoint and remove department heads, prepare and submit the budget, and who can also veto ordinances passed by the commission. With the obvious exception of single commissioner county government, county commissions in Georgia range in size from two to eleven commissioners (see Table 10.2).

TABLE 10.2
County Commission Sizes

No. of Commissioners	No. of Counties
1	13
3	18
4	2
5	98
6	12
7	10
8	3
9	1
11	2

Source: ACCG Survey on County Governments, 1995

With the exception of counties that have only one commissioner, 97 counties' commissioners serve staggered terms, while 49 serve concurrent terms.

The County Commission creates a budget to manage the services necessary to respond to citizen demands, such as road and bridge building, health services, law enforcement and legal services. Funding for these elementary services is primarily derived from property taxes on residents' habitations and owned lands. The Commissioners are responsible for setting the tax rate for property in the county, within state constitutional limits. They are also responsible for contracting to build roads, bridges, county facilities—including jails, libraries, hospitals, and other health facilities, as well as provision for fire protection, sanitation, and emergency and disaster relief.

Many other individuals charged with responsibility for implementation of the many functions of the county level of government are publicly elected, including the Clerk of the Superior Court, the Tax Commissioner, the Sheriff and the Judge of the Probate court. And of course the County Commissioners also hire a wide array of professionals to staff the bureaucracies and offices to meet the citizens' needs.

Though voters may not specifically be familiar with the broad allocation of powers given in the commission's charter, they are familiar, almost intuitively, with where responsibility rests; and at the county level blame and credit is quickly assessed in the voting booth. Success in budget and personnel power is reflected by repeated re-elections; while failure in either area is often reflected by rejection of a county commissioner or a county sheriff. For example, in the authors' home county, Lowndes, the entire county commission was defeated for reelection in 1996 in either the primary or the general election. Disgruntlement within the electorate over the manner in which the incumbent commissioners handled the financial and infrastructure arrangements for a new chemical plant to locate in Lowndes County resulted in this clean sweep.

City Government

Unlike some states, Georgia does not differentiate among its municipalities by labeling them as first, second, or third class according to population size. In general, all municipal corporations are treated equally, but occasionally the General Assembly may make laws that are applicable only to cities of a certain population size. Officially, all urban areas are simply called *municipalities* without the distinctions found in other states which designate municipal government as, for examples, towns, townships, boroughs, etc. Of course, many local officials like to call their home towns "cities," but that is a matter of local concern, and not a reflection of any state policy.

Local Government in Georgia

In ancient times, cities were often free and independent states, city-states exercising sovereign power. But in the modern world and certainly in Georgia, cities are mere creatures of the state. That is, local governments have no independent sovereignty, no right to exist independent of the authority and approval of the state government. The mechanism by which this authority is granted, and the precise powers and geographical scope of the city is the city charter. The city charters can be granted, and a new local government will come into existence.

An old standing joke in Georgia says that every town (remember that "town" is not a legal designation) is a county seat. Certainly most towns want to be known as viable and important centers of population and commerce. But if a town starts off well, but then declines in population, or fails to provide enough services to justify its continued existence, it may actually lose its charter. In Georgia, the state reviews local governments to make sure that municipal entities continue to be worthy of their charters.

138   Chapter Ten

The City Charter in Georgia

The city of Good Hope (pop. 181) in Walton County; Newborn (pop. 404) in Newtown County and Deepstep (pop. 120) in Washington County, are among the hundreds of small cities being examined to determine if they should have their municipal charters revoked. This review is conducted by a special government commission established by former governor Joe Frank Harris. A recent law passed by the state General Assembly authorized the Local Government Commission to survey small cities in rural Georgia to determine whether they remain viable. The criteria enacted require providing, or contracting for, a minimum of three municipal services: such as water, sewers or zoning (Osinski, 1994). If cities are losing too much population to be viable, and lapse on such services, they might be culled from the ranks of Georgia municipalities.

State officials say that problems that might lead to revocation of a city charter include not only declining population and dwindling services, but also cities which are inefficient, or providing duplicate services that could be provided by an alternative local government (Osinski, 1994). However, no one predicts the wholesale revocation of hundreds of city charters in Georgia. Where the commission does detect a problem, the city is formally notified and given at least a year to mend its ways or justify its existence. Given the loyalties many Georgians feel towards their hometowns, few observers expect that the commission will in fact recommend the demise of many cities. In fact, some of these cities, like Good Hope, have weathered the storm, and because they lie close to growing metropolitan areas, are becoming merged into suburban developments and soon can expect to start to grow again.

Riddleville: To Be or Not?

The town of Riddleville, a tiny town of 79 residents in Washington County, is facing possible extinction (Osinski, 1994). Like some 350 other small towns in Georgia, Riddleville is in danger of being declared dead. Local governments have no real independent sovereignty, no right to exist without the authority and approval of the state government. The mechanism granting the precise powers and scope of the city is the city charter. If granted, a new local government will come into existence. But if a town then declines in population, or fails to provide enough services to justify its continued existence, then it may lose its charter. This is Riddleville, Georgia.

City Government Forms

Throughout the United States there are four fundamental forms of city government. Georgia has examples of each of the major forms. The most basic form is some kind of a combination of a Mayor and Council Government. This form of government is the oldest in the United States, dating to its heritage from the

British system more than 400 years ago. This form has had many modifications over the centuries, but basically there are two versions, depending on whether the formal powers of the mayor are strong or weak.

Strong Mayor/(Weak) Council

In the strong mayor/council form of city government the mayor has major powers particularly associated with personnel and budget. The mayor can **"hire or fire"** city personnel without approval by the city's council—regardless of the number of the council or the employee's position in the city. However, rarely does this occur even in settings in which mayors are identified as **"strong."** Political havoc can occur; the mayor needs council support both publicly and politically. Thus, even with strong personnel powers granted by a city's charter, few mayors would consistently circumvent the powers delegated a city's council and risk losing wide-ranging public support over repeated elections. Atlanta is often depicted as a clearly identifiable **"strong"** mayor/council city, which like both Chicago and New York have a city charter giving both personnel and budgeting power to their mayors. Effectively, the publics' voices are limited to what the mayor perceives as essential to the city's needs. Council members in such cities must rely on either advocating or rejecting the mayor's position, and suffer the consequences of the public's interpretation of the mayor's impact on each area's resident's life. The standard type of organization chart for a strong mayor system is shown below in Figure 10.2.

The flow of power, the arrows, indicates the form of the cities' government, whether it is strong or weak mayor or council, or modifications where other elected positions intersect either budget, personnel, or both.

The City of Atlanta

Atlanta is the largest city in the State of Georgia, and in fact serves as a transportation, communication and cultural hub of the southeastern United States. The City of Atlanta serves as the state capitol, and with a total population of 396,052, ranks 37th in size among the nation's great cities.

During the political and constitutional reform movements in Georgia of the mid-1970's, the Atlanta city charter was redrafted, and various changes and improvements reforms took effect in 1974. The old Board of Aldermen was reorganized as a City Council, and a mayor/council form of government was instituted. Instead of electing all of the members at-large, two-thirds of the eighteen new city council members were elected (four year terms) from twelve districts to foster better urban representation; among the remaining six at large posts was the position of President of the Council, the former vice-mayor position, which today serves as the council's presiding legislative leader.

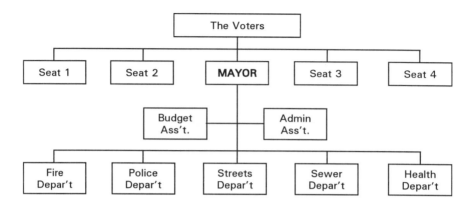

Mayor (elected at-large)
Council Members (at large or district member, or both)
Department Heads (Appointed)

FIGURE 10.2. Strong Mayor Organization Chart

As a political rule of thumb, the bigger the city, the stronger the mayor, and Atlanta is no exception to the rule. The mayoralty of Atlanta is a qualified **strong mayor**/city council system. The mayor operates as the city's chief executive officer, enjoys a veto power over council actions, and prepares the annual city budgets for the council's review and approval. Although in the past council members have not succeeded to the mayoralty position, that was changed when District Two Councilman Bill Campbell ran on a platform of **"make the system work"** and was inaugurated as mayor on January 3, 1994 (Campbell was re-elected in 1997).

Some of the complexity of local government functioning and intergovernmental relations is seen by the linkages between the city government and special purpose governments in the area. At the sub-local level, dozens of neighborhoods planning units are incorporated in the council districts, influencing the elections to the council and serving as a focus for the council's legislative focus and planning efforts. Expanding in geographical focus, the City Council also elects a number of its members to be directors and board members of various special purpose government authorities. These include such entities as the Atlanta Regional Commission (ARC), the Solid Waste Management Authority (SWMA), and the Metropolitan Atlanta Olympic Games Authority (MAOGA).

The Atlanta City Council meets twice a month. Citizens are invited to attend the sessions and to bring complaints, issues and sometimes even **"thank-you's"** to the council meetings. Here is local government in the raw: vital, emotional and sometimes characterized by hot tempered exchanges of opinion and viewpoint. Council members are assigned to various functional committees, which meet twice a month, and whose function is to review proposals, recommend legislation to the council, and oversee daily departmental operations. These committees are concerned with such areas as public utilities, finance, human resources, zoning and transportation. Members may serve on three or four such committees, including the Committee on Council, the executive committee of the city council. Of course, the exact powers of the mayor and the council will vary with the personalities of the people involved. A mayor with a strong personality and a canny political style will gain power even when the city council is designed to be dominant.

For their part-time but politically intensive jobs the city council members in Atlanta, in the early 1990's, received salaries of about twenty-two thousand dollars a year, and were responsible for the operation of the city and its annual budget of over a billion and a half dollars, including bonds and the capital construction projects of water and sewer connections under the streets and also the Airport Authority budget allotments. As is routine in Georgia, the mayor received a fractionally higher salary, about twenty-five thousand dollars. The city government exercises two types of legislative enactments: ordinances and resolutions. Ordinances are the ordinary laws of a city, binding on the citizens and business of daily life. In contrast, resolutions are non-binding, used to project a sense of the local government's feelings on various issues.

Weak Mayor/(Strong) Council

Mayor/council relationships are similar to the strong mayor/council, systems, but effectively the power of the government as identified in the city's charter is held in the hands of the city's council as a group instead of concentrated in the mayor's hands. Like any Governor, the Mayors of such cities must **"rule"** by political skill, charisma, or both. Cities with a weak mayor system have both personnel and funding power chartered to the city's council members. The Mayor can only seek public support politically, and seek to acquire support of the city's council members through use of political manipulation and personal charisma.

In this type of system, the organization chart is very similar to the strong mayor system, but the power of the mayor is considerably reduced. The mayor generally is little more than a typical council member, and all decisions must be by majority vote. The mayor must either submit to the council's decision, or seek to influence the council with personal charisma and political influence. In particular, the personnel and budgeting powers of the mayor are greatly reduced, and usually the mayor will not control the agenda of the meetings. Organizational depictions of this form of government will not reveal a general structural difference, but the flow of power will be significantly modified to the benefit of the council. Essentially, the weak mayor system results in a legislatively dominated political system.

There is little information from various municipalities in Georgia as to whether they have a strong mayor/council or a weak mayor council form of government. We do know, however, that regardless of the strength of the mayor, some form of mayor-council government is considerably more popular than any other type of municipal government in Georgia. In one study, 85% of the cities responding indicated that they had a mayor-council form (See Weeks and Hardy, Handbook for Georgia Mayors and Councilmembers, 1993). By contrast, fewer than thirteen percent of Georgia's cities employed the next most popular of the municipal government types, the council-manager form, although half of all responding larger cities (with more than 10,000 population) did.

Council-Manager Form of City Government

Moving to become one of the most popular forms of government after World War II, with expansion of expectations for professionalism by the public, the council-manager form of government rapidly increased. This form is also referred to as the **"corporate"** form of government, in that it splits the responsibility for directing policy-making and implementation of policy. Elected city leaders are charged with responsibility for making policy, while an individual they collectively hire, the city manager, is charged with implementing the mayor and council's policies.

The operation of this form of government is similar to the form of special district governments, especially school districts, which are discussed below; and it reflects the business management style of many major corporations. For instance, the council and mayor are comparable to the corporation's Board of Directors, as policymakers, while the city manager is comparable to the chief executive officer (CEO) of a corporation.

According to this model, the city manager does not make policy but only implements policies adopted by elected leaders. However, in reality, the city manager may acquire a substantial amount of power and be requested to provide major input to council members and the mayor in decisions associated with both personnel and budgets. Unfortunately, because the council and mayor must stand for election periodically, the city manager's position is subject to the stability of the council. When the council and/or mayor are changed in the majority that hired the manager, a high probability occurs that the manager will be terminated from his or her position; another hired, and the process continues.

The Council-Manager system may be popular today, but there was a time when it had to compete for popularity with a form of municipal government that is now all but extinct. That is the commission form of city government.

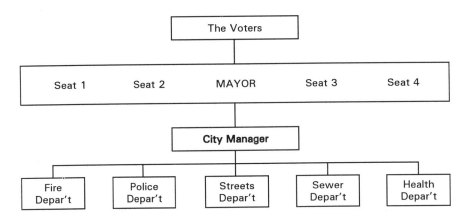

FIGURE 10.3. Council Manager Organization Chart

Commission

It is said that "necessity is the mother of invention", and that is no less true in government than elsewhere. A devastating flood destroyed Galveston, Texas in 1900. This disaster provided the opportunity for Galveston to experiment with a brand new form of local government, the commission. In the commission form of municipal government executive and legislative functions are entrusted to the same persons, who, in effect, wear two hats. When they're wearing their legislative hats, commissioners are policy-makers. But when they switch to their executive hats, they are department heads. Thus, one commissioner will head the Department of Public Safety, another the Public Works Department, a third will be mayor, and so on. The problem with this system is that there is relatively weak executive control. Today most former commission cities have abandoned that form. Georgia is no exception; in the study cited above, only three responding cities retained the commission form of government (less than one percent).

Americans in general and many Georgians treat politics and government with a wry sense of humor; they are a necessary evil and we can't live with them and we can't live without them. About the best thing we can do is to remember Winston Churchhills quip to the effect that democracies are the worst form of government, except that the alternatives are even worse! Politicians will always make more promises than they can keep, and we just have to grin and bear it.

FIGURE 10.4. Local Government Promises Revealed

Special District Governments

The State of Georgia has over 627 governments identified as **special districts.** Special district governments are governments associated with singular interests. Thus, special district governments may be seen throughout the state, both statewide and at regional levels, served by both appointed or elected boards. The forms of the boards vary as much as do the geographical areas and specialized topics they manage. Included in the varieties of special government districts are school districts, airports, sanitation, housing and soil conservation districts. An airport authority requires a big investment for construction and operation. As a general rule, the board or commission that is elected or appointed to manage the concern of the single purpose government is accorded a major degree of autonomy, but is usually cross-linked to adjoining city and county governments by appointed board memberships.

The special purpose form of government, focusing on a particular type of service, usually relies heavily on a professional ethic and organizational style. It is most similar to the council-manager form of government, and was first used in the nineteenth century to reform the Chicago school district by removing it from the corrupt political practices of the big city "party machine". In this form, the responsibility for directing policy-making is placed in an elected board, which then appoints an expert administrator for implementation of policy. Often the administrative director will dominate the board because of his or her expertise as well as the administrator's operational control. Figure 10.5 shows this type of organization.

Special District Funding

Each district also has independent local taxing power, judicial power, and executive power, in addition to its primary allocated lawmaking powers in its special purpose area or function. A high degree of growth in special districts has proliferated across the nation, as well as in Georgia. Much of the reason for the growth is linked to the so-called taxpayer revolt; citizens won't vote for general tax increases, but they understand and tolerate tax burdens for identifiable and needed services.

Today, there is a **"fad"** to create local special districts; it almost seems as if such fads come along periodically, with new types of special districts being established whenever opportunity to do so arises. (It is noted by the authors that rarely do the special districts *"go out of business"* even when the **"fad"** passes). The multiplicity of special districts throughout the state comprises another tier of taxing and governing entities. Each special entity carries responsibility to the people of Georgia both for service and for efficient use of public monies.

Educational Districts

It should be mentioned that school districts are a particular example of local special purpose governments. Traditionally, a distinction is made between the public schools offering of kindergarten through twelfth grade, and the higher educational, or college institutions. This division is reflected in two major bureaucracies: the State Board of Education and the State Board of Regents. These agencies and local governments are discussed in more detail in chapter nine.

FIGURE 10.5. Special Purpose Government Chart

Too Many Governments?

One frequently heard criticism of local government in Georgia and everywhere is that there are simply too many governments. Why do we need 159 counties, 534 municipalities, 187 school districts, and 421 other special districts? The simple answer is that we probably don't, but how do we get rid of governments that may no longer be necessary?

It is probably safe to say that no plan to eliminate or merge counties will succeed in Georgia. The attachment to county is just too strong. But annexation and consolidation are still possible approaches to the problem of too many governments. Georgia law provides for four methods of annexation, where one government absorbs people and property in immediate proximity to it. A municipal corporation can annex if its local legislative delegation can get the General Assembly to pass a local act, or if it passes a resolution to annex and holds a referendum in the to-be-annexed area or areas, or by one of two petition procedures. The first procedure allows the municipality to annex if all the owners of all of the land in the area to be annexed petition for annexation. The second procedure allows the municipality to annex land where sixty percent of the land owners and sixty percent of the others petition for annexation. In either case, there must be a public hearing and the passage of an ordinance for the annexation to be completed. In cases where a municipality completely surrounds an unincorporated area of fewer than fifty acres, the municipality may annex the "island."

Consolidation is a process by which a county, its municipalities, and perhaps its special districts become one government. Successful consolidation of school districts has taken place all over the country, with the number of independent school districts declining quite dramatically. Consolidation of counties, cities, and special districts, however, has been quite rare. Although there have been 27 proposals for city-county consolidation in Georgia between 1933 and 1997, only three have succeeded: Columbus-Muscogee County, Athens-Clarke County, and Augusta-Richmond County. Probably the principal obstacle to successful consolidation in Georgia is the requirement that there must be a majority vote in support of consolidation in each of the governmental entities to be consolidated, even if the overall vote is in favor of a merger. In 1987, for example, a proposed consolidation of Brunswick and Glynn County failed because the residents of Brunswick opposed it, even though a majority of the residents on the Islands (St. Simons, Sea Island, and Jekyll Island) supported it along with the residents of rural Glynn County. In fact, this was a "textbook case" of the failure of consolidation proposals. African Americans, who had established a power base in Brunswick, were reluctant to have that power diluted by merging with majority white unincorporated communities in the County. Arguments that consolidation would eliminate duplication of services and reduce expenses, and ultimately taxes, largely fell on deaf ears in the city.

Conclusion

Under America's "apple pie" system of federalism, there is no easy way to separate one government's functioning from another, as none functions independently. Yet, ultimately, each entity must also be viewed in isolation if we are to understand it. The complexity of viewing all levels of our state's government is properly the enterprise of a substantial number of books, and a substantial number of researchers; far more than the scope appropriate to this small volume on Georgia state government. In our hectic day and age, the need for strong local governments has been met by continued growth and evolution of local government forms, meeting the modern challenges.

FIGURE 11.1. Statue of Herman Eugene Talmadge

11

The State Constitution

Reflecting State Diversity

It is well known that much of Georgia's constitution reflects the political theories of an Englishman, John Locke, as adapted by the American experience after the British monarchy was rejected by the colonies over two hundred years ago. It is less well known and understood that Georgia's Constitution is also indebted to the French theorist Jean J. Rousseau, for his theory of the general will. Rousseau argued that in a democracy the structure of government, and its functioning and policies, should reflect the general will of all the people. This is the essential basis of democratic theory, that the government should represent the people and their desires. But the people often disagree, and in the worst scenarios, such as when we had three governors at one time, good constitutions should point the way to a solution. And if we had a simple society, and a simple undifferentiated economy, and if we had ethnic and cultural unity, then our constitution could be simple too. However, those are a lot of ifs, and none of them are true.

Georgia is in fact a large and complex state, the biggest east of the Mississippi River and with a correspondingly rich and complicated economy and multifaceted culture. Therefore we should expect that our constitution would be complex also, and it is. But underlying that political complexity is an orderly and rational system of government that reflects Georgia's civilization and culture, and the general will of its citizens. This chapter focuses on explaining how our system of government does reflect the will of the people of Georgia, but that it does so by reflecting the varied desires and policy preferences of many different groups of people, as they were described earlier in chapter three above. How can the wills and desires of different people, with different ideas, be incorporated into one government and one constitution? James Q. Wilson describes how a complicated government can have policies based on four basic types political action. These four types of policies are majoritarian, interest-group policies, client centered policies, and entrepreneurial policies.

Rousseau's concept of the general will is best expressed in majoritarian policies, ones that benefit all of the people, and are paid for all of the people. For example, the capitol building serves as our seat of government, and its construction and maintenance is paid for out of general revenues. In contrast, interest-group policies benefit one smaller group of people and are paid for only by that group of people, who thus incur both the costs and the benefits of that program. A good example can be found in the hunting and fishing laws of the state. Hunters and fishermen pay fees for their hunting and fishing licenses, and the money collected from them is used to regulate wildlife and to stock the forests and rivers with game. Few people seriously contest the equity of either the majoritarian or special-interest policies as described by Wilson.

However, the other two types of policies: client centered policies, and entrepreneurial policies, generate a great deal of controversy and constitutional activity. That is because both of them involve taking money or resources from one group of people and redistributing money or benefits to other groups of people. When government collects money from the majority of the people and gives to a small group of people, Professor Wilson calls it client politics. An example might be welfare programs, or food distribution programs, the larger part of society pays the cost of helping out a smaller part. On the other hand, when government collects money from a small group of people and uses it to give benefits to a larger group or to the majority, professor Wilson calls that entrepreneurial politics. An example might be taxes levied on businessmen who own manufacturing facilities which pollute our air and water, and then uses the money to protect the environment. Society wants strong industry of course, but we need good air and water too, so we tax the small number of big polluters and use the revenues to benefit society as a whole.

All of the different provisions of the Constitution of the State of Georgia can be looked at as policies which are so important that they have been lodged within the constitution to protect them from routine political maneuvering. And each policy generally falls into one of the four categories of policies described by professor Wilson, depending on who benefits from the policy, and who bears the cost of the policy. So while it is true that in a democratic society the will of the people usually determines the substantive policies and procedures of the state, it is also true that the politics of state government reflects all of the different interest groups, and so can sometimes be controversial and result in complex laws and constitutional provisions.

The more the variation in regions, industries, peoples and activities that a state encompasses, the more and varied the interest groups will be. In Georgia, they may be called lobbyists, interest groups, special interest groups, or pressure groups, but they are all concerned with pursuing their own agenda's and policy preferences. These interest groups have two major ways of pursuing their political goals: financing the political campaigns of their representatives and supporters, and lobbying for regulations, laws and constitutional amendments that institutionalize their policy preferences. Groups which are not effective in lobbying for their preferred policies are unlikely to be well served by the policies which are enacted. This chapter is not concerned with the variety of techniques interest groups use to influence policy making, but rather in describing the end results: the extent to which the Constitution is fundamentally majoritarian or not. Are the people of Georgia generally receiving their fair share of the state's budget? Have they succeeded in maintaining their democratic political influence, and changing the law and the state's Constitution to reflect their changing needs? As we discussed in chapter four, Georgia's General Assembly is quite sensitive to the needs of interest groups; but constitutional provisions require popular ratification, and an analysis of the policy types within the Constitution will enable us to determine the extent to which the people of the state favor majoritarian policies. The relative power of all of the contending interest groups in Georgia is reflected in the Constitution and its recent amendments.

The Constitution of 1983

The present Constitution of the State of Georgia, as ratified in 1983 and amended over the last fifteen years, is short, about 36,900 words as measured on a word processor. In structure, it consists of a preamble and eleven articles. Cursory overview of the constitution shows that most of it's provisions are intended to be majoritarian in conception and function. However, there are sections which seem to indicate that interest-group policies, client centered policies, and even some entrepreneurial policies exert significant influence in the Constitution.

The preamble is a short positive invocation expressing the hope of all Georgians that the Constitution will serve our needs and desires for freedom and justice. Article One of the Constitution of the State of Georgia begins basically as a Bill of Rights emphasizing the powers of the people and their rights and privileges vis-a-vis the government; it also has a second section on the origin and structure of government and a third section focusing on property rights. The basic organization of this article is clearly majoritarian oriented, as is Article II, which continues the theme of popular sovereignty, detailing the requirements of popular voting, elections for the most important state offices, and procedures for removal of public officials. Both of these articles are designed to benefit the majority of the population.

Articles III through VI, discussing the four branches of state government, also clearly convey the general intent that the government is designed to be under general popular control, and can thus be categorized as majoritarian as well. All of these articles illustrate the importance of the representatives of the people in framing the laws of the state, and reflecting the wills and desires of the people as a whole.

Article VII is a different story altogether. Article VII is the taxation article, granting the power to tax, the power to exempt from taxation, and it describes the purposes for which debt may be incurred. Let us look at the various sections of that article. Section One describes the general power of taxation, including taxes on tangible and intangible property (including the income tax). It should be noted that most of the language of this section is extremely detailed as to what types of tangible property are to be taxed, such as trailers, motor vehicles, real property and agricultural products. The specifications here, and the fact that the section provides allows the General Assembly to modify the tax rates and methods for these categories, indicates that interest group competition over policy is probably intense, and probably not simply majoritarian in operation.

A Philosophical View

Comment by Dr. Jack Waskey. The role of philosophy in political theory and constitutional law is not given enough credit. Many scholars argue that the United States was the first country in the world to be founded on philosophy rather than on religion. Plato's dialogue *The Laws* was the source for the idea that philosophy and purposes of law should be put forth before the law itself is stated.

We should also note that many political theories were rejected by the people of Georgia. Some of these include arguments that the government comes from the right of conquest (Thrasymachus) or by divine right (Robert Filmer) or by ethnic/racial superiority (Hitler). In Georgia we emphasize the rights of the people and insist that the government should not be all powerful, that it should exist to do only a limited number of things. Therefore, the people have rights that are beyond the authority of governmental officials to supervise.

This is even more noticeable in Section Two, which lists specific exemptions from the state's ad valorem taxation. There are primarily four categories of exemption: homesteads, locally granted exemptions, holdover exemptions from the prior constitution and laws, and an exemption for disabled veterans. These exemptions are clearly designed to benefit their respective groups, and are thus not majoritarian. The toleration for locally granted exemptions, when multiplied by the hundreds of governmental taxing entities in Georgia, makes it certain that interest-group policies, client centered policies, and entrepreneurial policies could be identified with a minimum of additional research. One definition of politics is that it is the process that determines who gets what, when, and how (Lasswell); it should be expanded to include: who is and who is not taxed.

Sections III and IV of Article VII provide explicit exceptions to the majoritarian principle. Section III creates the basic practice of putting all revenues in the state's general fund. However, it allows agricultural revenues to be treated differently and used for the promotion of agricultural produce, a clear example of interest-group policy. Of course, most people will agree that the special conditions and hazards of agricultural productivity and perishability justify this exception to the majoritarian principle. Section III also allows general revenue funds to be dispensed as grants to counties and municipalities, a clear example of client centered policy embedded in the Constitution. These are usually justified in terms of disaster relief programs and in promoting economic growth. Section IV, detailing the purposes and guarantees for public debt in Georgia, both at the state and local levels, by underwriting special programs and capital building projects, also creates a wide variety of client centered policies and expenditures. This section basically allows counties and other local entities to borrow money for large construction projects and public improvement programs. Although Article VII is obviously not simply majoritarian in its operation, it allows local flexibility in responding to the needs of the people of the State of Georgia, and so allows government to respond to needs on a priority basis.

Article VIII, concerning public education is, in monetary terms, the largest and most important function of state government. This article provides for the governance, administrative structure and for the financial support of public education at the elementary, secondary and college levels. Since it takes general revenue funds and allocates them to specific educational entities, school districts and colleges, it is clearly an example of client centered policy. And since some paragraphs allow the use of lottery money to support education, this article also provides an example of entrepreneurial policy, by taxing one group, the lottery gamblers, for the benefit of another group, students in the State of Georgia. As discussed in Chapter One of this textbook, Georgia's political culture is a blend of traditionalistic and individualistic elements, with a moralistic tinge, that would generally be hostile to state approved gambling activities. However, in this case the need to secure adequate levels of funding for education overrides minor moral considerations, and having gamblers pay a "sin tax" marks this entrepreneurial tax policy an understandable exception.

Article IX deals with counties and municipal corporations. Lacking sovereignty, these local governments are creatures of the state, and subject to the State Constitution and to state laws. The article describes the allowable structures, powers and governance of county, city and special purpose governments; and relations among these and between them and the state as a whole. In Wilson's typology, perhaps the essential significance of a multiplicity of little governments is that it allows small regional populations to control themselves, enjoying their own unique political and cultural lifestyles. In this view, the entire article is an example of interest group politics, centered not so much on financial policies, but upon other political values, primarily freedom and diversity. Home rule is a very comforting policy to many of the citizens of the State of Georgia. The Constitution clearly reflects our respect for individuals and local traditions.

The Amending Processes

Article X is the amending article. It allows amendments to the Constitution to be proposed either by the General Assembly or by a constitutional convention. It is based on the Madisonian idea that frequent elections to facilitate change is superior to suppressing dissent and subsequent risking of violent change. It provides for amendments to be submitted to the voters, with a majority of those voting necessary for ratification. In Wilson's typology, this article is clearly majoritarian in conception. It underscores Georgia's commitment to democratic governance, so that if it is the general will of the people to change their constitution, then they may do so through the ballot box.

Article X establishes identical procedures for either amending the existing Constitution or for replacing it with a totally new one. An amendment or a new constitution may be proposed either by a two-thirds vote on a resolution by both houses of the General Assembly or by a convention called by a two-thirds vote of the General Assembly. Under the 1983 Constitution, however, all amendments have been proposed by a two-thirds vote on a resolution in the General Assembly, not by a convention process.

Should a convention route be taken, the General Assembly determines the procedures by which it is called and the procedures by which it operates. Whichever process is used, once proposed, an amendment or a new constitution must be submitted to the electorate for ratification. A simple majority (50% + 1) of those actually voting in the first general election in an even numbered year following the proposal is all that is required for ratification. The governor has no veto power over amendments or new constitutions, so the decision of the people is final. Hopefully, only necessary amendments will ratified, otherwise the constitution may become cluttered up with frills that may look ridiculous.

Finally, Article XI is the effective implementing article for the effectuation of the 1983 Constitution, concluding in Paragraph VI: "this Constitution shall become effective on July 1, 1983; and except as otherwise provided in this Constitution, all previous Constitutions and all amendments thereto shall thereupon stand repealed."

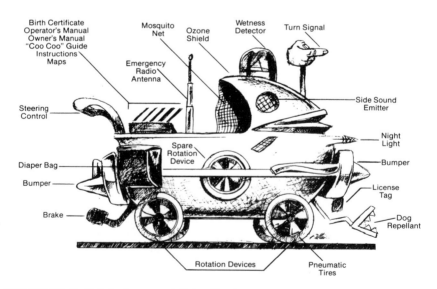

FIGURE 11.2. Safety Improved Baby Carriage

Constitutional Changes

What changes have been made in the Constitution of the State of Georgia since it was ratified in 1983? If the reader looks at the Constitution in the back of the textbook, it will be noted that some sections are in normal font, and others are in an italic font; the italic portions represent the new additions to the Constitution of Georgia ratified in 1983. The other normal font portions were in the original version of the 1983 Constitution (deleted and omitted portions are not shown in the appendix). What are the significant changes since 1983? This is not always easy to determine, because several of its sections have been amended as many as five times, so the individual provisions may vary from year to year, and sometimes even our elected officials have trouble keeping track. This is not surprising, because as researchers know, one of the many problems of identifying the law at any level is its lack of coherency (Elza, 162). However, every constitutional amendment is noted in the *Official Code of Georgia, Annotated,* affectionately known as the "mickey code" as a mnemonic for its publisher, the Michie company.

A perusal of the *Code* shows that in the last fifteen years a total of sixty-three (63) proposed amendments have been sent to the citizens for consideration. Of those, forty-eight (48) have been ratified, and the remaining fifteen (15) have been rejected. In percentage terms, the length of the Constitution has been increased by about twenty-eight (28) percent.

The following Table shows some of the major substantive changes in the Constitution since it was adopted in 1983. Of the eleven Articles, the ones most significantly amended were the voting Article II (80%) reflecting restricting the right to vote and serve in office of public offenders; the tax and finance Article VII (45%) detailing tax classifications and debt provisions; and Article III (40%) increasing the powers of the legislative branch of government.

Similar expansion of taxing and operational changes for boards of education (Article VIII); local government (Article IX); and the judicial branch (Article VI) were ratified. The trend of the last decade to improved education in Georgia were reflected in substantial increases in the powers of boards of education to impose taxes and issue bonds subject of course to voter approval.

Significant changes were also made in the area of special purpose districts and operations. Article IX was amended to allow the creation of local community improvement districts with local revenue sources; this built of other amendments that approved the creation of regional facilities such as industrial parks and re-development zones. Articles V (Executive) and X (Amending) were not changed. A summary depiction of the number of proposed amendments and the dates for their consideration by the voters and subsequent ratification is depicted on Table 11.2.

TABLE 11.1
Changes Listed by Sections

PORTION	TOPIC	# New Pages	% Change
ARTICLE I	Lottery Allowed	2 of 6	+ 30%
ARTICLE II	Ineligible Voters	4 of 5	+ 80%
ARTICLE III	Powers of Leg.	7 of 18	+ 40%
ARTICLE IV	Powers of Bds.	.5 of 4	+ 12%
ARTICLE V	no change — —	---	0%
ARTICLE VI "	Court Organization & jud. discipline)	3 of 10	+ 28%
ARTICLE VII " "	Classif. of Prop. & local options & public debt)	6 of 13	+ 45%
ARTICLE VIII "	Bds of Educat. & tax options	3 of 8	+ 36%
ARTICLE IX " " "	Re-devel. Zones Inter-gov't Relat. Regional Facil. Comm. Imp. Dist.	5.5 of 17	+ 32%
ARTICLE X — — — — ----------		---	0%
ARTICLE XI	Indust.Parks	.5 of 3	+ 15%
Totals:	all changes	27.5 of 97	+ 28%

Source: Compiled by authors.

TABLE 11.2
Amendments Listed by Years

Year	Proposed	Rejected	Ratified
1984	11	1	10
1986	9	1	8
1988	15	9	6
1990	9	1	8
1992	8	1	7
1994	6	1	5
1996	5	1	4
1998	5	2	3
Totals:	68	17	51

Source: L.A.Massey, *Constitution of the State of Georgia* (Atlanta: Office of the Secretary of State, 1998), at 72.

Summary Analysis

A casual inspection of Table 11.2 shows that the pace of amendment is slowing down, and that when the General Assembly has offered proposed amendments to the people the likelihood is that they will be ratified. Further analysis led the authors to conclude that many of the amendments are the sort of technical trivia that scholars love to criticize as being too minor to be elevated to constitutional status: restrictions on offenders as voters and office-holders, procedures for suspending indicted officials, punishments for accepting gratuities, and perhaps instructions on how to appoint replacements for vacant offices. Many others, such as the creation of re-development zones and community improvement districts do represent progress in creating new governmental entities and probably do belong in the constitution.

Other significant changes are the amendments establishing, in great detail, procedures for dealing with judges who have earned official sanctions and changing the structure of the courts by allowing the creation of special court projects. There were technical changes in the replacement appointive duties of the Governor to fill vacancies. On a more positive note, one amendment give increased power to local governments to contract with each other to provide services. By using memorandums of understanding (MoU's) and memoranda of agreement (MoA's) or simple contracts for services, the field of intergovernmental cooperation was much strengthened. In terms of intergovernmental relations, perhaps the single most interesting amendment to be ratified involved the amendment that established The Georgia State Finance and Investment Commission, the "super commission" responsible for approving general obligation bonds. The Constitutional Commission's members include the Governor, the Lt. Governor, The Speaker, The Attorney General the Commissioner of Agriculture and the State Auditor. See Article VII, Section IV, Paragraph VII, which passed on November 4,1986.

In terms of politics, some of the most interesting amendments are changes in the tax and appropriations provisions, intended for a variety of purposes. In main they allow for more flexible legislative appropriations for children, injured workers and indigent persons. They also allow more latitude for allotments to entrepreneurial efforts in technology, manufacturing and agriculture. Investment "seed capital" is offered for new small business ventures, as are provisions for a new agricultural crop fund. One hopes that the majority of these amendments will help to alleviate misery and to spur economic development. To enable readers to more easily identify these amendments, the sections of the Constitution which have been amended recently are italicized in the Appendix containing the Constitution of the State of Georgia.

Chapter Eleven

Recent Amendments

Ratification of an amendment to Article I, Section II, Paragraph VII (d), taking effect on and after January 1, 1995, now allows the holding of raffles by nonprofit organizations and repeals contrary laws enacted prior to January 1, 1995. Since the state government is allowed to hold a lottery, this gives other local governments and organizations the power to hold revenue raising raffles. This provision maintains the power of the state to regulate such activities by saying that laws which may be enacted by the General Assembly may restrict, regulate or prohibit the operation of such raffles.

Article III, Section VI was amended by adding Paragraph VII, on the regulation of alcoholic beverages, particularly in the counties and municipalities of the state for the purpose of regulating, restricting, or prohibiting the exhibition of nudity, partial nudity, or depictions of nudity in connection with the sale or consumption of alcoholic beverages. It provides delegated regulatory authority for the adoption and enforcement of regulatory ordinances by the counties and municipalities of this state.

Despite the fact that overall crime rates have been declining for years, the 'tough-on-crime' mentality continues to be a popular choice for some political elements. Article IV, Section II was amended restricting the powers of the courts and of the Board of Pardons and Paroles. The new Paragraph II (b) (2) provides that the General Assembly may by general law provide for minimum mandatory sentences and for sentences which are required to be served in their entirety for persons convicted of armed robbery, kidnapping, rape, aggravated child molestation, aggravated sodomy, or aggravated sexual battery. And sub-section (3) provides that the General Assembly may similarly provide for the imposition of sentences of life without parole for persons convicted of murder, and for anyone who is twice convicted of murder, armed robbery, kidnapping, rape, aggravated child molestation, aggravated sodomy, or aggravated sexual battery, the so-called 'two-strikes law'. When and if the General Assembly specifies, the board of pardons and parole shall not have the authority to consider such persons for pardon, parole, or commutation from any portion of such sentence.

The next Article was amended by a new paragraph. Paragraph X of Article VI, Section I, authorizes pilot projects in the courts. This substantially modifies the court structure of the state, by allowing the General Assembly to enact legislation providing for, as pilot programs of limited duration, courts which are not uniform within their classes in jurisdiction, powers, rules of practice and procedure, and also the selections, qualifications, terms, and discipline of judges for such pilot courts.

Article VIII, Section VI was modified so that boards of education may impose new sales and use taxes for educational purposes, as long as they are approved by a majority of the local voters. The voters have to be given information about which capital outlay projects the money is for, the maximum cost of such projects, with the maximum period of time not to exceed five years. Nothing in this amendment prohibits counties and municipalities from imposing additional taxes local sales and use taxes authorized by general law.

In these days of continued tax payer revolt, ways to finance public improvement without new taxes is leading to a variety of budget cutting and privatization initiatives. One amendment, altering Article IX, Section II, Paragraph VII authorized the General Assembly to provide for the creation of enterprise zones by counties or municipalities, or both. This allows for exemptions, credits, or reductions of any tax or taxes levied within such zones by the state, a county, or any municipality, or any combination thereof, if persons, firms, or corporations create job opportunities within the enterprise zone for unemployed, low, and moderate income persons.

Similarly Article IX, Section IV was amended to allow the creation of "regional facilities". These regional facilities mean industrial parks, business parks, conference centers, convention centers, airports, athletic facilities, recreation facilities, jails or correctional facilities, or other similar or related economic development facilities. Counties and municipalities are authorized to enter into contracts with contiguous counties for the purpose of allocating the proceeds of ad valorem taxes assessed and collected on real property for development purposes. And unless otherwise provided by law, the regional facilities can qualify for any income tax credits, regardless of where the business is located.

Finally, in one amendment that looks as if it were very narrowly drawn, Article XI, Section I was amended so that any person owning property in an industrial area may voluntarily remove the property from that industrial area, by filing a certificate to that effect with the clerk of the superior court in that county. Once the certificate is filed, the property described in the certificate, together with all public streets and public rights of way within the property, abutting the property, or connecting the property to property outside the industrial area may be annexed by an adjacent city.

Conclusions

By applying Wilson's classification of policy model, it can be confidently asserted that Georgia's State Constitution with its amendments is fundamentally majoritarian, except as tax and local options are structured to allow narrower interest-group policies to flourish for general economic improvement. While there are examples of client policies (taxing the many to benefit the few) and even entrepreneurial policies (taxing the few to benefit the many) these are generally justified in promoting the public good. Generally, the Constitution of the State of Georgia is an accurate reflection of the fundamental structure of the state's economics and politics. Unlike some states, with antiquated and outmoded government systems, the Georgia State Government, responding to the voice of the people in their varied interest groups, has attempted to create a modern flexible system of functional branches and specialized agencies to meet the growing needs of an increasingly sophisticated urban society. It is certain that the traditionalistic elements of our people are yielding to the disruptive demands of an increasingly individualistic economic and social setting. It is the genius of the State of Georgia that a regional leader can move into the age of mass bureaucracy, and yet retain the traditional graciousness and style that has always made the Peach State a symbol of well managed change.

Having already had ten constitutions in its history, it is unlikely that the 1983 constitution will be the last. It is the contention of the authors that the political culture of the state is evolving from traditionalistic to individualistic, with an increasing element of moral responsibility. This can be attributed in part to the large numbers of northern professionals and managers migrating southward to the Peach State, and in part to the undeniable modernization of the state's economy. Whatever the proportion, Georgia is in a state of transition. As a result, it can be expected that the current constitution will continue to gradually reflect the changing demographics of the state and will undergo such dichotomous amendment that within another two decades, or even sooner, it will need another complete revision.

The state is undergoing economic changes and new people are moving into Georgia, bringing their new ideas with them. The new emphasis on enterprise zones and redevelopment districts exemplifies the dramatic professionalization of our emerging administrative government; and merit systems have all but completely replaced the earlier system of political patronage. The 1998 session of the General Assembly hinted at the declining power of the "good old boy" legislative network and the emphatic participation by new, more professional legislators oriented to the Republican Party. The times are changing in Georgia. If history provides a lesson, it is this: When the times change in Georgia, so does the Constitution.

In 1998 voters approved three new amendments to the Georgia Constitution. Article One, section 2, paragraph VIII had a new section C added to the lottery language, providing for specific uses of lottery money, and that it be used to supplement, not supplant, other educational resources. This added 294 more words to the Constitution. Two amendments modified Article Three, section 9, paragraph VI. The first of these added sub-paragraph (k) allowing for additional penalties and fees for drunk driving convictions and to allocate such monies to a Brain and Spinal Cord Injury Trust Fund. This added another 143 new words to the Constitution. The second amendment in this section provided authority in another 129 words for the General Assembly to create a roadside enhancement and beautification fund, which may improve our economy by making tourists feel happier driving in our state and generally help to promote the interests and happiness of our citizens and families, as stated in the Preamble of the Constitution of the state of Georgia.

Appendix I
Georgia State Questions

General Test Bank

Chapter 1: Introduction to Georgia Politics

1. Which of the following is not a state power?
    a. Education
    b. Transportation
    c. Police protection
    d. Mail delivery

2. State laws
    a. Must be compatible with state Constitutions
    b. Must be compatible with the U.S. Constitution
    c. Must be compatible with federal laws
    d. Must be compatible with the U.N. charter

3. The U.S. Constitution
    a. Is longer than Georgia's
    b. Is shorter than Georgia's
    c. Has more amendments than Georgia's
    d. Has fewer amendments than Georgia's

4. Only one state has had more constitutions in its history than Georgia. That state is
    a. Alabama
    b. New York
    c. Louisiana
    d. Massachusetts

5. The current Georgia constitution can best be described as the
    a. Restoration Constitution
    b. Bureaucratic Constitution
    c. Secession Constitution
    d. Reconstruction Constitution

6. As of 1998, the number of amendments to Georgia's Constitution stood at
   a. 27
   b. 51
   c. 432
   d. 1000 plus

7. The body of the Georgia Constitution contains
   a. A preamble and eleven articles
   b. A preamble and seven articles
   c. A preamble and thirty-two articles
   d. Sixteen articles

8. Amendments to the Georgia Constitution are ratified by
   a. The county commissions
   b. County commissions and city councils
   c. The people in a referendum
   d. The Governor of Georgia

9. Georgia has a plural executive, which means:
   a. Georgia has two governors, one for domestic affairs, one for foreign affairs
   b. Georgia has a constitutional relationship between the Governor and the CEO's of major businesses like Coca-Cola
   c. Georgia has many independently elected chief executives
   d. The Georgia Governor appoints all the other officials to his cabinet

10. Which one of these is *not* an executive officer in Georgia
    a. Lieutenant Governor
    b. Attorney General
    c. Commissioner of Agriculture
    d. State auditor

11. Georgia is closest to which of Daniel Elazar's types of political culture?
    a. Traditionalistic
    b. Individualistic
    c. Moralistic
    d. All three

12. Where would one find Georgia's bill of rights?
    a. Georgia Declaration of the Rights of Man
    b. Article I of the Georgia Constitution
    c. Amendments I through XI of the Georgia Constitution
    d. Georgia has no written bill of rights

13. "Devolution" means
    a. Transferring power from the national government to the state governments
    b. Transferring power from the state governments to the national government
    c. Devil worship
    d. Transferring power from local governments to the national government
14. States are free
    a. To exceed federal constitutional protections
    b. To supercede federal constitutional protections
    c. To deny, disparage, or abuse peoples' rights
    d. To ignore the federal government whenever it suits them

Chapter 2: Civil Rights and Civil Liberties

1. The original purpose of the new British colony in Georgia was to provide a haven for:
   a. The poor
   b. Army veterans
   c. Religious minorities
   d. Convicts and criminals

2. Which of the following is not a major section in Article I of the Georgia Constitution?
   a. Civil liberties
   b. Origin and structure
   c. Limiting taxation
   d. General provisions

3. A majority of the paragraphs in Article I, Section I involve:
   a. Civil rights
   b. Civil liberties
   c. Popular government
   d. Intergovernmental relations

4. Which of the following possessions of a free citizen are not described in the first paragraph of Article I?
   a. Life
   b. Liberty
   c. Happiness
   d. Property

5. Which of the following are elements of due process?
   a. Notification of action
   b. An open and public hearing
   c. Benefit of legal counsel
   d. All of the above

6. Which of the these liberties are usually non-controversial?
   a. Right to assemble in groups
   b. Right to circulate petitions
   c. Right to send petitions to officials
   d. All of the above

7. In Georgia, the right to a jury trial includes all but:
   a. A jury of peers
   b. A jury of officials
   c. An impartial jury
   d. A speedy trial

Appendix I

8. The government's use of which of the following is limited:
   a. Searches
   b. Seizures
   c. Warrants
   d. All of the above

9. Which of the following are protected against a governments use of unreasonable searches?
   a. Persons
   b. Houses
   c. Papers
   d. All of the above

10. Accused persons must be given all of the following except:
    a. An opportunity to leave the state
    b. A copy of the accusation
    c. A list of witnesses
    d. A right to confront witnesses

11. Which of the following became a major civil rights figure?
    a. James Oglethorpe
    b. Martin Luther King
    c. Richard Jewell
    d. All of the above

12. The State of Georgia may do which of the following:
    a. Declare someone to be a noble
    b. Declare someone to be a peasant
    c. Declare someone to be a citizen
    d. Declare someone to be an aristocrat

13. Article I, Section II, Paragraph III names all but which of the following branches of government.
    a. Legislative
    b. Judicial
    c. Bureaucratic
    d. Executive

14. Which of the following statements are true under the Constitution of the State of Georgia?
    a. No money can be taken from the treasury for any church
    b. Each person has the right to worship in his or her own way
    c. No one should interfere with anyone's right of conscience
    d. All of the above

Chapter 3: Political Participation in Georgia

1. To win a general election in Georgia candidates must win what percentage of the votes?
   a. 33 1/3%
   b. 45%
   c. 50% + 1
   d. 66 2/3%

2. Georgia's voter registration system is
   a. Permanent
   b. Periodic
   c. Episodic
   d. Idiotic

3. The Democratic party in Georgia
   a. Controls theState House of Representatives
   b. Controls the Governorship
   c. Controls the Congressional delegation
   d. Controls the State Senate

4. Turnout in the Georgia gubernatorial election of 1994 was
   a. Less than 30%
   b. Less than 40%
   c. Less than 50%
   d. Over 50%

5. Which of the following can't vote in Georgia?
   a. Convicted felons
   b. Mental incompetents
   c. Persons under the age of 21
   d. Non-residents

6. Georgia Democrats
   a. Are liberal
   b. Are conservative
   c. Identify with the national Democratic party
   d. Liked Kennedy, Mondale and Dukakis

7. The political party systems in Georgia can best be described as
   a. Hierarchical
   b. Stratarchical
   c. Monarchical
   d. Polyarchical

8. Federal encroachments on states' prerogatives in the area of voting include
   a. The 15th Amendment
   b. The 26th Amendment
   c. The 1st Amendment
   d. The Voting Rights Act

9. Georgia has a system of interest groups that is considered
   a. Strong
   b. Weak
   c. Responsive
   d. Pro-labor

10. Powerful interest groups in Georgia include
    a. Medical Association of Georgia
    b. Queer Nation Atlanta
    c. Coca Cola
    d. Georgia Association of Educators

11. Political interest groups seek
    a. Access to political decision-makers
    b. To influence the outcome of public policy
    c. To elect public officials to office who are sympathetic
    d. To capture control of government

12. Democratic members of Congress include
    a. Bob Barr
    b. John Lewis
    c. Cynthia McKinney
    d. Newt Gingrich

13. Political interest groups in Georgia may
    a. Not contribute money to candidates for public office
    b. Contribute as much money as they wish to candidates for public office
    c. Contribute a maximum of $1,000 to candidates for local office and $2,500 to candidates for statewide office
    d. Contribute no more than $10,000 to any candidate for public office

14. As voter turnout in Georgia increases,
    a. National voter turnout decreases
    b. National voter turnout also increases
    c. National voter turnout remains about the same
    d. Voter turnout in Alabama and South Carolina is affected

Chapter 4: The Legislative Branch

1. Georgia's bicameral legislature consists of
    a. A Senate and a House of Delegates
    b. A Senate and a House of Burgesses
    c. A Senate and a House of Commons
    d. A Senate and a House of Representatives

2. Members of the General Assembly serve terms of
    a. Two years
    b. Four years
    c. Six years
    d. Two years for the lower house and six years for the upper house

3. The lower house of the General Assembly consists of
    a. Thirty members
    b. Fifty-six members
    c. One hundred fifty members
    d. One hundred eighty members

4. The upper house of the General Assembly consists of
    a. Thirty-six members
    b. Fifty-six members
    c. Seventy-six members
    d. Ninety-six members

5. The typical state legislature in Georgia is
    a. A black, Roman Catholic, female lawyer
    b. A white, Jewish, male farmer
    c. An hispanic, Methodist, female teacher
    d. A white, Baptist, male businessman

6. The Georgia State Senate's presiding officers are
    a. The Lt. Governor and the President Pro Tempore
    b. The Speaker of the House and the President Pro Tempore
    c. The Governor and the Lt. Governor
    d. The Governor and the Majority Leader

7. The General Assembly's lower house officials are
    a. The Speaker of the House and the Speaker Pro Tempore
    b. The Lt. Governor and the Speaker of the House
    c. The Governor and the Lt. Governor
    d. The Speaker of the House and the Secretary of State

8. The General Assembly usually meets
   a. All year long
   b. Every other year
   c. Forty working days in a year
   d. Only in August

9. Which of these is not a committee in the Georgia General Assembly?
   a. Sitting
   b. Standing
   c. Special
   d. Joint

10. If the Governor vetoes a bill, both houses of the General Assembly can override that veto by a vote of a
    a. Simple majority
    b. Two-thirds majority
    c. A three-fifths majority
    d. A three-fourths majority

11. The State of Georgia
    a. Must balance its operational budget
    b. Can spend as much as the Governor requests
    c. Can print more money if it runs out
    d. Has perpetual funding

12. Who presides over Georgia's State Senate?
    a. Governor
    b. Lieutenant Governor
    c. Senate Majority Leader
    d. Senate Majority Whip

13. "Junior Tuesday" is
    a. Presidential primary election day in Georgia
    b. Presidential general election day in Georgia
    c. In the week following "Super Tuesday"
    d. The nickname of the Georgia State Senate minority whip

14. *Miller v. Johnson*
    a. Abolished the "county unit system" in Georgia
    b. Declared the 11th Congressional District in Georgia unconstitutional
    c. Made Georgia create the 5th Congressional District
    d. Was Zell Miller's impeachment trial

Chapter 5: The Plural Executive of Georgia

1. The Governor of Georgia
   a. Has absolute control over the state's executive branch
   b. Shares power with other elected executive officials
   c. Is not ranked as an influential governor
   d. Appoints all members of state boards and commissions

2. When it comes to making laws, the Governor
   a. Is a significant player
   b. Has no role to play at all
   c. Is confined to signing or vetoing bills
   d. Has the sole legislative power

3. Georgia Governors can serve
   a. One four-year term
   b. One two-year term
   c. Two four-year terms
   d. As many terms as they are elected to in succession

4. To be elected Governor of Georgia
   a. A person must be a citizen of the U.S. and be at least 35 years old
   b. A person must be male
   c. A person must own property in Georgia and have been a resident for at least fifteen years
   d. A person must be a citizen of the U.S. for at least fifteen years, a legal resident of Georgia

5. The Georgia Attorney General heads
   a. The Department of Law
   b. The Justice Department
   c. The State Supreme Court
   d. The State National Guard

6. One of these is **not** an elected public official in Georgia
   a. State School Superintendent
   b. State Commissioner of Revenue
   c. State Commissioner of Insurance
   d. State Commissioner of Labor

7. The Georgia Governor does **not** serve as
   a. Top state bureaucrat
   b. The filler of vacancies
   c. Conservator of the peace
   d. Top state judge

8. The *Hope Scholarship Program* is funded
   a. By the General Assembly from the general fund
   b. By the Governor from license tag fees
   c. By proceeds from the lottery
   d. by the county governments in Georgia

9. If the Governor dies, resigns, or is permanently disabled,
   a. The Lieutenant Governor becomes the new Governor
   b. The Governor's wife becomes the new Governor
   c. A new election is called in thirty days
   d. The speaker of the House becomes the new Governor

10. The Governor acts as Chief Legislator by
    a. Convening special sessions
    b. Writing the annual appropriations bill
    c. Delivering the annual State of the State Address
    d. Serving as President of the Senate

11. Who is the chief of state of Georgia?
    a. Governor
    b. Lieutenant Governor
    c. Secretary of State
    d. Attorney General
    e. Speaker of the House

12. An elected State School Superintendent
    a. Is found in all 50 states
    b. Is unique to Georgia
    c. Is found in a majority of the states
    d. Is found in a minority of the states

13. The Georgia Board of Regents
    a. Has a non-line-itemed budget
    b. Consists of sixteen members appointed by the Governor
    c. Oversees the University System
    d. Serves ten-year terms

14. The so-called "flag issue" in the 1993 session of the General Assembly
    a. Was one of Governor Miller's greatest successes
    b. Was prompted by Governor Miller's support for flag burning
    c. Was a "no-win" situation for Governor Miller, who never brought it up again
    d. Saw Speaker Murphy and other legislative leaders flock to Governor Miller's side

Questions by Chapters   175

Chapter 6: Administration and Agencies

1. Max Weber's "succession crisis" is
   a. A typology of historical change in government organizations
   b. What happens when a newly appointed bureaucrat replaces one who is stepping down
   c. A model of bureaucratic inertia
   d. Probably the major problem with bureaucracies today

2. The Article of the Georgia Constitution that establishes the Bureaucracy is
   a. Article I
   b. Article II
   c. Article III
   d. Article IV

3. The Georgia Public Service Commission regulates
   a. The Insurance Industry
   b. Electric Power Companies
   c. Railroads
   d. All of the above

4. Members of the State Transportation Board
   a. Are appointed by the Governor
   b. Are chosen by the general assembly
   c. Are elected by the people
   d. Are appointed by their U.S. Congressmen

5. The State Board of Pardons and Paroles
   a. Has the power to grant reprieves, pardons, and paroles
   b. Has the power to commute sentences
   c. Has the power to impose sentences
   d. Has the power to build prisons

6. The State Personnel Board
   a. Consists of five members nominated by the Governor
   b. Sets policy for the State Merit System
   c. Selects its own chairman
   d. All of the above

7. Veterans Preference
   a. Means that veterans don't have to take state merit exams
   b. Means that veterans automatically get the state jobs for which they apply
   c. Means that veterans get bonus points on merit exams
   d. Means that veterans prefer public sector jobs to private sector jobs

8. The Georgia Board of Natural Resources
   a. Oversees Georgia's principal natural resources, its people
   b. Is charged with environmental protection
   c. Primarily engages in oil exploration
   d. Operates all the state's zoos
9. Special authorities are created
   a. To finance an enterprise to get around debt limitations
   b. To avoid raising taxes
   c. To serve the needs that cut across traditional governmental boundaries
   d. All of the above
10. The number of state bureaucrats in Georgia
    a. Is approximately 114,000
    b. Is approximately 184,000
    c. Is approximately 344,000
    d. Is in the millions
11. The Commissioner of Insurance
    a. Sets criteria for licensing insurance companies
    b. Sets standards for performance of insurance companies
    c. Sets rates for insurance policies
    d. All of the above
12. Who selects Georgia's State Superintendent of Schools?
    a. State Board of Education
    b. Governor
    c. General Assembly
    d. Voters
13. The Georgia Secretary of State
    a. Oversees the elections process
    b. Carries out Georgia's foreign policy
    c. Records financial statements from candidates for office
    d. Grants charters to corporations
14. The State Financing and Investment Commission
    a. Is an example of a "Super Commission"
    b. Includes among its members the Governor, Speaker of the House, Agriculture Commissioner
    c. Tries to ensure that Special Authorities contribute to efficient government
    d. Does not exist

Chapter 7: The Georgia State Judiciary

1. Courts of limited jurisdiction in Georgia include
   a. Magistrate
   b. Probate
   c. Juvenile
   d. Superior

2. A judge in Georgia may be removed from office by
   a. The Governor
   b. The General Assembly
   c. The Judicial Qualifications Commission
   d. All of the above

3. ALJ is an abbreviation for
   a. Alter Legis Judicium
   b. A legal joke
   c. Administrative Law Judge
   d. Another Lenient Judge

4. Each county in Georgia shall have at least one
   a. Supreme Court
   b. Superior Court
   c. Magistrate Court
   d. Probate Court

5. Two fraternity brothers hazing freshmen would be called
   a. Joint obligators
   b. Joint tort-feasors
   c. Joint co-signers
   d. Joint custodians

6. Judges may be removed for
   a. Willful misconduct
   b. Habitual intemperance
   c. Conviction of a crime involving moral turpitude
   d. All of the above

7. The number of inmates currently serving time in Georgia's prisons is approximately
   a. 3,700
   b. 37,000
   c. 370,000
   d. 3,700,000

8. The Georgia Court of Appeals consists of
   a. Five judges
   b. Nine judges
   c. Twelve judges
   d. Twenty-seven judges sitting three in a panel
9. The Georgia Supreme Court consists of
   a. Seven justices
   b. Nine justices
   c. Twelve justices
   d. 159 justices
10. The Chief Justice of the Georgia Supreme Court is
    a. Appointed by the Governor to be Chief Justice
    b. Elected by the people as Chief Justice
    c. Elected by the Supreme Court
    d. Appointed by the General Assembly
11. Which of the following Georgia courts has original jurisdiction?
    a. Supreme Court
    b. Court of Appeals
    c. Superior Court
    d. All of these
12. Members of Georgia's Supreme Court serve for how many years?
    a. 2 years
    b. 4 years
    c. 8 years
    d. Tenure for life
13. All other judges in Georgia must retire
    a. At age 55
    b. At age 65
    c. At age 75
    d. Never
14. Members of the Judicial Qualifications Commission
    a. Are all judges
    b. Are all state legislators
    c. Are judges, lawyers, and non-lawyer citizens
    d. May not be lawyers

Chapter 8: Budgeting and Finance

1. In Fiscal Year 1994 the total indebtedness of the State of Georgia was
    a. Over three billion dollars
    b. Nothing, because the State is required to pay as it goes
    c. Nearly three trillion dollars
    d. Approximately ten million dollars

2. The bulk of Georgia's revenue comes from
    a. Ad valorem taxes
    b. Income taxes
    c. Sales taxes
    d. The lottery

3. Comparatively, Georgia is considered
    a. A high-tax state
    b. A low-tax state
    c. A fair-tax state
    d. An unfair-tax state

4. A revenue bond
    a. Is retired with the revenues from money-making enterprises
    b. Is based on the "full faith and credit" of the state
    c. Is a tie that links a taxpayer to his state government
    d. Is usually a risky undertaking

5. The largest single expenditure in the Georgia State budget is
    a. Transportation
    b. Education
    c. Welfare
    d. Corrections

6. In 1998 the Georgia General Assembly "gave back" about _____ in tax relief to the people of Georgia.
    a. $100 million
    b. $200 million
    c. $300 million
    d. $400 million

7. Georgia's bond ratings are:
    a. Very high
    b. Very low
    c. Set by the General Assembly
    d. Dictated by the Governor

8. Income of over $7,000 a year is taxed in Georgia at a rate of:
   a. 6%
   b. 28%
   c. 35%
   d. 62%

9. Exempted from Georgia's sales tax are
   a. Bibles
   b. Food
   c. Fuel used to heat chicken houses
   d. Girl Scout cookies

10. Georgia's sales tax rate varies from
    a. 3–6%
    b. 4–7%
    c. 8–10%
    d. 11–15%

11. Georgia's fiscal (budget) year runs from:
    a. October to September
    b. January to December
    c. July to June
    d. May to September

12. A capital budget is:
    a. Used for maintenance of the capitol building
    b. Used to fund routine operations
    c. Used for expensive long-term building projects
    d. Used to fund capital death penalty appeals

13. By 1998 the Georgia lottery was producing $____ for education
    a. Over $100 million
    b. Over $500 million
    c. Over $1 billion
    d. Over $5 billion

14. Elementary, secondary, and higher education together consume what percent of the Georgia State annual budget?
    a. Nearly 40%
    b. Nearly 55%
    c. Nearly 75%
    d. Nearly 25%

Chapter 9: State Education Policy

1. The State Board of Education
   a. Makes policy for state education systems
   b. Sets standards for teacher education programs
   c. Certifies teachers
   d. All of the above

2. The number of public school systems in Georgia is
   a. 127
   b. 159
   c. 187
   d. 203

3. The Board of Regents of the University System of Georgia is
   a. Appointed by the Governor
   b. Appointed by the General Assembly
   c. Elected by the people
   d. Selected by the State Board of Education

4. The number of public institutions of higher learning in Georgia is
   a. 25
   b. 34
   c. 63
   d. 159

5. State School Board members
   a. Are all teachers
   b. Are appointed by the Governor and confirmed by the Senate
   c. Represent congressional districts
   d. Must have doctorates in education

6. The State School Superintendent is
   a. Appointed by the Governor
   b. Appointed by the Governor and confirmed by the Senate
   c. Elected by the people
   d. Appointed by the General Assembly

7. In the state budget passed in 1998, education received
   a. $10,000,000
   b. $1,000,000,000
   c. $3,500,000,000
   d. $6,500,000,000

8. Local School District Superintendents
   a. Are elected by the people
   b. Are appointed by the Governor
   c. Are appointed by the County Commission
   d. Are appointed by the local Board of Education
9. Georgia's University System
   a. Includes all public and private colleges and universities in Georgia
   b. Includes 34 public research universities, regional universities, four-year colleges, and two-year colleges
   c. Includes all colleges and technical schools in Georgia
   d. Includes only UGA, Georgia Tech, Georgia State University, and the Medical College of Georgia
10. The head of the University System of Georgia is called a
    a. President
    b. Chancellor
    c. Provost
    d. Professor
11. A voucher system for supporting private education
    a. Exists in Georgia
    b. Does not exist in Georgia
    c. Has been proposed in the General Assembly, but has failed
    d. Has never been considered by the General Assembly
12. The Hope Scholarship Program requires that a recipient
    a. Maintain a B average in college
    b. Make all A's
    c. Attend only a public institution in Georgia
    d. Be personally selected by comedian Bob Hope
13. The state appropriation for education in Georgia
    a. Is all the money that local school districts can spend
    b. Is a small percentage of the money that local school districts spend
    c. May be supplemented by local school districts
    d. Does not exist
14. Church-related schools in Georgia
    a. Are fully funded by the state's taxpayers
    b. Are illegal
    c. May only be operated by the Southern Baptist Convention
    d. None of the above

Chapter 10: Local Government

1. A Georgia county with a single member county commission is
   a. Fulton
   b. Cobb
   c. Bleckley
   d. Lowndes

2. The City of Atlanta is closest to this form of municipal government:
   a. Strong mayor/weak council
   b. Weak mayor/strong council
   c. Council-Manager
   d. Commission

3. Once granted, a municipal charter may:
   a. Never be revoked
   b. Be revoked only if population declines
   c. Be revoked if population declines and services stop
   d. Be revoked without cause

4. In 1994, the number of special districts in Georgia was about:
   a. 34
   b. 125
   c. 436
   d. 627

5. Local governments in Georgia are known as
   a. Counties
   b. Municipalities
   c. Special districts
   d. Townships

6. The number of counties in Georgia is
   a. 46
   b. 93
   c. 159
   d. 227

7. Each county in Georgia must elect
   a. A clerk of the Superior court
   b. A Sheriff
   c. A judge of the Probate court
   d. A dogcatcher

8. Which of the following services is a "special district" most likely to carry out?
   a. Provision of water utility service to a group of contiguous local communities
   b. Regulation of interstate commerce
   c. Administration of prison facilities for the state government
   d. Election of state legislators
9. What is the purpose of a special district?
   a. To provide services to several neighboring communities
   b. To decide disputes between city department heads
   c. To elect a delegate to a convention
   d. To serve as a state capital or county seat
10. The most common type of county government in Georgia is
    a. The commission-administrator form
    b. The traditional form
    c. The commission-manager form
    d. The single commissioner form
11. Consolidation of cities and counties in Georgia
    a. Is a very popular process
    b. Is never used
    c. Has been used three times in over 60 years
    d. Has been used 60 times in three years
12. What is "home rule"?
    a. The Principle that police need a warrant to search one's residence
    b. The Principle that any state should be able to secede
    c. The Principle that justifies geographic representation
    d. The Principle that local governments should be given substantial governing authority
13. The system of municipal government most like a Business Corporation is
    a. Council-Manager
    b. Weak mayor-Council
    c. Strong mayor-Council
    d. Commission
14. The City of Atlanta is
    a. A Class A City
    b. A Class I City
    c. A Class B City
    d. A municipality as is every other municipal corporation in Georgia

Chapter 11: The State Constitution

1. How many articles are there in the Georgia Constitution?
   a. Seven
   b. Eleven
   c. Seventeen
   d. Twenty-five

2. The present Constitution of the State of Georgia was basically written in:
   a. 1776
   b. 1860
   c. 1945
   d. 1983.

3. Which of the following constitutional statements is most true?
   a. John Locke is the exclusive source for basic theory
   b. Constitutional theory is extremely complex
   c. Jean Rousseau is the exclusive source for basic theory
   d. Georgia is a simple state and needs a simple constitution

4. Which of the following is not one of James Q. Wilson's types?
   a. Capitalistic Policies
   b. Majoritarian Policies
   c. Interest-Group Policies
   d. Entrepreneurial Policies

5. Which is a good example of Wilson's majoritarian policy?
   a. Welfare policy
   b. Hunting & fishing
   c. The Capitol Building
   d. Pollution taxes

6. Which is a good example of Wilson's client centered type?
   a. Welfare policy
   b. Hunting & fishing
   c. The Capitol Building
   d. Pollution Taxes

7. Which is a good example of Wilson's interest group type?
   a. Welfare policy
   b. Hunting & fishing
   c. The Capitol Building
   d. Pollution taxes

8. Which is a good example of Wilson's entrepreneurial type?
   a. Welfare policy
   b. Hunting & fishing
   c. The Capitol Building
   d. pollution taxes
9. In the Georgia Constitution, true majoritarian policies:
   a. Are the prevailing type
   b. exist only in the civil rights article
   c. Exist only in the taxation article
   d. Hardly exist at all
10. Belief that government should serve the general public is in:
    a. Client-Group Policies
    b. Majoritarian Policies
    c. Interest-Group Policies
    d. Entrepreneurial Policies
11. Generally, our Constitution rejects which of the following?
    a. Right of governing comes from conquest
    b. Right of governing comes from divine will
    c. Right of governing comes from ethnic superiority
    d. All of the above
12. Which of the following are emphasized in our Constitution?
    a. The rights of the people
    b. Limits on government power
    c. Limits on government officials
    d. all of the above
13. Since the present modern Georgia Constitution was adopted:
    a. Over sixty amendments were proposed
    b. Over sixty amendments were ratified
    c. Over sixty amendments were rejected
    d. All of the above
14. The _____ article of the Georgia Constitution is most amended.
    a. The Second
    b. The Fourth
    c. The Eighth
    d. The Last

Sample Final Examination

Georgia State Government   Name: _____

True/False Questions (2 points each)

___ 1. There are about 1,271 governments in the State of Georgia.
___ 2. The Speaker of the House is a major legislative official.
___ 3. There are 58 State Senators in the Georgia General Assembly.
___ 4. A Conference Committee is a special joint committee.
___ 5. Georgia has had over 40 constitutions in its history.
___ 6. Machiavelli said a Prince should act like a Lion and a Fox.
___ 7. Sovereign Immunity means legislators are free from arrest.
___ 8. Georgia lobbyists are required to wear identification badges.
___ 9. Equity Law decisions cannot be appealed to the State Supreme Court.
___ 10. Judicial review is a constitutional power in Georgia.

Multiple Choice Questions (2 points each)

___ 11. Georgia displays which of the following political cultures?
    a. Traditionalistic   b. Individualistic   c. Moralistic
    d. All of the above   e. None of the above

___ 12. In Georgia, the annual budget bill is drafted by the:
    a. Governor   b. Senate   c. House
    d. Courts   e. Popular referendum

___ 13. Who said that there are three basic political cultures?
    a. Hobbes   b. Locke   c. Rousseau
    d. Elazar   e. Burke

___ 14. The lower house of the General Assembly has how many members?
    a. 80   b. 180   c. 280
    d. 485   e. 535

___ 15. Which of the following budgets are used in Georgia?
    a. Operational   b. Capitol   c. Line-Item
    d. Off-line   e. All of the above

___ 16. Which of the following terms describe Georgia's bureaucracy?
    a. Effective   b. Expensive   c. Lovable
    d. Big   e. All of the above

___ 17. Among the characteristics of the Ideal Bureaucracy are all except:
    a. Hierarchy   b. Red Tape   c. Impersonality
    d. Destructiveness   e. Predictability

___ 18. Governor Zell Miller's Georgia Rebound program called for:
   a. Less money   b. More money   c. Personnel cutbacks
   d. Cutbacks of services e. More business regulation

___ 19. Which of the following are functions of the court system?
   a. Reservoir of Tradition b. Final Arbitrators   c. Balance Wheel
   d. Application of Laws   e. All of the above

___ 20. In the future, the Georgia Constitution is expected to change:
   a. Not at all   b. Just a little   c. Greatly in decades
   d. All of the above   e. None of the above

Fill-in-the-Blank Questions (2 points each)

___ 21. The Governor of Georgia is: _____.

___ 22. The total number of State Legislators _____.

___ 23. List four roles of the Governor not counting Commander-in-Chief.
   1. _____ 2. _____
   3. _____ 4. _____

___ 24. The right to abortion was set in: _____.

___ 25. Three extra rights in the Georgia Bill of Rights are:
   1. _____ 2. _____ 3. _____.

Matching Questions (1 point each)

___ 26. General Assembly   a) The power of the pen
___ 27. The Governor   b) One Hundred fifty-nine
___ 28. Bureaucracy   c) Has Home rule
___ 29. Courts   d) The Power of the purse
___ 30. Bill of Rights   e) Unique purposes
___ 31. Local Government   f) Are state agencies
___ 32. Special Districts   g) The power of the sword
___ 33. Authorities   h) Plural Executives
___ 34. Counties   i) Power of the people
___ 35. Commissions   j) The Power of expertise

Essay Question (Choose only 1; 30 points)

A. Discuss the significance of the Plural Executive in Georgia.

B. Explain the way in which a bill becomes a law. Be sure to include not only the committee system but also subsequent politics.

C. Describe the functioning of political parties in Georgia.

Appendix II
Georgia State Politics: The Constitutional Foundation

Preamble

To perpetuate the principles of free government, insure justice to all, preserve peace, promote the interest and happiness of the citizen and of the family, and transmit to posterity the enjoyment of liberty, we the people of Georgia, relying upon the protection and guidance of Almighty God, do ordain and establish this Constitution.

Article I
Bill of Rights

Section I
Rights of Persons

Paragraph I. Life, liberty, and property. No person shall be deprived of life, liberty, or property except by due process of law.

Paragraph II. Protection to person and property; equal protection. Protection to person and property is the paramount duty of government and shall be impartial and complete. No person shall be denied equal protection of the laws.

Paragraph III. Freedom of conscience. Each person has the natural and inalienable right to worship God, each according to the dictates of that person's own conscience; and no human authority should, in any case, control or interfere with such right of conscience.

Paragraph IV. Religious opinions; freedom of religion. No inhabitant of this state shall be molested in person or property or be prohibited from holding any public office or trust on account of religious opinions; but the right of freedom of religion shall not be constructed as to excuse acts of licentiousness or justify practices inconsistent with the peace and safety of the state.

Paragraph V. Freedom of speech and of the press guaranteed. No law shall be passed to curtail or restrain the freedom of speech or of the press. Every person may speak, write, publish sentiments on all subjects but shall be responsible for the abuse of that liberty.

Paragraph VI. Libel. In all civil or criminal actions for libel, the truth may be given in evidence; and, if it shall appear to the trier of fact that the matter charged as libelous is true, the party shall be discharged.

Paragraph VII. Citizens, protection of. All citizens of the United States, resident in this state, are hereby declared citizens of this state; and it shall be the duty of the General Assembly to enact such laws as will protect them in the full enjoyment of the rights, privileges, and immunities due to such citizenship.

Paragraph VIII. Arms, right to keep and bear. The right of the people to keep and bear arms shall not be infringed, but the General Assembly shall have the power to proscribe the manner in which arms may be borne.

Paragraph IX. Right to assemble and petition. The people have the right to assemble peaceably for their common good and to apply by petition or remonstrance to those vested with the powers of government for redress of grievances.

Paragraph X. Bill of attainder; ex post facto laws; and retroactive laws. No bill of attainer, ex post facto law, retroactive law, or laws impairing the obligation of contract or making irrevocable recant of special privileges or immunities shall be passed.

Paragraph XI. Right to trial by jury; number of jurors; selection and compensation of jurors.
  (a) The right to trial by jury shall remain inviolate, except that the court shall render judgement without the verdict of a jury in all civil cases where no issuable defense is filed and where a jury is not demanded in writing by either party. In criminal cases, the defendant shall have a public and speedy trial by an impartial jury; and the jury shall be the judges of the law and the facts.
  (b) A trial jury shall consist of 12 persons; but the General Assembly may prescribe any number, not less than six, to constitute a trial jury in the courts of limited jurisdiction and in superior courts in misdemeanor cases.
  (c) The General Assembly shall provide by law for the selection and compensation to persons to serve as grand jurors and trial jurors.

Paragraph XII. Rights to the courts. No person shall be deprived of the right to prosecute or defend, either in person or by an attorney, that person's own cause in any of the courts of this state.

Paragraph XIII. Searches, seizures, and warrants. The right of the people to be secure in their persons, houses, papers, and effects against unreasonable searches and seizures shall not be violated; and no warrant shall issue except under probable cause supported by oath or affirmation particularly describing the place or places to be searched and the persons or things to be seized.

Paragraph XIV. Benefit of counsel; accusation; list of witnesses; compulsory process. Every person charged with an offense against the laws of this state shall have the privilege and benefit of counsel; shall be furnished with a copy of the accusation or indictment and, on demand, with a list of witnesses on whose testimony such charge is founded, shall have the compulsory process to obtain the testimony of that person's own witnesses; and shall be confronted with the witnesses testifying against such person.

Paragraph XV. Habeas corpus. The writ of habeas corpus shall not be suspended unless, in case of rebellion or invasion, the public safety may require it.

Paragraph XVI. Self-incrimination. No person shall be compelled to give testimony tending in any manner to be self-incriminating.

Paragraph XVII. Bail; fines; punishment; arrest, abuse of prisoners. Excessive bail shall not be required, nor excessive fines imposed, nor cruel or unusual punishments inflicted; nor shall any person be abused in being arrested, while under arrest, or in prison.

Paragraph XVIII. Jeopardy of life or liberty more than once forbidden. No persons shall be put in jeopardy of life or liberty more than once for the same offense except when a new trial has been granted after conviction or in case of mistrial.

Paragraph XIX. Treason. Treason against the State of Georgia shall consist of insurrection against the state, adhering to the state's enemies, or giving them aid and comfort. No person shall be convicted of treason except on the testimony of two witnesses to the same overt act or confession in open court.

Paragraph XX. Conviction, effect of. No conviction shall work corruption of blood or forfeiture of estate.

Paragraph XXI. Banishment and whipping as punishment for crime. Neither banishment beyond the limits of the state nor whipping shall be allowed as punishment for crime.

Paragraph XXII. Involuntary servitude. There shall be no involuntary servitude within the State of Georgia except as a punishment for crime after legal conviction thereof or for contempt of court.

Paragraph XXIII. Imprisonment for debt. There shall be no imprisonment for debt.

Paragraph XXIV. Costs. No person shall be compelled to pay costs in any criminal case except after conviction on final trial.

Paragraph XXV. Status of the citizen. The social status of the citizen shall never be the subject of legislation.

Paragraph XXVI. Exemptions from levy and sale. The General Assembly shall protect by law from levy and sale by virtue of any process under the laws of this state a portion of the property of each person in an amount of not less than $1,600.00 and shall have authority to define to whom any such additional exemptions shall be allowed; to specify the amount of such exemptions; to provide for the manner of exempting such property and for the sale, alienation, and encumbrance thereof; and to provide for the waiver of said exemptions by the debtor.

Paragraph XXVII. Spouse's separate property. The separate property of each spouse shall remain the separate property of that spouse except as otherwise provided by law.

Paragraph XXVIII. Enumeration of rights not denial of others. The enumeration of rights herein contained as a part of this Constitution shall not be construed to deny to the people any inherent rights which they may have hitherto enjoyed.

Section II
Origin and Structure of Government

Paragraph I. Origin and foundation of government. All government, of right, originates with the people, is founded upon their will only, and is instituted solely for the good of the whole. Public officers are the trustees and servants of the people and are at all times amenable to them.

Paragraph II. Object of government. The people of this state have the inherent right of regulating their internal government. Government is instituted for the protection, security, and benefit of the people; and at all times they have the right to alter or reform the same whenever the public good may require it.

Paragraph III. Separation of legislative, judicial, and executive powers. The legislative, judicial, and executive powers shall forever remain separate and distinct; and no person discharging the duties of one shall at the same time exercise the function of either of the others except as herein provided.

Paragraph IV. Contempts. The power of the courts to punish for contempt shall be limited by legislative acts.

Paragraph V. What acts void. Legislative acts in violation of this Constitution or the Constitution of the United States are void, and the judiciary shall so declare them.

Paragraph VI. Superiority of civil authority. The civil authority shall be superior to the military.

Paragraph VII. Separation of church and state. No money shall ever be taken from the public treasury, directly or indirectly, in aid of any church, sect, cult, or religious denomination or of any sectarian institution.

Paragraph VIII. Lotteries and nonprofit bingo games.
- (a) *except as herein specifically provided in this Paragraph VIII, all lotteries, and the sale of lottery tickets, and all forms of parimutuel betting and casino gambling are hereby prohibited; and this prohibition shall be enforced by penal laws.*
- (b) *The General Assembly may by law provide that the operation of a nonprofit bingo game shall not be a lottery and shall be legal in this state. The General Assembly may by law define a nonprofit bingo game and provide for the regulation of nonprofit bingo games.*
- (c) *The general Assembly may by law provide that the operation and regulation of a lottery or lotteries by or on behalf of the state and for any matters relating to the purposes or provisions of this subparagraph. Proceeds derived from the lottery or lotteries operated by or on behalf of the state shall be used to pay the operating expenses of the lottery or lotteries, including all prizes, without any appropriations required by law, and for educational programs and purposes hereinafter provided. Lottery proceeds shall not be subject to Article VII, Section III, Paragraph II; Article III, Section IX, Paragraph VI(a); or Article III, Section IX, Paragraph IV(c), except that the net proceeds after payment of such operating expenses shall be subject to Article VII, Section III, Paragraph II. Net proceeds after payment of such operating expenses shall be separately accounted for and shall be specifically identified by the Governor in his annual budget presented to the General Assembly as a separate budget category entitled 'Lottery Proceeds' and the governor shall make specific recommendations as to educational programs and educational purposes to which said net proceeds shall be appropriated. In the General Appropriations Act adopted by the General Assembly, the General Assembly shall appropriate all net proceeds of the lottery or lotteries by such separate budget category to educational programs and educational purposes. Such net proceeds shall be used to support improvements and enhancements for educational programs and purposes and such net proceeds shall be used to supplement, not supplant, non-lottery educational resources for educational programs and purposes. The educational programs and educational purposes for which proceeds may be so appropriated shall include only the following:*
    - (1) *Tuition grants, scholarships, or loans to citizens of this state to enable such citizens to attend colleges and universities located within this state, regardless of whether such colleges or universities are operated by the board of regents, or to attend institutions operated under the authority of the Department of Technical and Adult Education;*
    - (2) *Voluntary pre-kindergarten;*
    - (3) *One or more educational shortfall reserves in a total amount of not less than 10 percent of the net proceeds of the lottery for the preceding fiscal year;*

(4) *Costs of providing to teachers at accredited public institutions who teach levels K–12, personnel at public postsecondary technical institutes under the authority of the Department of Technical and Adult Education, and professors and instructors within the University System of Georgia the necessary training in the use and application of computers and advanced electronic instructional technology to implement interactive learning environments in the classroom and to access the statewide distance learning network; and*

(5) *Capital outlay projects for educational facilities; provided, however, that no funds shall be appropriated for the items listed in paragraphs (4) and (5) of this subsection until all persons eligible for and applying for assistance as provided in paragraph (1) of this subsection have received such assistance, all approved prekindergarten programs provided for in paragraph (2) of this subsection have been fully funded, and the education shortfall reserve or reserves provided for in paragraph (3) of this subsection have been fully funded.* (Amendment approved Nov. 3, 1998, CVIG.).

(d) *On and after January 1, 1995, the holding of raffles by nonprofit organizations shall be lawful and shall not be prohibited by any law enacted prior to January 1, 1995. Laws enacted on or after January 1, 1994, however, may restrict, regulate or prohibit the operation of such raffles.* (Source: Sec.St. 1997).

Paragraph IX. Sovereign immunity and waiver thereof; claims against the state and its departments, agencies, officers and employees.

(a) *The General Assembly may waive the state's sovereign immunity from suit by enacting a State Tort Claims Act, in which the General Assembly may provide by law for procedures for the making, handling, and disposition of actions or claims against the state and its departments, agencies, offices, and employees, upon such terms and subject to such conditions and limitations as the General Assembly may provide.*

(b) *The General Assembly may also provide by law for the processing and disposition of claims against the state which do not exceed such maximum amount as provided therein.*

(c) *The states defense of sovereign immunity is hereby waived as to any action ex contractu for the breach of any written contract now existing or hereafter entered into by the state or its departments and agencies.*

(d) *Except as specifically provided by the General Assembly in a State Tort Claims Act, all officers and employees of the state or its departments and agencies may be subject to suit and may be liable for injuries and damages caused by the negligent performance of, or negligent failure to perform, their ministerial functions and may be liable for injuries and damages if they act with actual malice or with actual intent to cause injury to the performance of their official functions. Except as provided in this subparagraph, officers and employees of the state or its departments and agencies shall not be subject to suit or liability, and no judgment shall be entered against them, for the performance or nonperformance of their official functions. The provision of this subparagraph shall not be waived.*

(e) *Except as specifically provided in this paragraph, sovereign immunity extends to the state and all of its departments and agencies. The sovereign immunity of the state and its departments and agencies can only be waived by an Act of the General Assembly which specifically provides that sovereign immunity is thereby waived and the extent of such waiver.*

(f) *No waiver of sovereign immunity under this paragraph shall be construed as a waiver of any immunity provided to the state or its departments, agencies, officers, or employees by the United States Constitution.* (Authority: OLC, pages 44–45).

Section III
General Provisions

Paragraph I. Eminent domain.
(a) Except as otherwise provided in this Paragraph, private property shall not be taken or damaged for public purposes without just and adequate compensation being first paid.
(b) When private property is taken or damaged by the state or the counties or municipalities of the state for public road or street purposes, or for public transportation purposes, or for any other public purpose as determined by the General Assembly, just and adequate compensation therefor need not be paid until the same has been finally fixed and determined as provided by law; but such just and adequate compensation shall then be paid in preference to all other obligations except bonded indebtedness.
(c) The General Assembly may by law require the condemnor to make prepayment against adequate compensation as a condition precedent to the exercise of the right of eminent domain and provide for the disbursement of the same to the end that the rights and equities of the property owner, lien holders, and the state and its subdivisions may be protected.
(d) The General Assembly may provide by law for the payment by the condemnor of reasonable expenses, including attorney's fees, incurred by the condemnee in determining just and adequate compensation.
(e) Notwithstanding any other provision of the Constitution, the General Assembly may provide by law for relocation assistance and payments to persons displaced through the exercise of the power of eminent domain or because of public projects or programs; and the powers of taxation may be exercised and public funds expended in furtherance thereof.

Paragraph II. Private ways. In case of necessity, private ways may be granted upon just and adequate compensation being first paid by the applicant.

Paragraph III. Tidewater titles confirmed. The Act of the General Assembly approved December 16, 1902, which extends the title of ownership of lands abutting on tidal water to low water mark, is hereby ratified and confirmed.

Article II
Voting and Elections

Section I
Method of Voting; Right to Register and Vote

Paragraph I. Method of voting. Elections by the people shall be by secret ballot and shall be conducted in accordance with procedures provided by law.

Paragraph II. Right to register and vote. Every person who is a citizen of the United States and a resident of Georgia as defined by law, who is at least 18 years of age and not disenfranchised by this article, and who meets minimum residency requirements as provided by law shall be entitled to vote at any election by the people. The General Assembly shall provide by law for the registration of electors.

Paragraph III. Exceptions to right to register and vote.
(a) No person who has been convicted of a felony involving moral turpitude may register, remain registered, or vote except upon completion of the sentence.
(b) No person who has been judicially determined to be mentally incompetent may register, remain registered, or vote unless the disability has been removed.

Section II
General Provisions

Paragraph I. Procedures to be provided by law. The General Assembly shall provide by law for a method of appeal from the decision to allow or refuse to allow any person to register or vote and shall provide by law for a procedure whereby returns of all elections by the people shall be made to the Secretary of State.

Paragraph II. Run-off election. A run-off election shall be a continuation of the general election and only persons who were entitled to vote in the general election shall be entitled to vote therein; and only those votes cast for the persons designated for the runoff shall be counted in the tabulation and canvass of the voters cast.

Paragraph III. Persons not eligible to hold office. *No person who is not a registered voter or who has been convicted of a felony involving moral turpitude, unless that person's civil rights have been restored and at least ten years have elapsed from the date of the completion of the sentence without a subsequent conviction of another felony involving moral turpitude, or who is the holder of public funds illegally shall be eligible to hold any office or appointment of honor or trust in this state. Additional conditions of eligibility to hold office for persons elected on a write-in vote and for persons holding offices or appointments of honor or trust other than elected offices created by this Constitution may be provided by law.* (Authority: OLC, page 56).

Paragraph IV. Recall of public officials holding elective office. *The General Assembly is hereby authorized to provide by general law for the recall of public officials who hold elective office. The procedures, grounds, and all other matters relative to such recall shall be provided for in such law.*

Paragraph V. Vacancies created by elected officials qualifying for other office. *The office of any state, county, or municipal elected official shall be declared vacant upon such elected official qualifying, in a general primary or general election, or special primary or special election, for another state, county, or municipal elective office or qualifying for the House of Representatives or the Senate of the United States if the term of the office for which such official is qualifying for begins more than 30 days prior to the expiration of such official's present term of office. The vacancy created in any such office shall be filled as provided by this Constitution or any general or local law. This provision shall not apply to any elected official seeking or holding more than one elective office when the holding of such offices simultaneously is specifically authorized by law.* (Authority: OLC, page 58).

Section III
Suspension and Removal of Public Officials

Paragraph I. Procedures for and effect of suspending or removing public officials upon felony indictment.
  (a) *As used in this paragraph, the term "public official" means the Governor, the Lieutenant Governor, the Secretary of State, the Attorney General, the State School Superintendent, the Commissioner of Insurance, the Commissioner of Agriculture, the Commissioner of Labor, and any member of the General Assembly.*
  (b) *Upon indictment for a felony by a grand jury of this state or by the United States which felony indictment relates to the performance or activities of the office of any public official, the Attorney General or district attorney shall transmit a certified copy of the indictment to the Governor or, if the indicted public official is the Governor, to the Lieutenant Governor who shall, subject to subparagraph (d) of this Paragraph, appoint a review commission. If the indicted public official is the Governor, the commission shall be*

composed of the Attorney General, the Secretary of State, the State School Superintendent, the Commissioner of Insurance, the Commissioner of Agriculture, and the Commissioner of Labor. If the indicted public official is the Attorney General, the commission shall be composed of three other public officials who are not members of the General Assembly. If the indicted public official is not the Governor, the Attorney General, or a member of the General Assembly, the commission shall be composed of the Attorney General and two other public officials who are not members of the General Assembly. If the indicted public official is a member of the General Assembly, the commission shall be composed of the Attorney General and one member of the Senate and one member of the House of Representatives. If the Attorney General brings the indictment against the public official, the Attorney General shall not serve on the commission. In place of the Attorney General, the Governor shall appoint a retired Supreme Court Justice or a retired Court of Appeals Judge. The commission shall provide a speedy hearing, including notice of the nature and cause of the hearing, process for obtaining witnesses, and the assistance of counsel. Unless a longer period of time is granted by the appointing authority, the commission shall make a written report within 14 days. If the commission determines that the indictment relates to and adversely affects the administration of the office of the indicted public official and that the rights and interests of the public are adversely affected thereby, the Governor or, if the Governor is the indicted public official, the Lieutenant Governor shall suspend the public official immediately and without further action pending the final disposition of the case or until the expiration of the officer's term of office, whichever occurs first. During the term of office to which such officer was elected and in which the indictment occurred, if a nolle prosequi is entered, if the public official is acquitted, or if after conviction the conviction is later overturned as a result of any direct appeal or application for a writ of certiorari, the officer shall be immediately reinstated to the office from which he was suspended. While a public official is suspended under this paragraph and until initial conviction by the trial court the officer shall continue to receive the compensation from his office. After initial conviction by the trial court, the officer shall not be entitled to receive any compensation from his office. If the officer is reinstated to office, he shall be entitled to receive any compensation withheld under the provisions of this Paragraph.

(c) Unless the Governor is the public officer under suspension, for the duration of any suspension under this Paragraph, the Governor shall appoint a replacement officer except in the case of a member of the General Assembly. If the Governor is the public officer under suspension, the provisions of Article V, Section I, Paragraph V of this constitution shall apply as if the Governor were temporarily disabled. Upon a final conviction with no appeal or review pending, the office shall be declared vacant and a successor to that office shall be chosen as provided in this constitution or the laws enacted in pursuance thereof.

(d) No commission shall be appointed for a period of 14 days from the day the indictment was received. This period of time may be extended by the Governor. During this period of time, the indicted public official may, in writing, authorize the Governor or, if the Governor is the indicted public official, the Lieutenant Governor to suspend him from office. Any such voluntary suspension shall be subject to the same conditions for review, reinstatement, or declaration of vacancy as are provided in this Paragraph for nonvoluntary suspension.

(e) After any suspension is imposed under this paragraph, the suspended public official may petition the appointing authority for a review. The Governor or, if the indicted public official is the Governor, the Lieutenant Governor may reappoint the commission to review the suspension. The commission shall make a written report within 14 days. If the com-

mission recommends that the public official be reinstated, he shall immediately be reinstated to office.
(f) The report and records of the commission and the fact that the public official has or has not been suspended shall not be admissible in evidence in any court for any purpose. The report and record of the commission shall not be open to the public.
(g) The provisions of this Paragraph shall not apply to any indictment handed down prior to January 1, 1985.
(h) If a public official who is suspended from office under the provisions of this Paragraph is not first tried at the next regular or special term following the indictment, the suspension shall be terminated and the public official shall be reinstated to office. The public official shall not be reinstated under this subparagraph if he is not so tired based on a continuance granted upon a motion by the defendant. (Authority: OLC, pages 59–61).

Paragraph II. Suspension upon felony conviction. Upon initial conviction of any public official designated in Paragraph I of this section for any felony in a trial court of this state or the United States, regardless of whether the officer had been suspended previously under Paragraph I of this section, such public official shall be immediately and without further action suspended from office. While a public official is suspended from office under this Paragraph, he shall not be entitled to receive the compensation from his office. If the conviction is later overturned as a result of any direct appeal or application for a writ of certiorari, the public official shall be immediately reinstated to the office from which he was suspended and shall be entitled to receive any compensation withheld under the provisions of this Paragraph. Unless the Governor is the public official under suspension, for the duration of any suspension under this Paragraph, the Governor shall appoint a replacement official except in the case of a member of the General Assembly. If the Governor is the public officer under suspension, the provisions of Article V, Section I, Paragraph V of this Constitution shall apply as if the Governor were temporarily disabled. Upon a final conviction with no appeal or review pending, the office shall be declared vacant and a successor to that office shall be chosen as provided in this Constitution or the laws enacted in the pursuance thereof. The provisions of this Paragraph shall not apply to any conviction rendered prior to January 1, 1987. (Authority: OLC, pages 61–62).

Article III
Legislative Branch

Section I
Legislative Power

Paragraph I. Power vested in General Assembly. The Legislative power of the state shall be vested in a General Assembly which shall consist of a Senate and a House of Representatives.

Section II
Composition of General Assembly

Paragraph I. Senate and House of Representatives.
(a) The Senate shall consist of not more than 56 Senators, each of whom shall be elected from single member districts.
(b) The House of Representatives shall consist of not fewer than 180 Representatives apportioned among representative districts of the state.

Paragraph II. Apportionment of General Assembly. The General Assembly shall apportion the Senate and House districts. Such districts shall be composed of contiguous territory. The apportionment of the Senate and of the House of Representatives shall be changed by the General Assembly as necessary after each United States decennial census.

Paragraph III. Qualifications of members of General Assembly.
(a) At the time of their election, the members of the Senate shall be citizens of the United States, shall be at least 25 years of age, shall have been citizens of this state for at least two years, and shall have been legal residents of the territory embraced within the district from which elected for at least one year.
(b) At the time of their election, the members of the House of Representatives shall be citizens of the United States, shall be at least 21 years of age, shall have been citizens of this state for at least two years, and shall have been legal residents of the territory embraced within the district from which elected for at least one year.

Paragraph IV. Disqualifications.
(a) No person on active duty with any branch of the armed forces of the United States shall have a seat in either house unless otherwise provided by law.
(b) No person holding any civil appointment or office having any emolument annexed thereto under the United States, this state, or any other state shall have a seat in either house.
(c) No Senator or Representative shall be elected by the General Assembly or appointed by the Governor to any office or appointment having any emolument annexed thereto during the time for which such person shall have been elected unless the Senator or Representative shall first resign the seat to which elected; provided, however, that, during the term for which elected, no Senator or Representative shall be appointed to any civil office which has been created during such term.

Paragraph V. Election and term of office.
(a) The members of the General Assembly shall be elected by the qualified electors of their respective districts for a term of two years and shall serve until the time fixed for the convening of the next General Assembly.
(b) The members of the General Assembly in office on June 30, 1983, shall serve out the remainder of the terms to which elected.
(c) The first election for members of the General Assembly under this Constitution shall take place on Tuesday after the first Monday in November, 1984, and subsequent elections biennially on that day until the day of election is changed by law.

Section III
Officers of the General Assembly

Paragraph I. President and President Pro Tempore of the Senate
(a) The Presiding officer of the Senate shall be styled the President of the Senate.
(b) A President Pro Tempore shall be elected by the Senate from among its members. The President Pro Tempore shall act as President in case of the temporary disability of the President. In case of the death, resignation, or permanent disability of the President or in the event of the succession of the President to the executive power, the President Pro Tempore shall become President and shall receive the same compensation and allowances as the Speaker of the House of Representatives. The General Assembly shall provide by law for the method of determining disability as provided in this paragraph.

Paragraph II. Speaker and Speaker Pro Tempore of the House of Representatives.
(a) The presiding officer of the House of Representatives shall be styled the Speaker of the House of Representatives and shall be elected by the House of Representatives from among its members.
(b) A Speaker Pro Tempore shall be elected by the House of Representatives from among its members. The Speaker Pro Tempore shall become Speaker in case of the death, resignation, or permanent disability of the Speaker and shall serve until a Speaker is elected. Such election shall be held as provided in the rules of the House. The General Assembly shall provide by law for the method of determining disability as provided in this paragraph.

Paragraph III. Other officers of the two houses. The other officers of the two houses shall be a Secretary of the Senate and a Clerk of the House of Representatives.

Section IV
Organization and procedure of the General Assembly

Paragraph I. Meeting, time limit and adjournment.
(a) The Senate and House of Representatives shall organize each odd-numbered year and shall be a different General Assembly for each two-year period. The General Assembly shall meet in regular session on the second Monday in January of each year, or otherwise as provided by law, and may continue in session for a period of no longer than 40 days in the aggregate each year. By concurrent resolution, the General Assembly may adjourn any regular session to such later date as it may fix for reconvening. Separate periods of adjournment may be fixed by one or more such concurrent resolutions.
(b) Neither house shall adjourn during a regular session for more than three days or meet in any place other than the state capitol without the consent of the other. Following the fifth day of a special session, either house may adjourn not more than twice for a period not to exceed seven days for such adjournment. In the event either house, after the thirtieth day of any session, adopts a resolution to adjourn for a specified period of time and such resolution and any amendments thereto are not adopted by both houses by the end of the legislative day on which adjournment was called for in such resolution, the governor may adjourn both houses for a period of time not to exceed ten days.
(c) If an impeachment trial is pending at the end of any session, the House shall adjourn and the Senate shall remain in session until such trial is completed.

Paragraph II. Oath of members. Each Senator and Representative, before taking the seat to which elected, shall take the oath or affirmation prescribed by law.

Paragraph III. Quorum. A majority of the members to which each house is entitled shall constitute a quorum to transact business. A smaller number may adjourn from day to day and compel the presence of its absent members.

Paragraph IV. Rules of procedure; employees; interim committees. Each house shall determine its rules of procedure and may provide for its employees. Interim committees may be created by or pursuant to the authority of the General Assembly or of either house.

Paragraph V. Vacancies. When a vacancy occurs in the General Assembly, it shall be filled as provided by this constitution and by law. The seat of a member of either house shall be vacant upon the removal of such member's legal residence from the district from which elected.

Paragraph VI. Salaries. The members of the General Assembly shall receive such salary as shall be provided for by law, provided that no increase in salary shall become effective prior to the end of the term during which such change is made.

Paragraph VII. Election and returns; disorderly conduct. Each house shall be the judge of the election, returns, and qualifications of its members and shall have power to punish them for disorderly behavior or misconduct by censure, fine, imprisonment, or expulsion; but no member shall be expelled except by a vote of two-thirds of the members of the house to which such member belongs.

Paragraph VIII. Contempts, how punished. Each house may punish by imprisonment, not extending beyond the session, any person not a member who shall be guilty of a contempt by disorderly behavior in its presence or who shall rescue or attempt to rescue any person arrested by order of either house.

Paragraph IX. Privilege of members. The members of both houses shall be free from arrest during sessions of the General Assembly, or committee meetings thereof, and in going thereto or returning therefrom, except for treason, felony, or breach of the peace. No member shall be liable to answer in any other place for anything spoken in either house or in any committee meeting of either house.

Paragraph X. Elections by either house. All elections by either house of the General Assembly shall be by recorded vote, and the vote shall appear on the respective journal of each house.

Paragraph XI. Open meetings. The sessions of the General Assembly and all standing committee meetings thereof shall be open to the public. Either house may by rule provide for exceptions to this requirement.

Section V
Enactment of Laws

Paragraph I. Journals and laws. Each house shall keep and publish after its adjournment a journal of its proceedings. The original journals shall be the sole, official records of the proceedings of each house and shall be preserved as provided by law. The General Assembly shall provide for the publication of the laws passed at each session.

Paragraph II. Bills for revenue. All bills for raising revenue, or appropriating money, shall originate in the House of Representatives.

Paragraph III. One subject matter expressed. No bill shall pass which refers to more than one subject matter or contains matter different from what is expressed in the title thereof.

Paragraph IV. Statutes and sections of Code, how amended. No law or section of the Code shall be amended or repealed by mere reference to its title or to the number of the section of the Code; but the amending or repealing Act shall distinctly describe the law or Code section to be amended or repealed as well as the alteration to be made.

Paragraph V. Majority of members to pass bill. No bill shall become law unless it shall receive a majority of the votes of all the members to which each house is entitled, and such vote shall so appear on the journal of each house.

Paragraph VI. When roll-call vote taken. In either house, when ordered by the presiding officer or at the desire of one-fifth of the members present or a lesser number if so provided by the rules of either house, a roll-call vote on any question shall be taken and shall be entered on the journal. The yeas and nays in each house shall be recorded and entered on the journal upon the passage or rejection of any bill or resolution appropriating money and whenever the Constitution requires a vote of two-thirds of either or both houses for the passage of a bill or resolution.

Paragraph VII. Reading of general bills. The title of every general bill and of every resolution intended to have the effect of general law or to amend this Constitution or to propose a new constitution shall be read three times and on three separate days in each house before such bill or resolution shall be voted upon; and the third reading of such bill and resolution shall be in their entirety when ordered by the presiding officer or by a majority of the members voting on such question in either house.

Paragraph VIII. Procedure for considering local legislation. The General Assembly may provide by law for the procedure for considering local legislation. The title of every local bill and every resolution intended to have the effect of local law shall be read at least once before such bill or resolution shall be voted upon; and no such bill or resolution shall be voted upon prior to the second day following the day of introduction.

Paragraph IX. Advertisement of notice to introduce local legislation. The General Assembly shall provide by law for the advertisement of notice of intention to introduce local bills.

Paragraph X. Acts signed. All Acts shall be signed by the President of the Senate and the Speaker of the House of Representatives.

Paragraph XI. Signature of Governor. No provision in this Constitution for a two-thirds' vote of both houses of the General Assembly shall be construed to waive the necessity for the signature of the Governor as in any other case, except in the case of the two-thirds' vote required to override the veto or to submit proposed constitutional amendments or a proposal for a new Constitution.

Paragraph XII. Rejected bills. No bill or resolution intended to have the effect of law which shall have been rejected by either house shall again be proposed during the same regular or special session under the same or any other title without the consent of two-thirds of the house by which the same was rejected.

Paragraph XIII. Approval, veto, and override of veto of bills and resolutions.
(a) All bills and all resolutions which have been passed by the General Assembly intended to have the effect of law shall become law if the Governor approves or fails to veto the same within six days from the date any such bill or resolution is transmitted to the Governor unless the General Assembly adjourns sine die or adjourns for more than 40 days prior to the expiration of said six days. In the case of such adjournment sine die or of such adjournment for more than 40 days, the same shall become law if approved or not vetoed by the Governor within 40 days from the date of any such adjournment.
(b) During sessions of the General Assembly or during any period of adjournment of a session of the General Assembly, no bill or resolution shall be transmitted to the Governor after passage except upon request of the Governor or upon order of two-thirds of the membership of each house. A local bill which is required by the Constitution to have a referendum election conducted before it shall become effective shall be transmitted immediately to the Governor when ordered by the presiding officer of the house wherein the bill shall have originated or upon order of two-thirds of the membership of such house.
(c) The Governor shall have the duty to transmit any vetoed bill or resolution, together with the reasons for such veto, to the presiding officer of the house wherein it originated within three days from the date of veto if the General Assembly is in session on the day of transmission. If the General Assembly adjourns sine die or adjourns for more than 40 days, the Governor shall transmit any vetoed bill or resolution, together with the reasons for such veto, to the presiding officer of the house wherein it originated within 60 days of the date of such adjournment.
(d) During sessions of the General Assembly, any vetoed bill or resolution may upon receipt be immediately considered by the house wherein it originated for the purpose of overriding the veto. If two-thirds of the members to which such house is entitled vote to override the veto of the Governor, the same shall be immediately transmitted to the other

house where it shall be immediately considered. Upon the vote to override the veto by two-thirds of the members to which such other house is entitled, such bill or resolution shall become law. All bills and resolutions vetoed during the last three days of the session and not considered for the purpose of overriding the veto and all bills and resolutions vetoed after the General Assembly has adjourned sine die may be considered at the next session of the General Assembly for the purpose of overriding the veto in the manner herein provided. If either house shall fail to override the Governor's veto, neither house shall again consider such bill or resolution for the purpose of overriding such veto.

(e) The Governor may approve any appropriation and veto any other appropriation in the same bill, and any appropriation vetoed shall not become law unless such veto is overridden in the manner herein provided.

Paragraph XIV. Jointly sponsored bills and resolutions. The General Assembly may provide by law for the joint sponsorship of bills and resolutions.

Section VI
Exercise of Powers

Paragraph I. General powers. The General Assembly shall have the power to make all laws not inconsistent with this Constitution, and not repugnant to the Constitution of the United States, which it shall deem necessary and proper for the welfare of the state.

Paragraph II. Specific powers.
(a) Without limitation of the powers granted under Paragraph I, the General Assembly shall have the power to provide by law for:
   (1) Restrictions upon land use in order to protect and preserve the natural resources, environment, and vital areas of this state.
   (2) A militia and for the trial by courts-martial and nonjudicial punishment of its members, the discipline of whom, when not in federal service, shall be in accordance with law and the directives of the Governor acting as commander in chief.
   (3) The participation by the state and political subdivisions and instrumentalities of the state in federal programs and the compliance with laws relating thereto, including but not limited to the powers, which may be exercised to the extent and in the manner necessary to effect such participation and compliance, to tax, to expend public money, to condemn property, and to zone property.
   (4) The continuity of state and local governments in periods of emergency resulting from disasters caused by enemy attack including but not limited to the suspension of all constitutional legislative rules during such emergency.
   (5) The participation by the state with any county, municipality, nonprofit organization, or any combination thereof in the operation of any of the facilities operated by such agencies for the purpose of encouraging and promoting tourism in this state.
   (6) The control and regulation of outdoor advertising devices adjacent to federal and interstate and primary highways and for the acquisition of property or interest therein for such purposes and may exercise the powers of taxation and provide for the expenditure of public funds in connection therewith.
(b) The General Assembly shall have the power to implement the provisions of Article I, Section III, Paragraph I(2.); Article IV, Section VIII, Paragraph II; Article IV, Section VIII, Paragraph III; and Article X, Section II, Paragraph XII of the Constitution of 1976 in force and effect on June 30, 1983; and all laws heretofore adopted thereunder and valid at the time of their enactment shall continue in force and effect until modified or repealed.

(c) The distribution of tractors, farm equipment, heavy equipment, new motor vehicles, and parts therefor in the State of Georgia vitally affects the general economy of the state and the public interests and public welfare. Notwithstanding the provisions of Article I, Section I, Paragraphs I, II, and III or Article III, Section VI, Paragraph V(c) of this constitution, the General Assembly in the exercise of its police power shall be authorized to regulate tractor, farm equipment, heavy equipment, and new vehicle manufactures, distributors, dealers, and their representatives doing business in Georgia, including agreements among such parties, in order to prevent frauds, unfair business practices, unfair methods of competition, impositions, and other abuses upon its citizens. Any law enacted by the General Assembly shall not impair the obligation of an existing contract but may apply with respect to the renewal of such a contract after the effective data of such law. (Source GA.L. 1992. Page 3342).

Paragraph III. Powers not to be abridged. The General Assembly shall not abridge its powers under this Constitution. No law enacted by the General Assembly shall be construed to limit its powers.

Paragraph IV. Limitations on special legislation.
(a) Laws of a general nature shall have uniform operation throughout this state and no local or special law shall be enacted in any case for which provision has been made by an existing general law, except that the General Assembly may by general law authorize local governments by local ordinance or resolution to exercise police powers which do not conflict with general laws.
(b) No population bill, as the General Assembly shall define by general law, shall be passed. No bill using classification by population as a means of determining the applicability of any bill or law to any political subdivision or group of political subdivisions may expressly or impliedly amend, modify, supersede, or repeal the general law defining a population bill.
(c) No special law relating to the rights or status of private persons shall be enacted.

Paragraph V. Specific limitations.
(a) The General Assembly shall not have the power to grant incorporation to private persons but shall provide by general law the manner in which private corporate powers and privileges may be granted.
(b) The General Assembly shall not forgive the forfeiture of the charter of any corporation existing on August 13, 1945, nor shall it grant any benefit to or permit any amendment to the charter of any corporation except upon the condition that the acceptance thereof shall operate as a novation of the charter and that such corporation shall thereafter hold its charter subject to the provisions of this Constitution.
(c) The General Assembly shall not have the power to authorize any contract or agreement which may have the effect of or which is intended to have the effect of defeating or lessening competition, or encouraging a monopoly, which are hereby declared to be unlawful and void.
(d) The General Assembly shall not have the power to regulate or fix charges of public utilities owned or operated by any county or municipality of this state except as authorized by this Constitution.
(e) No municipal or county authority is authorized to construct, improve, or maintain any road or street on behalf of, pursuant to a contract with, or through the use of taxes or other revenues of a county or municipal corporation shall be created by any local Act or pursuant to any general Act nor shall any law specifically relating to any such authority be amended unless the creation of such authority or the amendment of such law is conditioned upon the approval of a majority of the qualified voters of the county or municipality corporation affected voting in a referendum thereon. This subparagraph shall not apply to or affect any state authority. (Authority: OLC, pages 70–71).

Paragraph VI. Gratuities.
(a) Except as otherwise provided in the Constitution, (1) the General Assembly shall not have the power to grant any donation or gratuity or to forgive any debt or obligation owing to the public, and (2) the General Assembly shall not grant or authorize extra compensation to any public officer, agent, or contractor after the service has been rendered or the contract entered into.
(b) All laws heretofore adopted under Article III, Section VIII, Paragraph XII of the Constitution of 1976 in force and effect on June 30, 1983, shall continue in force and effect and may be amended if such amendments are consistent with the authority granted to the General Assembly by said provisions of said Constitution.
(c) The General Assembly may provide by law and may expend or authorize the expenditure of public funds for a health insurance plan or program for persons and the spouses and dependent children of persons who are retired former employees of public schools or public school systems of this state.
(d) The General Assembly may provide by law for indemnification with respect to licensed emergency management rescue specialists who are or have been killed or permanently disabled in the line of duty on or after January 1, 1991, and publicly employed emergency medical technicians who are or have been killed or permanently disabled in the line of duty on or after January 1, 1987.
(e) The General Assembly may provide by law for a program of indemnification with respect to the death or permanent disability of any law enforcement officer, fireman, prison guard, or publicly employed emergency medical technician who is or at any time in the past was killed or permanently disabled in the line of duty. Funds shall be appropriated as necessary for payment of such indemnification or for the purchase of insurance for such indemnification or both.
(f) The General Assembly is authorized to provide by law for compensating innocent victims of crimes which occur on and after July 1, 1989. The General Assembly is authorized to define the types of victims eligible to receive compensation and to vary the amounts of compensation according to need. The General Assembly shall be authorized to allocate certain funds, to appropriate funds, to provide for a continuing fund, or to provide for any combination thereof for the purpose of compensating innocent victims of crime and for the administration of any laws enacted for such purpose. (Authority: OLC, pages 72–73).

Paragraph VII. Regulation of alcoholic beverages. The State of Georgia shall have full and complete authority to regulate alcoholic beverages and to regulate, restrict, or prohibit activities involving alcoholic beverages. This regulatory authority of the state shall include all such regulatory authority as is permitted to the states under the Twenty-First Amendment to the United States Constitution. This regulatory authority of the state is specifically delegated to the counties and municipalities of the state for the purpose of regulating, restricting, or prohibiting the exhibition of nudity, partial nudity, or depictions of nudity in connection with the sale or consumption of alcoholic beverages; and such delegated regulatory authority may be exercised by the adoption and enforcement of regulatory ordinances by the counties and municipalities of this state. A general law exercising such regulatory authority shall control over conflicting provisions of any local ordinance but shall not preempt any local ordinance provisions not in direct conflict with general law. (Source: Sec.St. 1997).

Section VII
Impeachments

Paragraph I. Power to impeach. The House of representatives shall have the sole power to vote impeachment charges against any executive or judicial officer of this state or any member of the General Assembly.

Paragraph II. Trial of impeachments. The Senate shall have the sole power to try impeachments. When sitting for that purpose, the Senators shall be on oath, or affirmation, and shall be presided over by the Chief Justice of the Supreme Court. Should the Chief Justice be disqualified, then the Presiding Justice shall preside. Should the Presiding Justice be disqualified, then the Senate shall select a Justice of the Supreme Court to preside. No person shall be convicted without concurrence of two-thirds of the members to which the Senate is entitled.

Paragraph III. Judgements in impeachment. In cases of impeachment, judgments shall not extend further than removal from office and disqualification to hold and enjoy any office of honor, trust, or profit within this state or to receive a pension therefrom, but no such judgment shall relieve any party from any criminal or civil liability.

Section VIII
Insurance Regulation

Paragraph I. Regulation of insurance. Provision shall be made by law for the regulation of insurance.

Paragraph II. Issuance of licenses. Insurance licenses shall be issued by the Commissioner of Insurance as required by law.

Section IX
Appropriations

Paragraph I. Public money, how drawn. No money shall be drawn from the treasury except by appropriation made by law.

Paragraph II. Preparation, submission, and enactment of general appropriations bills.
(a) The Governor shall submit to the General Assembly within five days after its convening in regular session each year a budget message and a budget report, accompanied by a draft of a general appropriations bill, in such form and manner as may be prescribed by statute, which shall provide for the appropriation of the funds necessary to operate all the various departments and agencies and to meet the current expenses of the state for the next fiscal year.
(b) The General Assembly shall annually appropriate those state and federal funds necessary to operate all the various departments and agencies. To the extent that federal funds received by the state for any program, project, activity, purpose, or expenditure are changed by federal authority or exceed the amount or amounts appropriated in the general appropriations Act or supplementary appropriations Act or Acts, or are not anticipated, such excess, changed or unanticipated federal funds are hereby continually appropriated for the purposes authorized and directed by the federal government in making the grant. In those instances where the conditions under which the federal funds have been made available do not provide otherwise, federal funds shall first be used to replace state funds that were appropriated to supplant federal funds in the same state fiscal year. The fiscal year of the state shall commence on the first day of July of each year and terminate on the thirtieth of June following.
(c) The General Assembly shall by general law provide for the regulation and management of the finance and fiscal administration of the state.

Paragraph III. General appropriations bill. The general appropriations bill shall embrace nothing except appropriations fixed by previous laws; the ordinary expenses of the executive, legislative, and judicial departments of the government; payment of the public debt and interest thereon; and for support of the public institutions and educational interests of the state. All other appropriations shall be made by separate bills, each embracing but one subject.

Paragraph IV. General appropriations Act.
(a) Each general appropriations Act, now of force or hereafter adopted with such amendments as are adopted from time to time, shall continue in force and effect for the next fiscal year after adoption and it shall then expire, except for the mandatory appropriations required by this Constitution and those required to meet contractual obligations authorized by this Constitution and the continued appropriation of federal grants.
(b) The General Assembly shall not appropriate funds for any given fiscal year which, in aggregate, exceed a sum equal to the amount of unappropriated surplus expected to have accrued in the state treasury at the beginning of the fiscal year together with an amount not greater than the total treasury receipts from existing revenue sources anticipated to be collected in the fiscal year, less refunds, as estimated in the budget report and amendments thereto. Supplementary appropriations, if any, shall be made in the manner provided in Paragraph V of this section of the Constitution; but in no event shall a supplementary appropriations Act continue in force and effect beyond the expiration of the general appropriations Act in effect when such supplementary appropriations Act was adopted and approved.
(c) All appropriated state funds, except for the mandatory appropriations required by this constitution, remaining unexpended and not contractually obligated at the expiration of such general appropriations Act shall lapse.
(d) Funds appropriated to or received by the State Housing Trust Fund for the Homeless shall not be subject to the provisions of Article III, Section IX, Paragraph IV(c), relative to the lapsing of funds, and may be expended for programs of purely public charity for the homeless, including programs involving the participation of churches and religious institutions, notwithstanding the provisions of Article I, Section II, Paragraph VII. (Authority: OLC, page 76).

Paragraph V. Other or supplementary appropriations. In addition to the appropriations made by the general appropriations Act and amendments thereto, the General Assembly may make additional appropriations by Acts, which shall be known as supplementary appropriation Acts, provided no such supplementary appropriation shall be available unless there is an unappropriated surplus in the state treasury or the revenue necessary to pay such appropriation shall have been provided by a tax laid for such purpose and collected into the general fund of the state treasury. Neither house shall pass a supplementary appropriation bill until the general appropriations Act shall have been finally adopted by both houses and approved by the Governor.

Paragraph VI. Appropriations to be for specific sums.
(a) Except as hereinafter provided, the appropriation for each department, officer, bureau, board, commission, agency, or institution for which appropriation is made shall be for a specific sum of money; and no appropriation shall allocate to any object the proceeds of any particular tax or fund or a part or percentage thereof.
(b) An amount equal to all money derived from motor fuel taxes received by the state in each of the immediately preceding fiscal years, less the amount of refunds, rebates, and collection costs authorized by law, is hereby appropriated for the fiscal year beginning July 1, of each year following, for all activities incident to providing and maintaining an adequate system of public roads and bridges in this state, as authorized by laws enacted by the General Assembly of Georgia, and for grants to counties by law authorizing road construction and maintenance, as provided by law authorizing such grants. Said sum is hereby appropriated for, and shall be available for, the aforesaid purposes regardless of whether the General Assembly enacts a general appropriations Act; and said sum need not be specifically stated in any general appropriations Act passed by the General Assembly in order to be available for such purposes. However, this shall not preclude the

General Assembly from appropriating for such purposes an amount greater than the sum specified above for such purposes. The expenditure of such funds shall be subject to all the rules, regulations, and restrictions imposed on the expenditure of appropriations by provisions of the Constitution and laws of this state, unless such provisions are in conflict with the provisions of this paragraph. And provided, however, that the proceeds of the tax hereby appropriated shall not be subject to budgetary reduction. In the event of invasion of this state by land, sea, or air or in case of a major catastrophe so proclaimed by the Governor, said funds may be utilized for defense or relief purposes on the executive order of the Governor.

(c) *A trust fund for use in the reimbursement of a portion of an employer's workers' compensation expenses resulting to an employee from the combination of a previous disability with subsequent injury incurred in employment may be provided for by law. As authorized by law, revenues raised for purposes of the fund may be paid into and disbursed from the trust without being subject to the limitations of sub-paragraph (a) of this Paragraph or of Article VII, Section III, Paragraph II.*

(d) *As provided by law, additional penalties may be assessed in any case in which any court in this state imposes a fine or orders the forfeiture of any bond in the nature of the penalty for all offenses against the criminal and traffic laws of this state or of the political subdivisions of this state. The proceeds derived from such additional penalty assessments may be allocated for the specific purpose of meeting any and all costs, or any portion of the cost, of providing training to law enforcement officers and to prosecuting officials.*

(e) *The General Assembly may by general law approved by a three-fifths' vote of both houses designate any part or all of the proceeds of any state tax now or hereafter levied and collected on alcoholic beverages to be used for prevention, education, and treatment relating to alcohol and drug abuse.*

(f) *The General Assembly is authorized to provide by law for the creation of a State Children's Trust Fund from which funds shall be disbursed for child abuse and neglect prevention programs. The General Assembly is authorized to appropriate moneys to such fund and such moneys paid into the fund shall not be subject to the provisions of Article III, Section IX, Paragraph IV(c), relative to the lapsing of funds.*

(g) *The General Assembly is authorized to provide by law for the creation of a Seed-Capital Fund from which funds shall be disbursed at the direction of the Advanced Technology Department Center of the University System of Georgia to provide equity and other capital to small, young, entrepreneurial firms engaged in innovative work in the areas of technology, manufacturing, or agriculture. Funds shall be disbursed in the form of loans or investments which shall provide for repayment, rents, dividends, royalties, or other forms of return on investments as provided by law. Moneys received from returns on loans or investments shall be deposited in the Seed-Capital Fund for further disbursement. The General Assembly is authorized to appropriate moneys to such fund and such moneys paid into the fund shall not be subject to the provisions of Article III, Section IX, Paragraph IV(c), relative to the lapsing of funds. The General Assembly shall be authorized to provide by law for any matters relating to the purpose or provisions of this subparagraph.*

(h) *The General Assembly is authorized to provide by general law for additional penalties or fees in any case in any court in this state in which a person is adjudged guilty of an offense against the criminal or traffic laws of this state or an ordinance of a political subdivision of this state. The General Assembly is authorized to provide by general law for the allocation of such additional penalties or fees for the construction, operation, and staffing of jails, correctional institutions, and detentional facilities by counties.*

(i) *The General Assembly is authorized to provide by general law for the creation of an Indigent Care Trust Fund. Any hospital, hospital authority, county, or municipality is authorized to contribute to the fund and any person or entity specified by the General Assembly* may also contribute to the fund. Moneys in the fund shall be exclusively appropriated to expand Medicaid eligibility to persons and for services which would otherwise not be eligible for Medicaid coverage to provide for indigent care with programs for rural and disproportionate indigent care providers, and primary care health programs for indigent citizens of this State. Any appropriation from the Indigent Care Trust Fund shall be void. Contributions to the fund shall not lapse and shall not be subject to the limitations of subparagraph (a) of this Paragraph or of Article VII, Section III, Paragraph II. Moneys in the fund which are not appropriated as required by this subparagraph shall be refunded pro rata to the contributors thereof, as provided by the General Assembly. (Source: GA.L., page 3333).

(j) The General Assembly is authorized to provide by general law for the creation of an emerging crops fund from which to pay interest on loans made to farmers to enable such farmers to produce certain crops on Georgia farms and thereby promote economic development. The General Assembly is authorized to appropriate moneys to such fund and moneys so appropriated shall not be subject to the provisions of Article III, Section IX, Paragraph IV(c), relative to the lapsing of appropriated funds. Interest on loans made to farmers shall be paid from such fund pursuant to such terms, conditions, and requirements as the General Assembly shall provide by general law. The General Assembly may provide by general law for the administration of such fund by such state agency or public authority as the General Assembly shall determine. (Authority: OLC, pages 77–80).

(k) The General Assembly is authorized to provide by general law for additional penalties or fees in any case in any court in this state in which a person is adjudged guilty of an offense involving driving under the influence of alcohol or drugs. The General Assembly is authorized to provide by general law for the allocation of such additional penalties or fees to the Brain and Spinal Injury Trust Fund, as provided by law, for the specified purpose of meeting any and all costs, or any portion of the costs, of providing care and rehabilitative services to citizens of the state who have survived neurotrauma with head or spinal cord injuries. Moneys appropriated for such purposes shall not lapse. The General Assembly may provide by general law for the administration of such fund by such authority as the General Assembly shall determine.

(l) The General Assembly is authorized to provide by general law for the creation of a roadside enhancement and beautification fund from whcih funds shall be disbursed for enhancement and beautification of public rights of way; for allocation and dedication of revenue from tree and other vegetation trimming or removal permit fees, other related assessments, and special and distinctive wildflower motor vehicle license plate fees to such fund; that moneys paid into the fund shall not lapse, the provisions of Article III, Section IX, Paragraph IV(c) notwithstanding; and for any matters relating to the purpose or provisions of this subparagraph. An Act creating such fund and making such provisions effective January 1, 1999, or later may originate or have originated in the Senate or the House of Representatives. (Constitutional amendments approved Nov. 3, 1998, CVIG.)

Paragraph VII. Appropriations void, when. Any appropriation made in conflict with any of the foregoing provisions shall be void.

Section X
Retirement Systems

Paragraph I. Expenditure of public funds authorized. Public funds may be expended for the purpose of paying benefits and other costs of retirement and pension systems for public officers and employees and their beneficiaries.

Paragraph II. Increasing benefits authorized. Public funds may be expended for the purpose of increasing benefits being paid pursuant to any retirement or pension system wholly or partially supported from public funds.

Paragraph III. Retirement systems covering employees of county boards of education. Notwithstanding Article IX, Section II, Paragraph III(a)(14), the authority to establish or modify heretofore existing local retirement systems covering employees of county boards of education shall continue to be vested in the General Assembly.

Paragraph IV. Firemen's Pension System. The powers of taxation may be exercised by the state through the General Assembly and the counties and municipalities for the purpose of paying pensions and other benefits and costs under a firemen's pension system or systems. The taxes so levied may be collected by such firemen's pension system or systems and disbursed therefrom by authority of the General Assembly for the purposes therein authorized.

Paragraph V. Funding standards. It shall be the duty of the General Assembly to enact legislation to define funding standards which will assure the actuarial soundness of any retirement or pension system supported wholly or partially from public funds and to control legislative procedures so that no bill or resolution creating or amending any such retirement or pension system shall be passed by the General Assembly without concurrent provisions for funding in accordance with the defined funding standards.

Paragraph V-A. Limitation on involuntary separation benefits for Governor of the State of Georgia. Any other provisions of this constitution notwithstanding, no past, present, or future Governor of the State of Georgia who ceases or ceased to hold office as Governor for any reason, except for medical disability, shall receive a retirement benefit based on involuntary separation from employment as a result of ceasing to hold office as Governor. The provisions of any law in conflict with this Paragraph are null and void effective January 1, 1985. (Authority: OLC, page 81).

Paragraph VI. Involuntary separation; part-time service.
  (a) Any public retirement or pension system provided for by law in existence prior to January 1, 1985, may be changed by the General Assembly for any one or more of the following purposes.
   (1) To redefine involuntary separation from employment; or
   (2) To provide additional or revise existing limitations or restrictions on the right to qualify for a retirement benefit based on involuntary separation from employment.
  (b) The General Assembly by law may define or redefine part-time service, including but not limited to service as a member of the General Assembly, for the purposes of any public retirement or pension system presently existing or created in the future and may limit or restrict the use of such part-time service as creditable service under any such retirement or pension system.
  (c) Any law enacted by the General Assembly pursuant to subparagraph (a) or (b) of this Paragraph may affect persons who are members of public retirement or pension systems on January 1, 1985, and who became members at any time prior to that date.
  (d) Any law enacted by the General Assembly pursuant to Subparagraph (a) or (b) of this Paragraph shall not be subject to any law controlling legislative procedures for the consideration of retirement or pension bills, including but not limited to, any limitations on the sessions of the General Assembly at which retirement or pension bills may be introduced.
  (e) No public retirement or pension system created on or after January 1, 1985, shall grant any person whose retirement is based on involuntary separation from employment a retirement or pension benefit more favorable than the retirement or pension benefit granted to a person whose separation from employment is voluntary. (Authority: OLC, pages 81–82).

Article IV
Constitutional Boards and Commissions

Section I
Public Service Commission

Paragraph I. Public Service Commission
(a) There shall be a Public Service Commission for the regulation of utilities which shall consist of five members who shall be elected by the people. The Commissioners in office on June 30, 1983, shall serve until December 31, after the general election at which the successor of each member is elected. Thereafter, all succeeding terms of members shall be for six years. Members shall Serve until their successors are elected and qualified. A chairman shall be selected by the members of the commission from its membership.
(b) The Commission shall be vested with such jurisdiction, powers, and duties as provided by law.
(c) The filling of vacancies and manner and time of election of members of the commission shall be as provided by law.

Section II
State Board of Pardons and Paroles

Paragraph I. State Board of Pardons and Paroles. There shall be a State Board of Pardons and Paroles which shall consist of five members appointed by the Governor, subject to confirmation by the Senate. The members of the board in office on June 30, 1983, shall serve out the remainder of their respective terms, providing that the expiration date of the term of any such member shall be December 31 of the year in which the member's term expires. As each term of office expires, the Governor shall appoint a successor as herein provided. All such members shall be for seven years. A chairman shall be selected by the members of the board from its membership.

Paragraph II. Powers and authority.
(a) Except as otherwise provided in this Paragraph, the State Board of Pardons and Paroles shall be vested with the power of executive clemency, including the powers to grant reprieves, pardons, and paroles; to commute penalties; to remove disabilities imposed by law; and to remit any part of a sentence for any offense against the state after conviction.
(b) (1) When a sentence of death is commuted to life imprisonment, the board shall not have the authority to grant a pardon to the convicted person until such person has served at least 25 years in the penitentiary; and such person shall not become eligible for parole at any time prior to serving at least 25 years in the penitentiary.
  (2) *The General Assembly may by general law approved by two-thirds of the members elected to each branch of the General Assembly in a roll-call vote provide for minimum mandatory sentences and for sentences which are required to be served in their entirety for persons convicted of armed robbery, kidnapping, rape, aggravated child molestation, aggravated sodomy, or aggravated sexual battery and, when so provided by such Act, the board shall not have the authority to consider such persons for pardon, parole, or commutation during that portion of the sentence.*
  (3) *The General Assembly may by general law approved by two-thirds of the members elected to each branch of the General Assembly in a roll-call vote provide for the imposition of sentences of life without parole for persons convicted of murder and for persons who having been previously convicted of murder, armed robbery, kidnapping, rape, aggravated child molestation, aggravated sodomy, or aggravated sexual battery or having been previously convicted under the laws of any other*

state or of the United States of a crime which if committed in this state would be one of these offenses and, when so provided by such Act, the board shall not have the authority to consider such persons for pardon, parole, or commutation from any portion of such sentence.

        (4) Any general law previously enacted by the General Assembly providing for life without parole or for mandatory service of sentence without suspension, probation, or parole is hereby ratified and approved but such provisions shall be subject to amendment or repeal by general law. (Source: Sec.St. 1997).

(c) Notwithstanding the provisions of subparagraph (b) of this Paragraph, the General Assembly, by law, may prohibit the board from granting and may prescribe the terms and conditions for the board's granting a pardon or parole to:
    (1) Any person incarcerated for a second or subsequent time for any offense for which such person could have been sentenced to life imprisonment; and
    (2) Any person who has received consecutive life sentences as the result of offenses occurring during the same series of acts.

(d) The chairman of the board, or any other member designated by the board, may suspend the execution of a sentence of death until the full board shall have an opportunity to hear the application of the convicted person for any relief within the power of the board.

(e) Notwithstanding any other provisions of this Paragraph, the State Board of Pardons and Paroles shall have the authority to pardon any person convicted of a crime who is subsequently determined to be innocent of said crime *or to issue a medical reprieve to an entirely incapacitated person suffering a progressively debilitating terminal illness or parole any person who is age 62 or older.* (Source: Sec.St. 1997).

Section III
State Personnel Board

Paragraph I. State Personnel Board

(a) There shall be a State Personnel Board which shall consist of five members appointed by the Governor, subject to confirmation by the Senate. The members of the board in office on June 30, 1983, shall serve out the remainder of their respective terms. As each term of office expires, the Governor shall appoint a successor as herein provided. All such terms of members shall be for five years. Members shall serve until their successors are appointed and qualified. A member of the State Personnel Board may not be employed in any other capacity in state government. A chairman shall be selected by the members of the board from its membership.

(b) The board shall provide policy direction for a State Merit System of Personnel Administration and may be vested with such additional powers and duties as provided by law. State personnel shall be selected on the basis of merit as provided by law.

Paragraph II. Veterans preference. Any veteran who has served as a member of the armed forces of the United States during the period of a war or armed conflict in which any branch of the armed force of the United States engaged, whether under United States command or otherwise, and was honorably discharged therefrom, shall be given such veterans preference in any civil service program established in state government as may be provided by law. Any such law must provide at least ten points to a veteran having at least a 10 percent service connected disability as rated and certified by the Veterans Administration, and all other such veterans shall be entitled to at least five points.

Section IV
State Transportation Board

Paragraph I. State Transportation Board; Commissioner.
(a) There shall be a State Transportation Board composed of as many members as there are congressional districts in the state. The member of the board from each congressional district shall be elected by a majority vote of the members of the House of Representatives and Senate whose respective districts are embraced or partly embraced within such congressional district meeting in caucus. The members of the board in office on June 30, 1983, shall serve out the remainder of their respective terms. The General Assembly shall provide by law the procedure for the election of members and for filling vacancies on the board. Members shall serve for terms of five years and until their successors are elected and qualified.
(b) The State Transportation Board shall select a commissioner of transportation, who shall be the chief executive officer of the Department of Transportation and who shall have such powers and duties as provided by law.

Section V
Veterans Service Board

Paragraph I. Veterans Service Board; Commissioner.
(a) There shall be a State Department of Veterans Service and Veterans Service Board which shall consist of seven members appointed by the Governor, subject to confirmation by the Senate. The members of the board in office on June 30, 1983, shall serve out the remainder of their respective terms. As each term of office expires, the Governor shall appoint a successor as herein provided. All such terms of members shall be for seven years. Members shall serve until their successors are appointed and qualified.
(b) The board shall appoint a commissioner who shall be the executive officer of the department. All members of the board and the commission shall be veterans of some war or armed conflict in which the United States has engaged. The board shall have such control, duties, powers, and jurisdiction of the State Department of Veterans Service as shall be provided by law.

Section VI
Board of Natural Resources

Paragraph I. Board of Natural Resources.
(a) There shall be a Board of Natural Resources which shall consist of one member from each congressional district in the state and five members from the state at large, one of whom must be from one of the following named counties: Chatham, Bryan, Liberty, Macintosh, Glynn, or Camden. All members shall be appointed by the Governor, subject to confirmation by the Senate. The members of the board in office on June 30, 1983, shall serve out the remainder of their respective terms. As each term of office expires, the Governor shall appoint a successor as herein provided. All such terms of members shall be for seven years. Members shall serve until their successors are appointed and qualified. Insofar as it is practicable, the members of the board shall be representative of all areas and functions encompassed within the Department of Natural Resources.
(b) The board shall have such powers and duties as provided by law.

Section VII
Qualifications, Compensation, Removal from Office, and Powers and Duties of Members of Constitutional Boards and Commissions

Paragraph I. Qualifications, compensation, and removal from office. The qualifications, compensation, and removal from office of members of constitutional boards and commissions provided for in this article shall be as provided by law.

Paragraph II. Powers and duties. The powers and duties of members of constitutional boards and commissions provided for in this article, except the Board of Pardons and Paroles, shall be as provided by law.

Article V
Executive Branch

Section I
Election of Governor and Lieutenant Governor

Paragraph I. Governor; term of office; compensation and allowances. There shall be a Governor who shall hold office for a term of four years and until a successor shall be chosen and qualified. Persons holding the office of Governor may succeed themselves for one four-year term of office. Persons who have held the office of Governor and have succeeded themselves as hereinbefore provided shall not again be eligible to be elected to that office until after the expiration of four years from the conclusion of their term as governor. The compensation and allowances of the governor shall be as provided by law.

Paragraph II. Election for Governor. An election for Governor shall be held on Tuesday after the first Monday in November of 1986, and the Governor-elect shall be installed in office at the next session of the General Assembly. An election for Governor shall take place quadrennially thereafter on said date unless another date be fixed by the General Assembly. Said election shall be held at the places of holding general elections in the several counties of this state, in the manner prescribed for the election of members of the General Assembly, and the electors shall be the same.

Paragraph III. Lieutenant Governor. There shall be a Lieutenant Governor, who shall be elected at the same time, for the same term, and in the same manner as the Governor. The Lieutenant Governor shall be the President of the Senate and shall have such executive duties as prescribed by the Governor and as may be prescribed by law not inconsistent with the powers of the governor or other provisions of this Constitution. The compensation and allowances of the Lieutenant Governor shall be as provided by law.

Paragraph IV. Qualifications of the Governor and Lieutenant Governor. No person shall be eligible for election to the office of Governor or Lieutenant Governor unless such person shall have been a citizen of the United States 15 years and a legal resident of the state six years immediately preceding the election and shall have attained the age of 30 years by the date of assuming office.

Paragraph V. Succession to executive power.
(a) In case of the temporary disability of the Governor as determined in the manner provided in Section IV of this article, the Lieutenant Governor shall exercise the powers and duties of the Governor and receive the same compensation as the Governor until such time as the temporary disability of the Governor ends.

(b) In case of the death, resignation, or permanent disability of the Governor or the Governor-elect, the Lieutenant Governor or the Lieutenant Governor-elect, upon becoming the Lieutenant Governor, shall become the Governor until a successor shall be elected and qualified as hereinafter provided. A successor to serve for the unexpired term shall be elected at the next general election; but if such death, resignation, or permanent disability shall occur within 30 days of the next general election or if the term will expire within 90 days after the next general election, the Lieutenant Governor shall become Governor for the unexpired term. No person shall be elected or appointed to the office of Lieutenant Governor for the unexpired term in the event the Lieutenant Governor shall become Governor as herein provided.

(c) In case of the death, resignation, or permanent disability of both the Governor or the Governor-elect, and the Lieutenant Governor or the Lieutenant Governor-elect, or in case of the death, resignation, or permanent disability of the Governor and there shall be no Lieutenant Governor, the Speaker of the House of representatives shall exercise the powers and duties of the Governor until the election and qualification of a Governor at a special election, which shall be held within 90 days from the date on which the Speaker of the House of representatives shall have assumed the powers and duties of the Governor, and the person elected shall serve out the unexpired term.

Paragraph VI. Oath of Office. The Governor and Lieutenant Governor shall, before entering on the duties of office, take such oath or affirmation as prescribed by law.

Section II
Duties and Powers of Governor

Paragraph I. Executive Powers. The chief executive powers shall be vested in the Governor. The other executive officers shall have such powers as may be prescribed by this Constitution and by law.

Paragraph II. Law Enforcement. The Governor shall take care that the laws are faithfully executed and shall be the conservator of the peace throughout the state.

Paragraph III. Commander in Chief. The Governor shall be commander in chief of the military forces of this state.

Paragraph IV. Veto power. Except as otherwise provided in this Constitution, before any bill or resolution shall become law, the Governor shall have the right to review such bill or resolution intended to have the effect of law which has been passed by the General Assembly. The Governor may veto, approve, or take no action on any such bill or resolution. In the event the Governor vetoes any such bill or resolution, the General Assembly may, by a two-thirds vote, override such veto as provided in Article III of this Constitution.

Paragraph V. Writs of Election. The Governor shall issue writs of election to fill all vacancies that may occur in the Senate and House of Representatives.

Paragraph VI. Information and recommendations to the General Assembly. At the beginning of each regular session and from time to time, the Governor may give the General Assembly information on the state of the state and recommend to its consideration such measures as the Governor may deem necessary or expedient.

Paragraph VII. Special sessions of the General Assembly.
(a) The Governor may convene the General Assembly in special session by proclamation which may be amended by the Governor prior to the convening of the special session or amended by the Governor with the approval of three-fifths of the members of each house

after the special session has convened; but no laws shall be enacted at any such special session except those which relate to the purposes stated on the proclamation or in any amendment thereto.

(b) The Governor shall convene the General Assembly in special session for all purposes whenever three-fifths of the members to each house is entitled certify to the governor in writing, with a copy to the Secretary of State, that in their opinion an emergency exists in the affairs of the state. The General Assembly may convene itself if, after receiving such certification, the Governor fails to do so within three days, excluding Sundays.

(c) Special sessions of the General Assembly shall be limited to a period of 40 days unless extended by three-fifths vote of each house and approved by the Governor or unless at the expiration of such period an impeachment trial of some officer of state government is pending, in which event the House shall adjourn and the Senate shall remain in session until such trial is completed.

Paragraph VIII. Filling vacancies.

(a) When any public office shall become vacant by death, resignation, or otherwise, the Governor shall promptly fill such vacancy unless otherwise provided by this Constitution or by law; and persons so appointed shall serve for the unexpired term unless otherwise provided by this Constitution or by law.

(b) In case of the death or withdrawal of a person who received a majority of votes cast in an election for the Office of Secretary of State, Attorney General, State School Superintendent, Commissioner of Insurance, Commissioner of Agriculture, or Commissioner of Labor, the Governor elected at the same election, upon becoming Governor, shall have the power to fill such office by appointing, subject to the confirmation of the Senate, an individual to serve until the next general election and until a successor for the balance of the unexpired term shall have been elected and qualified.

Paragraph IX. Appointments by Governor. The Governor shall make such appointments as are authorized by this Constitution or by law. If a person whose confirmation is required by the Senate is once rejected by the Senate, that person shall not be renominated by the Governor for appointment to the same office until the expiration of a period of one year from the date of such rejection.

Paragraph X. Information from officers and employees. The Governor may require information in writing from constitutional officers and all other officers and employees of the executive branch on any subject relating to the duties of their respective offices or employment.

Section III
Other Elected Executive Officers

Paragraph I. Other executive officers, how elected. The Secretary of State, Attorney General, State School Superintendent, Commissioner of Insurance, Commissioner of Agriculture, or Commissioner of Labor shall be elected in the manner prescribed for the elections of members of the General Assembly and the electors shall be the same. Such executive officers shall be elected at the same time and hold their officers for the same term as the Governor.

Paragraph II. Qualifications.

(a) No person shall be eligible to the offices of the Secretary of State, Attorney General, State School Superintendent, Commissioner of Insurance, Commissioner of Agriculture, or Commissioner of Labor unless such person shall have been a citizen of the United States for ten years and a legal resident of the state for four years immediately preceding election or appointment and shall have attained the age of 25 years by the date of assuming office. All of said officers shall take such oath and give bond and security, as prescribed by law, for the faithful discharge of their duties.

(b) No person shall be Attorney General unless such person shall have been an active-status member of the State Bar of Georgia for seven years.

Paragraph III. Powers, duties, compensation, and allowances of other executive officers. Except as otherwise provided in this Constitution, the General Assembly shall prescribe the powers, duties, compensation, and allowances of the above executive officers and provide assistance and expenses necessary for the operation of the department of each.

Paragraph IV. Attorney General; duties. The Attorney General shall act as the legal advisor of the executive department, shall represent the state in the Supreme Court in all capital felonies and in all civil and criminal cases in any court when required by the Governor, and shall perform such other duties as shall be required by law.

Section IV
Disability of Executive Officers

Paragraph I. "Elected constitutional executive officer," how defined. As used in this section, the term "elected constitutional executive officer" means the Governor, the Lieutenant Governor, the Secretary of State, the Attorney General, the State School Superintendent, the Commissioner of Insurance, the Commissioner of Agriculture, and the Commissioner of Labor.

Paragraph II. Procedure for determining disability. Upon a petition of any four of the elected constitutional officers to the Supreme Court of Georgia that another elected constitutional executive officer is unable to perform the duties of office because of a physical or mental disability, the Supreme Court shall by appropriate rule provide for a speedy and public hearing on such matter, including notice of the nature and cause of the accusation, process for obtaining witnesses, and assistance of counsel. Evidence at such hearing shall include testimony from not fewer than three qualified physicians in private practice, one of whom must be a psychiatrist.

Paragraph III. Effect of determination of disability. If, after hearing the evidence on disability, the Supreme Court determines that there is a disability and that such disability is permanent, the office shall be declared vacant and the successor to that office shall be chosen as provided in this Constitution or the laws enacted in pursuance thereof. If it is determined that the disability is not permanent, the Supreme Court shall determine when the disability has ended and when the officer shall resume the exercise of powers of office. During the period of temporary disability, the powers of such office shall be exercised as provided by law.

Article VI
Judicial Branch

Section I
Judicial Power

Paragraph I. Judicial power of the state. The judicial power of the state shall be vested exclusively in the following classes of courts: magistrate courts, probate courts, juvenile courts, state courts, superior courts, Court of Appeals, and Supreme Court. Magistrate courts, probate courts, juvenile courts, and state courts shall be courts of limited jurisdiction. In addition, the general assembly may establish or authorize the establishment of municipal courts and may authorize administrative agencies to exercise quasi-judicial powers. Municipal courts shall have jurisdiction over *ordinance violations and such other jurisdiction as provided by law. Except as provided in this paragraph and in Section X, municipal courts, county recorder's courts and civil courts in existence on June 30, 1983, and administrative agencies shall not be subject to the provisions of this article. The General Assembly shall have the authority to confer "by law" jurisdiction upon municipal courts to try state offenses.* (Authority: OLC, page 86).

Paragraph II. Unified judicial system. All courts of the state shall comprise a unified judicial system.

Paragraph III. Judges; exercise of power outside own court; scope of term "judge." Provided the judge is otherwise qualified, a judge may exercise judicial power in any court upon the request and with the consent of the judges of that court and the judge's own court under rules prescribed by law. The term "judge" as used in this article, shall include Justices, judges, senior judges, magistrates, and every other such judicial office of whatever name existing or created.

Paragraph IV. Exercise of judicial power. Each court may exercise such powers as necessary in aid of its jurisdiction or to protect or effectuate its judgments; but only the superior and appellate courts shall have the power to issue process in the nature of mandamus, prohibition, specific performance, quo warranto, and injunction. Each superior court, state court, and other courts of record may grant new trials on legal grounds.

Paragraph V. Uniformity of jurisdiction, powers, etc. Except as otherwise provided in this constitution, the courts of each class shall have uniform jurisdiction, powers, rules of practice and procedure, and selection, qualifications, terms, and discipline of judges. The provisions of this Paragraph shall be effected by law within 24 months of the effective date of this Constitution.

Paragraph VI. Judicial circuits; courts in each county; court sessions. The state shall be divided into judicial circuits, each of which shall consist of not less than one county. Each county shall have at least one superior court, magistrate court, a probate court, and, where needed, a state court and a juvenile court. The General Assembly may provide by law that the judge of the probate court may also serve as the judge of the magistrate court. In the absence of a state court or a juvenile court, the superior court shall exercise that jurisdiction. Superior courts shall hold court at least twice each year in each county.

Paragraph VII. Judicial circuits, courts and judgeships, law changed. The General Assembly may abolish, create, consolidate, or modify judicial circuits and courts and judgeships; but no circuit shall consist of less than one county.

Paragraph VIII. Transfer of cases. Any court shall transfer to the appropriate court in the state any civil case in which it determines that jurisdiction or venue lies elsewhere.

Paragraph IX. Rules of evidence; law prescribed. All rules of evidence shall be as prescribed by law.

Paragraph X. Authorization for pilot projects. The General Assembly may by general law approved by a two-thirds majority of the members of each house enact legislation providing for, as pilot programs of limited duration, courts which are not uniform within their classes in jurisdiction, powers, rules of practice and procedure, and selections, qualifications, terms, and discipline of judges for such pilot courts and other matters relative thereto. Such legislation shall name the political subdivision, judicial circuit, and existing courts affected and may, in addition to any other power, grant to such court created as a pilot program the power to issue process in the nature of mandamus, prohibition, specific performance, quo warranto, and injunction. The General Assembly shall provide by general law for a procedure for submitting proposed legislation relating to such pilot programs to the Judicial Council of Georgia or its successor. Legislation enacted pursuant to this Paragraph shall not deny equal protection of the laws to any person in violation of Article I, Section I, Paragraph II of this constitution. (Source: Sec.St. 1997).

Section II
Venue

Paragraph I. Divorce Cases. Divorce cases shall be tried in the county where the defendant resides, if a resident of this state; if the defendant is not a resident of this state, then in the county in which the plaintiff resides; provided, however, a divorce case may be tried in the county of residence of the plaintiff if the defendant has moved from that same county within six months from the date of the filing of the divorce action and said county was the site of the marital domicile at the time of the separation of the parties, and provided further, that any person who has been a resident of any United States army post or military reservation within the State of Georgia for one year next preceding the filing of the petition may bring an action for divorce in any county adjacent to said United States army post or military reservation. (Authority: OLC, page 89).

Paragraph II. Land titles. Cases respecting titles to land shall be tried in the county where the land lies, except where a single tract is divided by a county line, in which case the superior court of either county shall have jurisdiction.

Paragraph III. Equity cases. Equity cases shall be tried in the county where a defendant resides against whom substantial relief is prayed.

Paragraph IV. Suits against joint obligers, copartners, etc. Suits against joint obligers, joint tort-feasors, joint promisors, copartners, or joint trespassers residing in different counties may be tried in either county.

Paragraph V. Suits against maker, endorser, etc. Suits against the maker and endorser of promissory notes, or drawer, acceptor, and endorser of foreign or inland bills of exchange, or like instruments, residing in different counties, shall be tried in the county where the maker or acceptor resides.

Paragraph VI. All other cases. All other civil cases, except juvenile court cases as may otherwise be provided by the Juvenile Court Code of Georgia, shall be tried in the county where the defendant resides; venue as to corporations, foreign and domestic, shall be as provided by law; and all criminal cases shall be tried in the county where the crime was committed, except cases in the superior court where the judge is satisfied that an impartial jury cannot be obtained in the such county.

Paragraph VII. Venue in third-party practice. The General Assembly may provide by law that venue is proper in a county other than the county of residence of a person or entity impleaded into a pending civil case by a defending party who contends that such person or entity is or may be liable to said defending party for all or part of the claim against said defending party.

Paragraph VIII. Power to change venue. The power to change the venue in civil and criminal cases shall be vested in the superior courts to be exercised in such manner as has been, or shall be, provided by law.

Section III
Classes of Courts of Limited Jurisdiction

Paragraph I. Jurisdiction of classes of courts of limited jurisdiction. The magistrate, juvenile and state courts shall have uniform jurisdiction as provided by law. Probate courts shall have such jurisdiction as now or hereafter provided by law, without regard to uniformity.

Section IV
Superior Courts

Paragraph I. Jurisdiction of Superior Courts. The superior courts shall have jurisdiction in all cases, except as otherwise provided in this Constitution. They shall have exclusive jurisdiction over trials in all felony cases, except in the case of juvenile offenders as provided by law; in cases respecting title to land; in divorce cases; and in equity cases. The superior courts shall have such appellate jurisdiction, either alone or by circuit or district, as may be provided by law.

Section V
Court of Appeals

Paragraph I. Composition of Court of Appeals; Chief Judge. The Court of Appeals shall consist of not less than nine judges who shall elect from among themselves a Chief Judge.

Paragraph II. Panels as proscribed. The Court of Appeals may sit in panels of not less than three Judges as prescribed by law or, if none, by its rules.

Paragraph III. Jurisdiction of Court of Appeals; decisions binding. The Court of Appeals shall be a court of review and shall exercise appellate and certiorari jurisdiction in all cases not reserved to the Supreme Court or conferred on other courts by law. The decisions of the Court of Appeals insofar as not in conflict with those of the Supreme Court shall bind all courts except the Supreme Court as precedents.

Paragraph IV. Certification of question to Supreme Court. The Court of Appeals may certify a question to the Supreme Court for instruction, to which it shall then be bound.

Paragraph V. Equal division of Court. In the event of an equal division of the Judges when sitting as a body, the case shall be immediately transmitted to the Supreme Court.

Section VI
Supreme Court

Paragraph I. Composition of Supreme Court; Chief Justice; Presiding Justice; quorum, substitute judges. The Supreme Court shall consist of not more than nine Justices who shall elect from among themselves a Chief Justice as the chief presiding and administrative officer of the court and a Presiding Justice to serve if the Chief Justice is absent or is disqualified. A majority shall be necessary to hear and determine cases. If a Justice is disqualified in any case, a substitute judge may be designated by the remaining Justices to serve.

Paragraph II. Exclusive appellate jurisdiction of Supreme court. The Supreme Court shall be a court of review and shall exercise exclusive appellate jurisdiction in the following cases:
- (1) All cases involving the construction of a treaty or of the Constitution of the State of Georgia or of the United States and all cases in which the constitutionality of a law, ordinance, or constitutional provision has been drawn in question; and
- (2) All cases of election contest.

Paragraph III. General appellate jurisdiction of Supreme Court. Unless otherwise provided by law, the Supreme Court shall have appellate jurisdiction of the following classes of cases:
 (1) Cases involving title to land;
 (2) All equity cases;
 (3) All cases involving wills;
 (4) All habeas corpus cases;
 (5) All cases involving extraordinary remedies;
 (6) All divorce and alimony cases;
 (7) All cases certified to it by the Court of Appeals; and
 (8) All cases in which a sentence of death was imposed or could be imposed.
Review of all cases shall be as provided by law.

Paragraph IV. Jurisdiction over questions of law from state or federal appellate courts. The Supreme Court shall have jurisdiction to answer any question of law from any state or federal appellate court.

Paragraph V. Review of cases in Court of Appeals. The Supreme Court may review by certiorari cases in the Court of Appeals which are of gravity or great public importance.

Paragraph VI. Decisions of Supreme Court binding. The decisions of the Supreme Court shall bind all other courts as precedents.

Section VII
Selection, Term, Compensation, and Discipline of Judges

Paragraph I. Election, term of office. All superior court and state court judges shall be elected on a nonpartisan basis for a term of four years. All justices of the Supreme Court and the Judges of the Court of Appeals shall be elected on a nonpartisan basis for a term of six years. The terms of all judges thus elected shall begin the next January 1 after their election. All other judges shall continue to be selected in the manner and for the term they were selected on June 30, 1983, until otherwise provided by local law.

Paragraph II. Qualifications.
 (a) Appellate and superior court judges shall have been admitted to practice law for seven years.
 (b) State and juvenile court judges shall have been admitted to practice law for five years.
 (c) Probate and magistrate judges shall have such qualifications as provided by law.
 (d) All judges shall reside in the geographical area in which they are selected to serve.
 (e) The General Assembly may provide by law for additional qualifications, including but not limited to, minimum residency requirements.

Paragraph III. Vacancies. Vacancies shall be filled by appointment of the Governor except as otherwise provided by law in the magistrate, probate and juvenile courts.

Paragraph IV. Period of service of appointees. An appointee to an elective office shall serve until a successor is duly selected and qualified and until January 1 of the year following the next general election which is more than six months after such person's appointment.

Paragraph V. Compensation and allowances of Judges. All judges shall receive compensation and allowances as provided by law; county supplements are hereby continued and may be granted or changed by the General Assembly. County governing authorities which had the authority on June 30, 1983, to make county supplements shall continue to have such authority under this Constitution. An incumbent's salary, allowance or supplement shall not be decreased during the incumbent's term of office.

Paragraph VI. Judicial Qualifications Commission; power; composition. The power to discipline, remove, and cause involuntary retirement of judges shall be vested in the Judicial Qualifications Commission. It shall consist of seven members, as follows:
(1) Two judges of any court of record, selected by the Supreme Court;
(2) Three members of the State Bar of Georgia who shall have been active status members of the state bar for at least ten years and who shall be elected by the Board of Governors of the State bar; and
(3) Two citizens, neither of whom shall be a member of the state bar, who shall be appointed by the Governor.

Paragraph VII. Discipline, removal, and involuntary retirement of judges.
(a) Any judge may be removed, suspended, or otherwise disciplined for willful misconduct in office, or for willful and persistent failure to perform the duties of office, or for habitual intemperance, or for conviction of a crime involving moral turpitude, or for conduct prejudicial to the administration of justice which brings the judicial office into disrepute. Any judge may be retired for disability which constitutes a serious and likely permanent interference with the performance of the duties of office. The Supreme Court shall adopt rules of implementation.
(b) (1) Upon indictment for a felony by a grand jury of this state or by a grand jury of the United States of any judge, the Attorney General or district attorney shall transmit a certified copy of the indictment to the Judicial Qualifications Commission. The commission shall, subject to subparagraph (b)(2) of this Paragraph, review the indictment, and, if it determines that the indictment relates to and adversely affects the administration of the office of the indicted judge and that the rights and interests of the public are adversely affected thereby, the commission shall suspend the judge immediately and without further action pending the final disposition of the case or until the expiration of the judge's term of office, whichever occurs first. During the term of office to which such judge was elected and in which the indictment occurred, if a nolle prosequi is entered, if the public official is acquitted, or if after conviction the conviction is later overturned as a result of any direct appeal or application for a writ of certiorari, the judge shall be immediately reinstated to the office from which he was suspended. While a judge is suspended under this subparagraph and until initial conviction by the trial court, the judge shall continue to receive the compensation from his office. After initial conviction by the trial court, the judge shall not be entitled to receive the compensation from his office. If the judge is reinstated to office, he shall be entitled to receive any compensation withheld under the provisions of this subparagraph. For the duration of any suspension under this subparagraph, the Governor shall appoint a replacement judge. Upon a final conviction with no appeal or review pending, the office shall be declared vacant and a successor to that office shall be chosen as provided in this Constitution or the laws enacted in pursuance thereof.
(2) The commission shall not review the indictment for a period of 14 days from the day the indictment is received. This period of time may be extended by the commission. During this period of time, the indicted judge may, in writing, authorize the commission to suspend him from office. Any such voluntary suspension shall be subject to the same conditions for review, reinstatement, or declaration of vacancy as are provided in this subparagraph for a nonvoluntary suspension.
(3) After any suspension is imposed under this subparagraph, the suspended judge may petition the commission for a review. If the commission determines that the judge should no longer be suspended, he shall immediately be reinstated to office.
(4) The findings and records of the commission and the fact that the public official has or has not been suspended shall not be admissible on evidence in any court for any purpose. The findings and records of the commission shall not be open to the public.

(5) The provisions of this subparagraph shall not apply to any indictment handed down prior to January 1, 1985.

(6) If a judge who is suspended from office under the provision of this subparagraph is not first tried at the next regular or special term following the indictment, the suspension shall be terminated and the judge shall be reinstated to office. The judge shall not be reinstated under this provision if he is not so tried based on a continuance granted upon a motion made only by the defendant.

(c) Upon initial conviction of any judge for any felony in a trial court of this state or the United States, regardless of whether the judge has been suspended previously under subparagraph (b) of this Paragraph, such judge shall be immediately and without further action suspended from office. While a judge is suspended from office under this subparagraph, he shall not be entitled to receive the compensation from his office. If the conviction is later overturned as a result of any direct appeal or application for a writ of certiorari, the judge shall be immediately reinstated to the office from which he was suspended and shall be entitled to receive any compensation withheld under the provisions of this subparagraph. For the duration of any suspension under this subparagraph, the Governor shall appoint a replacement judge. Upon a final conviction with no appeal or review pending, the office shall be declared vacant and a successor to that office shall be chosen as provided in this Constitution or the laws enacted in pursuance thereof. The provisions of this subparagraph shall not apply to any conviction rendered prior to January 1, 1987. (Authority: OLC, pages 105–107).

Paragraph VIII. Due process; review by Supreme Court. No action shall be taken against a judge except after hearing and in accordance with due process of law. No removal or involuntary retirement shall occur except upon order of the Supreme Court after review.

Section VIII
District Attorneys

Paragraph I. District attorneys; vacancies; disqualification; compensation; duties; immunity.

(a) There shall be a district attorney for each judicial circuit, who shall be elected circuit-wide for a term of four years. The successors of present and subsequent incumbents shall be elected by the electors of their respective circuits at the general election held immediately preceding the expiration of their respective terms. District attorneys shall serve until their successors are duly elected and qualified. Vacancies shall be filled by appointment of the governor.

(b) No person shall be a district attorney unless such person shall have been an active-status member of the State Bar of Georgia for three years immediately preceding such person's election.

(c) The district attorneys shall receive such compensation and allowances as provided by law and shall be entitled to receive such local supplements to their compensation and allowances as may be provided by law.

(d) It shall be the duty of the district attorney to represent the state in all criminal cases in the superior court of such district attorney's circuit and in all cases appealed from the superior court and the juvenile courts of that circuit to the Supreme Court and the Court of Appeals and to perform such other duties as shall be required by law.

(e) District attorneys shall enjoy immunity from private suit for actions arising from the performance of their duties.

Paragraph II. Discipline, removal, and involuntary retirement of district attorneys. Any district attorney may be disciplined, removed or involuntarily retired as provided by general law.

Section VIII
General Provisions

Paragraph I. Administration of the judicial system; uniform court rules; advice and consent of councils. The judicial system shall be administered as provided in this Paragraph. Not more than 24 months after the effective date hereof, and from time to time thereafter by amendment, the Supreme Court shall, with the advice and consent of the council of the affected class or classes of trial courts, by order adopt and publish uniform court rules and record-keeping rules which shall provide for the speedy, efficient and inexpensive resolution of disputes and prosecutions. Each council shall be comprised of all of the judges of the courts of that class.

Paragraph II. Disposition of cases. The Supreme Court and the Court of Appeals shall dispose of every case at the term for which it is entered on the court's docket for hearing or at the next term.

Section X
Transition

Paragraph I. Effect of ratification. On the effective date of this article:
(1) Superior Courts shall continue as superior courts.
(2) State courts shall continue as state courts.
(3) Probate courts shall continue as probate courts.
(4) Juvenile courts shall continue as juvenile courts.
(5) Municipal courts not otherwise named herein, of whatever name, shall continue as and be denominated municipal courts, except that the City Court of Atlanta shall retain its name. Such municipal courts, county recorder's courts, and Civil Courts of Richmond and Bibb counties, and administrative agencies having quasi-judicial powers shall continue with the same jurisdiction as such courts and agencies have on the effective date of this article until otherwise provided by law.
(6) Justice of the peace courts, small claims courts, and magistrate courts operating on the effective date of this Constitution and the County Court of Echols County shall become and be classified as magistrate courts. The County Court of Baldwin County and the County Court of Putnam County shall become and be classified as state courts, with the same jurisdiction and powers as other state courts.

Paragraph II. Continuation of judges. Each judge holding office on the effective date of this article shall continue in office until the expiration of the term of office, as a judge of the court having the same or similar jurisdiction. Each court not named herein shall cease to exist on such date or at the expiration of the term of the incumbent judge, whichever is later; and its jurisdiction shall automatically pass to the new court of the same or similar jurisdiction, in the absence of which court it shall pass to the superior court.

Article VII
Taxation and Finance

Section I
Power of Taxation

Paragraph I. Taxation; limitations on grants of tax powers. The state may not suspend or irrevocably give, grant, limit, or restrain the right of taxation and all laws, grants, contracts, and other acts to effect any of these purposes are null and void. Except as otherwise provided in this Constitution, the right of taxation shall always be under the complete control of the state.

Paragraph II. Taxing power limited.
(a) The annual levy of state ad valorem taxes on tangible property for all purposes, except for defending the state in an emergency, shall not exceed one-forth mill on each dollar of the assessed value of the property.
(b) So long as the method of taxation in effect on December 31, 1980, for the taxation of shares of stock of banking corporations and other monied capital coming into competition with such banking corporations continues in effect, such shares and other monied capital may be taxed at an annual rate not exceeding five mills on each dollar of the assessed value of the property.

Paragraph III. Uniformity; classification of property; assessment of agricultural land; utilities.
   (a) *All taxes shall be levied and collected under general laws and for public purposes only. Except as otherwise provided in subparagraphs (c), (d), and (e), all taxation shall be uniform upon the same class of subjects within the territorial limits of the authority levying the tax.*
   (b) (1) *Except as otherwise provided in this subparagraph (b), classes of subjects for taxation of property shall consist of tangible property and one or more classes of intangible personal property including money.*
       (2) *Subject to the conditions and limitations specified by law, each of the following types of property may be classified as a separate class of property for ad valorem property tax purposes and different rates, methods, and assessment dates may be provided for such properties:*
          (A) *Trailers.*
          (B) *Mobile homes other than those mobile homes which qualify the owner of the home for a homestead exemption from ad valorem taxation.*
          (C) *Heavy-duty equipment motor vehicles owned by non-residents and operated in this state.*
       (3) *Motor vehicles may be classified as a separate class or property for ad valorem tax purposes, and such class may be divided into separate subclasses for ad valorem tax purposes. The General Assembly may provide by general law for the ad valorem taxation of motor vehicles including, but not limited to, providing for different rates, methods, assessment dates, and taxpayer liability for such class and for each of its subclasses and need not provide for uniformity of taxation with other classes of property or between or within its subclasses. the General Assembly may also determine what proportion of any ad valorem tax on motor vehicles will be retained by the state. As used in this subparagraph, the term 'motor vehicles' means all vehicles which are self-propelled.* (Source: ga.l. 1992, page 3336).
   (c) *Tangible real property, but not more than 2,000 acres of any single property owner, which is devoted to bona fide agricultural purposes shall be assessed for ad valorem taxation purposes at 75 percent of the value which other tangible real property is assessed. No property shall be entitled to receive the preferential assessment provided for in this*

subparagraph if the property which would otherwise receive such assessment would result in any person who has a beneficial interest in such property, including any interest in the nature of stock ownership, receiving the benefit of such preferential assessment as to more than 2,000 acres. No property shall be entitled to receive the preferential assessment provided for in this subparagraph unless the conditions set out below are met:

(1) The property must be owned by:
  (A) (i) One or more natural or naturalized citizens;
      (ii) An estate of which the devisee or heirs are one or more natural or natralized citizens; or
      (iii) A trust of which the beneficiaries are one or more natural or naturalized citizens; or
  (B) A family-owned farm corporation, the controlling interest of which is owned by individuals related to each other within the fourth degree of civil reckoning, or which is owned by an estate of which the devisee or heirs are one or more natural or naturalized citizens, or which is owned by a trust of which the beneficiaries are one or more natural or naturalized citizens, and such corporation derived 80 percent or more of its gross income from bona fide agricultural pursuits within this state within the year immediately preceding the year in which eligibility is sought.

(2) The General Assembly shall provide by law:
  (A) For a definition of the term "bona fide agricultural purposes," but such term shall include timber production;
  (B) For additional minimum conditions of eligibility which such properties must meet in order to qualify for the preferential assessment provided for herein, including, but not limited to, the requirement that the owner be required to enter into a covenant with the appropriate taxing authorities to maintain the use of the properties in bona fide agricultural purposes for a period of not less than ten years and for appropriate penalties for the breach of any such covenant.

(3) In addition to the specific conditions set forth in this subparagraph (c), the General Assembly may place further restrictions upon, but may not relax, the conditions of eligibility for the preferential assessment provided for herein.

(d) The General Assembly shall be authorized by general law to establish as a separate class of property for ad valorem tax purposes any tangible real property which is listed in the National Register of Historic Places or in a state historic register authorized by general law. For such purposes, the General Assembly is authorized by general law to establish a program by which certain properties within such class may be assessed for taxes at different rates or valuations in order to encourage the preservation of such historic properties and to assist in the revitalization of historic areas.

(e) The General Assembly shall provide by general law:
  (1) For the definition and methods of assessment and taxation, such methods to include a formula based on current use, annual productivity, and real property sales data, of: "bona fide conservation use property," to include bona fide agricultural and timber land not to exceed 2,000 acres of a single owner; and "bona fide residential transitional property" to include private single-family residential owner occupied property located in transitional developing areas not to exceed five acres of any single owner. Such methods of assessment and taxation shall be subject to the following conditions:
    (A) A property owner desiring the benefit of such methods of assessment and taxation shall be required to enter into a covenant to continue the property in bona fide conservation use or bona fide residential transitional use; and

(B) A breach of such covenant within ten years shall result in a recapture of the tax savings resulting from such methods of assessment and taxation and may result in other appropriate penalties.

(2) That standing timber shall be assessed only once, and such assessment shall be made following its harvest or sale and on the basis of its fair market value at the time of harvest or sale. Said assessments shall be two and one-half times the assessed percentage of value fixed by law for other real property taxed under the uniformity provisions of subparagraph (a) of this Paragraph but in on event greater than its fair market value; and for a method of temporary supplementation of the property tax digest of any county if the implementation of the method of taxing timber reduces the tax digest by more than 20 percent, such supplemental assessed value to be assigned to the properties otherwise benefiting from such method of taxing timber.

(f) The General Assembly may provide for a different method and time of returns, assessments, payment, and collection of ad valorem taxes of public utilities, but not on a greater assessed percentage of value or at a higher rate of taxation than other properties, except that property provided for in subparagraph (c), (d), or (e). (Authority: OLC, pages 112–115).

Section II
Exemptions from Ad Valorem Taxation

Paragraph I. Unauthorized tax exemptions void. Except as authorized in or pursuant to this Constitution, all laws exempting property from ad valorem taxation are void.

Paragraph II. Exemptions from taxation of property.
(a) (1) Except as otherwise provided in this Constitution, no property shall be exempted from ad valorem taxation unless the exemption is approved by two-thirds of the members elected to each branch of the General Assembly in a roll-call vote and by a majority of the qualified electors of the state voting in a referendum thereon.

(2) Homestead exemptions from ad valorem taxation levied by local taxing jurisdiction may be granted by local law conditioned upon approval by a majority of the qualified electors residing within the limits of the local taxing jurisdiction voting in a referendum thereon.

(3) Laws subject to the requirement of a referendum as provided in this subparagraph (a) may originate in either the Senate or the House of Representatives.

(4) The requirements of this subparagraph shall not apply with respect to a law which codifies or recodifies an exemption previously authorized in the Constitution of 1976 or an exemption authorized pursuant to this Constitution.

(b) The grant of any exemptions from ad valorem taxation shall be subject to the conditions, limitations, and administrative procedures specified by law.

Paragraph III. Exemptions which may be authorized locally.
(a) (1) The governing authority of any county or municipality, subject to the approval of a majority of the qualified electors of such political subdivision voting in a referendum thereon, may exempt from ad valorem taxation, including all such taxation levied for educational purposes and for state purposes, inventories of goods in the process of manufacture or production, and inventories, of finished goods.

(2) Exemptions granted pursuant to this subparagraph (a) may only be revoked by a referendum election called and conducted as provided by law. The call for such referendum shall not be issued within five years from the date such exemptions were first granted and, if the results of the election are in favor of the revocation of such

exemptions, then such revocation shall be effective only at the end of a five-year period from the date of such referendum.
(3) The implementation, administration, and revocation of the exemptions authorized in this subparagraph (a) shall be provided for by law. Until otherwise provided by law, the grant of the exemption shall be subject to the same conditions, limitations, definitions, and procedures provided for the grant of such exemption in the Constitution of 1976 on June 30, 1983.
(b) Repealed.

Paragraph IV. Current property tax exemptions preserved. Those types of exemptions from ad valorem taxation provided for by law on June 30, 1983, are hereby continued in effect as statutory law until otherwise provided for by law. Any law which reduces or repeals any homestead exemption in existence on June 30, 1983, or created thereafter must be approved by two-thirds of the members elected to each branch of the General Assembly in a roll-call vote and by a majority of the qualified electors of the state or the affected local taxing jurisdiction voting in a referendum thereon. Any law which reduces or repeals exemptions granted to religious or burial grounds or institutions of purely public charity must be approved by two-thirds of the members elected to each branch of the General Assembly.

Paragraph V. Disabled veteran's homestead exemption. *Except as otherwise provided in this paragraph, the amount of the homestead exemption granted to disabled veterans shall be the greater of $32,500.00 or the maximum amount which may be granted to a disabled veteran under Section 802 of Title 38 of the United States Code as hereafter amended. Such exemptions shall be granted to: those persons eligible for such exemptions on June 30, 1983; to disabled American veterans of any war or armed conflict who are disabled due to loss or loss of use of one lower extremity together with the loss or loss of use of one upper extremity which so effects the function of balance or propulsion as to preclude locomotion without the aid if braces, crutches, canes, or a wheelchair; and to disabled veterans hereafter becoming eligible for assistance in acquiring housing under Section 801 of the United States Code as hereafter amended. The General Assembly may by general law provide for a different amount or a different method of determining the amount of or eligibility for the homestead exemption granted to disabled veterans. Any such law shall be enacted by a simple majority of the votes of all the members to which each house is entitled and may become effective without referendum. Such law may provide that the amount of or eligibility for the exemption shall be determined by reference to laws enacted by the United States Congress.* (Authority: OLC, page 118).

Section III
Purposes and Method of State Taxation

Paragraph I. Taxation; purpose for which powers may be exercised.
(a) Except as otherwise provided in this Constitution, the power of taxation over the whole state may be exercised for any purpose authorized by law. Any purpose for which the powers of taxation over the whole state could have been exercised on June 30, 1983, shall continue to be a purpose for which such powers may be exercised.
(b) Subject to conditions and limitations as may be provided by law, the power of taxation may be exercised to make grants for tax relief purposes to persons for sales tax paid and not otherwise reimbursed on prescription drugs. Credits or relief provided hereunder may be limited only to such reasonable classifications of taxpayers as may be specified by law.

Paragraph II. Revenue to be paid into general fund.
(a) Except as otherwise provided in this Constitution, all revenue collected from taxes, fees, and assessments for state purposes, as authorized by revenue measures enacted by the General Assembly, shall be paid into the general fund of the state treasury.
(b) (1) As authorized by law providing for the promotion of any one or more types of agricultural products, fees, assessments, and other charges collected on the sale or processing of agricultural products need not be paid into the general fund of the state treasury. The uniformity requirement of this article shall be satisfied by the application of the agricultural promotion program upon the affected products.
(2) As used in this subparagraph, "agricultural products" includes, but is not limited to, registered livestock and livestock products, poultry and poultry products, timber and timber products, fish and seafood, and the products of the farms and forests of this state.

Paragraph III. Grants to counties and municipalities. State funds may be granted to counties and municipalities within the state. The grants authorized by this Paragraph shall be made in such manner and form and subject to the procedures and conditions specified by law. The law providing for any such grant may limit the purposes for which the grant funds may be expended.

Section IV
State Debt

Paragraph I. Purposes for which debt may be incurred. The state may incur:
(a) Public debt without limit to repel invasion, suppress insurrection, and defend the state in time of war.
(b) Public debt to supply a temporary deficit in the state treasury in any fiscal year created by a delay in collecting the taxes of that year. Such debt shall not exceed, in the aggregate, 5 percent of the total revenue receipts, less funds, of the state treasury in the fiscal year immediately preceding the year in which such debt is incurred. The debt incurred shall be repaid on or before the last day of the fiscal year in which it is incurred out of taxes levied for that fiscal year. No such debt may be incurred in any fiscal year under the provisions of this subparagraph (b) if there is then outstanding unpaid debt from any previous fiscal year which was incurred to supply a temporary deficit in the state treasury.
(c) General obligation debt to acquire, construct, develop, extend, enlarge, or improve land, waters, property, highways, buildings, structures, equipment, or facilities of the state, its agencies, departments, institutions, and of those state authorities which were created and activated prior to November 8, 1960.
(d) General obligation debt to provide educational facilities for county and independent school systems and to provide public library facilities for county and independent school systems, counties, municipalities and boards of trustees of public libraries or boards of trustees of public library systems, and, when the construction of such educational or library facilities has been completed, the title of such facilities shall be vested in the respective local boards of education, counties, municipalities, or public library boards of trustees for which such facilities were constructed.
(e) General obligation debt in order to make loans to counties, municipal corporations, political subdivisions, local authorities, and other local government entities for water or sewerage facilities or systems. It shall not be necessary for the state or a state authority to hold title to or otherwise be the owner of such facilities or systems. General obligation debt for these purposes may be authorized and incurred for administration and disbursement by a state authority created and activated before, on, or after November 8, 1960.

(f) Guaranteed revenue debt by guaranteeing the payment of revenue obligations issued by an instrumentality of the state if such revenue obligations are issued to finance:
  (1) Toll bridges or toll roads.
  (2) Land public transportation facilities or systems.
  (3) Water facilities or systems.
  (4) Sewage facilities or systems.
  (5) Loans to, and load programs for, citizens of the state for educational purposes.
  (6) Regional or multijurisdictional solid waste recycling or solid waste facilities or systems. (Source: GA.L. 1992, page 3329).

Paragraph II. State general obligation debt and guaranteed revenue debt; limitations.
(a) As used in this Paragraph and Paragraph III of this section, "annual debt service requirements" means the total principle and interest coming due in any state fiscal year. With regard to any issue of debt incurred wholly or in part on a term basis, "annual debt service requirements" means an amount equal to the total principal and interest payment required to retire such issue in full divided by the number of years from its issue date to its maturity date.
(b) No debt may be incurred under subparagraphs (c), (d), and (e) of Paragraph I of this section or Paragraph V of this section at any time when the highest aggregate annual debt service requirements for the then current year or any subsequent year for outstanding general obligation debt and guaranteed revenue debt, including the proposed debt, and the highest aggregate annual payments for the then current year or any subsequent fiscal year of the state under all contracts then in force to which the provisions of the second paragraph of Article IX, Section VI, Paragraph I(a) of the Constitution of 1976 are applicable, exceed 10 percent of the total revenue receipts, less refunds of the state treasury in the fiscal year immediately preceding the year in which any such debt is to be incurred.
(c) No debt may be incurred under subparagraphs (c) and (d) of Paragraph I of this section at any time when the term of the debt is in excess of 25 years.
(d) No guaranteed revenue debt may be incurred to finance water or sewage treatment facilities or systems when the highest aggregate annual debt service requirements for the then current year or any subsequent fiscal year of the state for outstanding or proposed guaranteed revenue debt for water facilities or systems or sewage facilities or systems exceed 1 percent of the total revenue receipts less refunds, of the state treasury in the fiscal year immediately preceding the year in which any such debt is to be incurred.
(e) The aggregate amount of guaranteed revenue debt incurred to make loans for educational purposes that shall be outstanding at any time shall not exceed $18 million, and the aggregate amount of guaranteed revenue debt incurred to purchase, or to lend or deposit against the security of, loans for educational purposes that may be outstanding at any time shall not exceed $72 million.

Paragraph III. State obligation debt and guaranteed revenue debt; conditions upon issuance; sinking funds and reserve funds.
(a) (1) General obligation debt may not be incurred until legislation is enacted stating the purposes, in general or specific terms, for which such issue of debt is to be incurred, specifying the maximum principal amount of such issue and appropriating an amount at least sufficient to pay the highest annual debt service requirements for such issue. All such appropriations for debt service purposes shall not lapse for any reason and shall continue in effect until the debt for which such appropriation was authorized shall have been incurred, but the General Assembly may repeal any such appropriation at any time prior to the incurring of such debt. The General Assembly shall raise by taxation and appropriate each fiscal year, in addition to the sum necessary to make all payments required under contracts entitled to the protection of the second paragraph of Paragraph I(a), Section VI, Article IX of the

Constitution of 1976, such amounts as are necessary to pay debt service requirements in such fiscal year on all general obligation debt.

(2) (A) The General Assembly shall appropriate to a special trust fund to be designated "State of Georgia General Obligation Debt Sinking Fund" such amounts as are necessary to pay annual debt service requirements on all general obligation debt. The sinking fund shall be used solely for the retirement of general obligation debt payable from the fund. If for any reason the monies in the sinking fund are insufficient to make, when due, all payments required with respect to such general obligation debt, the first revenues thereafter received in the general fund of the state shall be set aside by the appropriate state fiscal officer to the extent necessary to cure the deficiency and shall be deposited by the fiscal officer into the sinking fund. The appropriate state fiscal officer may be required to set aside and apply such revenues at the suit of any holder of any general obligation debt incurred under this section.

(B) The obligation to make sinking fund deposits are provided in subparagraphs (2)(A) shall be subordinate to the obligation imposed upon the fiscal officers of the state pursuant to the provisions of the second paragraph of Paragraph I(a) of Section VI of Article IX of the Constitution of 1976.

(b) (1) Guaranteed revenue debt may not be incurred until legislation has been enacted authorizing the guarantee of the specific issue of revenue obligations then proposed, reciting that the General Assembly has determined such obligations will be self-liquidating over the life of the issue (which determination shall be conclusive), specifying the maximum principal amount of such issue and appropriating an amount at

(2) least equal to the highest annual debt service requirements for such issue.

(A) Each appropriation made for the purposes of subparagraph (b)(1) shall be paid upon the issuance of the said obligation into a special trust fund to be designated "State of Georgia Guaranteed Revenue Debt Common Reserve Fund" to be held together with all other sums similarly appropriated as a common reserve for any payment which may be required by virtue of any guarantee entered into in connection with any issue of guaranteed revenue obligations. No appropriations for the benefit of guaranteed revenue debt shall lapse unless repealed prior to the payment of the appropriation into the common reserve fund.

(B) If any payments are required to be made from the common reserve fund to meet debt service requirements on guaranteed revenue obligations by virtue of an insufficiency of revenues, the amount necessary to cure the deficiency shall be paid from the common reserve fund by the appropriate state fiscal officer. Upon such payment, the common reserve fund shall be reimbursed from the general funds of the state within ten days following the commencement of any fiscal year of the state for any amounts so paid; provided, however, the obligation to make any such reimbursements shall be subordinate to the obligation imposed upon the fiscal officers of the state pursuant to the second paragraph of Paragraph I(a) of section VI, Article IX of the Constitution of 1976 and shall also be subordinate to the obligation to make sinking fund deposits for the benefit of general obligation debt. The appropriate state fiscal officer may be required to apply such funds as provided in this subparagraph (b)(2)(B) at the suit of any holder of any such guaranteed revenue obligations.

(C) The amount to the credit to the common reserve fund shall at all times be at least equal to the aggregate highest annual debt service requirements on all outstanding guaranteed revenue obligations entitled to the benefit of the fund. If at the end of any fiscal year of the state the fund is in excess of the required amount, the appropriate state fiscal officer, as designated by law, shall transfer the excess amount to the general funds of the state free of said trust.

(c) The funds in the general obligation debt sinking fund and the guaranteed revenue debt common reserve fund shall be as fully invested as is practicable, consistent with the requirements to make current principal and interest payments. Any such investment shall be restricted to obligations constituting direct and general obligations of the United States government or obligations unconditionally guaranteed as to the payment of principal and interest by the United States government, maturing no longer than 12 months from the date of purchase.

Paragraph IV. Certain contracts prohibited. The state, and all state institutions, departments, and agencies of the state are prohibited from entering into any contract, except contracts pertaining to guaranteed revenue debt, with any public agency, public corporation, authority, or similar entity if such contract is intended to constitute security for bonds or other obligations issued by any such public agency, public corporation, or authority and, in the event any contract between the state, or any state institution, department or agency of the state and any public agency, public corporation, authority or similar entity, or any revenues from any such contract, is pledged or assigned as security for the repayment of bonds or other obligations, then and in either such event, the appropriation or expenditure of any funds of the state for the payment of obligations under any such contract shall likewise be prohibited.

Paragraph V. Refunding of debt. The state may incur general obligation debt or guaranteed revenue debt to fund or refund any such debt or to fund or refund any obligations issued upon the security of contracts to which the provisions of the second paragraph of Paragraph I(a), Section VI, Article IX of the Constitution of 1976 are applicable. The issuance of any such debt for the purposes of said funding or refunding shall be subject to the 10 percent limitation in Paragraph II(b) of this section to the same extent as debt incurred under Paragraph I of this section; provided, however, in making such computations the annual debt service requirements and annual contract payments remaining on the debt or obligations being funded or refunded shall not be taken into account. The issuance of such debt may be accomplished by resolution of the Georgia State Financing and Investment Commission without any action on the part of the General Assembly and any appropriation made or required to be made with respect to the debt or obligation being funded or refunded shall immediately attach and inure to the benefit of the obligation to be issued in connection with such funding or refunding. Debt incurred in connection with any such funding or refunding shall be the same as the originally authorized by the General Assembly, except that the general obligation debt may be incurred to fund or refund obligations issued upon the security of contracts to which the provisions of the second paragraph of Paragraph I(a), Section VI, Article IX of the Constitution of 1976 are applicable and the continuing appropriations required to be made under this Constitution shall immediately attach and inure to the benefit of the obligation to be issued in connection with such funding or refunding with the same force and effect as though said obligations so funded or refunded had originally been issued as a general obligation debt authorized hereunder. The term of a funding or refunding issue pursuant to this Paragraph shall not extend beyond the term of the original debt or obligation and the total interest on the funding or refunding issue shall not exceed the total interest to be paid on such original debt or obligation. The principal amount of any debt issued in connection with such funding or refunding may exceed the principal amount being funded or refunded to the extent necessary to provide for the payment of any premium thereby incurred.

Paragraph VI. Faith and credit of state pledged debt may be validated. The full faith, credit, and taxing power of the state are hereby pledged to the payment of all public debt incurred under this article and all such debt and the interest on the debt shall be exempt from taxation. Such debt may be validated by judicial proceedings in the manner provided by law. Such validation shall be incontestable and conclusive.

Paragraph VII. Georgia State Financing and Investment Commission; duties.
(a) There shall be a Georgia State Financing and Investment Commission. The commission shall consist of the Governor, the President of the Senate, the Speaker of the House of

Representatives, the State Auditor, the Attorney General, the director, Fiscal Division, Department of Administrative Services, or such other officer as may be designated by law, and the Commissioner of Agriculture. The commission shall be responsible for the issuance of all public debt and for the proper application, as provided by law, of the proceeds of such debt to the purposes for which it is incurred; provided, however, the proceeds from guaranteed revenue obligations shall be paid to the issuer thereof and such proceeds and the application thereof shall be the responsibility of such issuer. Debt to be incurred at the same time for more than one purpose may be combined in one issue without stating the purpose separately but the proceeds thereof must be allocated, disbursed and used solely in accordance with the original purpose and without exceeding the principal amount authorized for each purpose set forth in the authorization of the General Assembly and to the extent not so used to purchase and retire public debt. The commission shall be responsible for the investment of all proceeds to be administered by it and, as provided by law, the income earned on any such investments may be used to pay operating expenses of the commission or placed in a common debt retirement fund and used to purchase and retire any public debt, or any bonds or obligations issued by any public agency, public corporation or authority which are secured by a contract to which the provisions of the second paragraph of Paragraph I(a) of Section VI, Article IX of the Constitution of 1976 are applicable. The commission shall have such additional responsibilities, powers, and duties as are provided by law.

(b) Notwithstanding subparagraph (a) of this Paragraph, proceeds from general obligation debt issued for making loans to local government entities for water or sewerage facilities or systems as provided in Paragraph I(e) of this section shall be paid or transferred to and administered and invested by the unit of state government or state authority made responsible by law for such activities, and the proceeds and investment earnings thereof shall be applied and disbursed by such unit or authority. (Source: GA.L. 1992, page 3329).

Paragraph VIII. State aid forbidden. Except as provided in this Constitution, the credit of the state shall not be pledged or loaned to any individual, company, corporation, or association. The state shall not become a joint owner or stockholder in or with any individual, company, association, or corporation.

Paragraph IX. Construction. Paragraphs I through VIII of this section are for the purpose of providing an effective method of financing the state's needs and their provisions and any law now or hereafter enacted by the General Assembly in furtherance of their provisions shall be liberally constructed to effect such purpose. Insofar as any such provisions or any such law may be inconsistent with any other provisions of this Constitution or of any other law, the provisions of such Paragraphs and laws enacted in furtherance of such Paragraphs shall be controlling; provided, however, the provisions of such Paragraphs shall not be so broadly construed as to cause the same to be unconstitutional and in connection with any such construction such Paragraphs shall be deemed to contain such limitations as shall be required to accomplish the foregoing.

Paragraph X. Assumption of debts forbidden; exceptions. The state shall not assume the debt, or any part thereof, of any county, municipality, or other political subdivision of the state, unless such debt be contracted to enable the state to repel invasion, suppress civil disorders or insurrection, or defend itself in time of war.

Paragraph XI. Section not to unlawfully impair contracts or revive obligations previously voided. The provisions of this section shall not be construed so as to:
  (a) Unlawfully impair the obligation of any contract in effect on June 30, 1983.
  (b) Revive or permit the revival of the obligation of any bond or security declared to be void by the Constitution of 1976 or any previous Constitution of this state.

Article VIII
Education

Section I
Public Education

Paragraph I. Public education; free public education prior to college or postsecondary level; support by taxation. The provision of an adequate public education for the citizens shall be a prime obligation of the State of Georgia. Public education for the citizens prior to the college or postsecondary level shall be free and shall be provided for by taxation. The expense of other public education shall be provided for in such a manner and in such amount as may be provided by law.

Section II
State Board of Education

Paragraph I. State Board of Education.
(a) There shall be a State Board of Education which shall consist of one member from each congressional district in the state appointed by the Governor and confirmed by the Senate. The Governor shall not be a member of said board. The ten members in office on June 30, 1983, shall serve out the remainder of their respective terms. As each term of office expires, the Governor shall appoint a successor as herein provided. The terms of office of all members appointed after the effective date of this Constitution shall be for seven years. Members shall serve until their successors are appointed and qualified. In the event of a vacancy on the board by death, resignation, removal, or any reason other than expiration of a member's term, the Governor shall fill such vacancy; and the person so appointed shall serve until confirmation by the Senate and, upon confirmation, shall serve for the unexpired term of office.
(b) The State Board of Education shall have such powers and duties as provided by law.
(c) The State Board of Education may accept bequests, donations, grants, and transfers of land, buildings, and other property for the use of the state educational system.
(d) The qualifications, compensation, and removal from office of the members of the board of education shall be as provided by law.

Section III
State School Superintendent

Paragraph I. State School Superintendent. There shall be a State School Superintendent, who shall be the executive officer of the State Board of Education, elected at the same time and in the same manner and for the same term as that of the Governor. The State School Superintendent shall have such qualifications and shall be paid such compensation as may be fixed by law. No member of the State Board of Education shall be eligible for election as State School Superintendent during the time for which such member shall have been appointed.

Section IV
Board of Regents

Paragraph I. University System of Georgia; board of regents.
(a) There shall be a Board of Regents of the University System of Georgia which shall consist of one member from each congressional district in the state and five additional members from the state at large, appointed by the Governor and confirmed by the Senate. The Governor shall not be a member of said board. The members in office on June 30, 1983, shall serve out the remainder of their respective terms. As each term of office expires, the Governor shall appoint a successor as herein provided. All such terms of membership shall be for seven years. Members shall serve until their successors are appointed and qualified. In the event of a vacancy on the board by death, resignation, removal, or any reason other than the expiration of a member's term, the Governor shall fill such vacancy; and the person so appointed shall serve until confirmed by the Senate and, upon confirmation, shall serve for the unexpired term of office.
(b) The board of regents shall have the exclusive authority to create new public colleges, junior colleges, and universities in the State of Georgia, subject to approval by majority vote in the House of Representatives and the Senate. Such vote shall not be required to change the status of a college, institution or university existing on the effective date of this Constitution. The government, control, and management of the University System of Georgia and all of the institutions in said system shall be vested in the Board of Regents of the University System of Georgia.
(c) All appropriations made for the use of any or all institutions in the university system shall be paid to the board of regents in a lump sum, with the power and authority in said board to allocate and distribute the same among the institutions under its control in such a way and manner and in such amounts as will further an efficient and economical administration of the university system.
(d) The board of regents may hold, purchase, lease, sell, convey, or otherwise dispose of public property, execute conveyances thereon, and utilize the proceeds arising therefrom; may exercise the power of eminent domain in the manner provided by law; and shall have such other powers and duties as provided by law.
(e) The board of regents may accept bequests, donations, grants, and transfers of land, buildings, and other property for the use of the University System of Georgia.
(f) The qualifications, compensation, and removal from office of the members of the board of regents shall be as provided by law.

Section V
Local School Systems

Paragraph I. School systems continued; consolidation of school systems authorized; new independent school systems prohibited. Authority is granted to county and area boards of education to establish and maintain public schools within their limits. Existing county and independent school systems shall be continued, except that the General Assembly may provide by law for the consolidation of two or more county school systems, independent school systems, portions thereof, or any combination thereof into a single county or area school systems under the control and management of a county or area board of education, under such terms and conditions as the General Assembly may prescribe; but no such consolidation shall become effective until approved by a majority of the qualified voters voting thereon in each separate school system proposed to be consolidated. No independent school system shall hereafter be established.

Paragraph II. Boards of education. Each school system shall be under the management and control of a board of education, the members of which shall be elected or appointed as provided by law. School board members shall reside within the territory embraced by the school system and shall have such compensation and additional qualifications as may be provided by law. *Any board of education to which the members are appointed as of December 31, 1992, shall continue as an appointed board of education through December 31, 1993, and the appointed members of such board of education who are in office on December 31, 1992, shall continue in office as members of such appointed board until December 31, 1993, on which date the terms of office of all appointed members shall end.* (Source: GA.L. 1991, page 2032).

Paragraph III. School superintendents. There shall be a school superintendent of each system appointed by the board of education who shall be the executive officer of the board of education and shall have such qualifications, powers, and duties as provided by general law. *Any elected school superintendent in office on January 1, 1993, shall continue to serve out the remainder of his or her respective terms of office and shall be replaced by an appointee of the board of education at the expiration of such term.* (Source: GA.L. 1991, page 2032).

Paragraph IV. Reserved. (Source: GA.L. 1991, page 2032).

Paragraph V. Power of boards to contract with each other.
(a) Any two or more boards of education may contract with each other for the care, education, and transportation of pupils and for such other activities as they may be authorized by law to perform.
(b) The General Assembly may provide by law for the sharing of facilities or services by and between local boards of education under such joint administrative authority as may be authorized.

Paragraph VI. Power of boards to accept bequests, donations, grants, and transfers. The board of education of each school system may accept bequests, donations, grants, and transfers of land, buildings, and other property for the use of such system.

Paragraph VII. Special schools.
(a) The General Assembly may provide by law for the creation of special schools in such areas as may require them and may provide for the participation of local boards of education in the establishment of such schools under such terms and conditions as it may provide; but no bonded indebtedness may be incurred nor a school tax levied for the support of special schools without the approval of the majority of the qualified voters voting thereon in each of the systems affected. Any special schools shall be operated in conformity with regulations of the State Board of Education pursuant to provisions of law. The state is authorized to expend funds for the support and maintenance of special schools in such amount and manner as may be provided by law.
(b) Nothing containing herein shall be construed to affect the authority of local boards of education or of the state to support and maintain special schools created prior to June 30, 1983.

Section VI
Local Taxation for Education

Paragraph I. Local taxation for education.
(a) The board of education of each school system shall annually certify to its fiscal authority or authorities a school tax not greater than 20 mills per dollar for the support and maintenance of education. Said fiscal authority or authorities shall annually levy said tax upon the assessed value of all taxable property within the territory served by said

school system, provided that the levy made by an area board of education, which levy shall not be greater than 20 mills per dollar, shall be in such amount and within such limits as may be prescribed by local law applicable thereto.

(b) School tax funds shall be expended only for the support and maintenance of public schools, public vocational-technical schools, public education, and activities necessary or incidental thereto, including school lunch purposes.

(c) The 20 mill limitation provided for in subparagraph (a) of this Paragraph shall not apply to those school systems which are authorized on June 30, 1983, to levy a school tax in excess thereof.

(d) The method of certification and levy of the school tax provided for in the subparagraph (a) of this Paragraph shall not apply to those systems that are authorized on June 30, 1983, to utilize a different method of certification and levy of such tax; but the General Assembly may by law require that such systems be brought into conformity with the method of certification and levy herein provided.

Paragraph II. Increasing or removing tax rate. The mill limitation in effect on June 30, 1983, for any school system may be increased or removed by action of the respective boards of education, but only after such action has been approved by a majority of the qualified voters voting thereon in the particular school system to be affected in the manner provided by law.

Paragraph III. School tax collection reimbursement. The General Assembly may by general law require local boards of education to reimburse the appropriate governing authority for the collection of school taxes, provide that any rate established may be reduced by local act.

Paragraph IV. Sales tax for educational purposes.

(a) The Board of education of each school district in a county in which no independent school district is located may by resolution and the board of education of each county school district and the board of education of each independent school district located within such county may by concurrent resolutions impose, levy, and collect a sales and use tax for educational purposes of such school districts conditioned upon approval by a majority of the qualified voters residing within the limits of the local taxing jurisdiction voting in a referendum thereon. This tax shall be at the rate of 1 percent and shall be imposed for a period of time not to exceed five years, but in all other respects, except as otherwise provided for by Article 3 of Chapter 8 of Title 48 of the Official Code of Georgia Annotated, relating to the special county 1 percent sales and use tax, as now or hereafter amended. Proceedings for the reimposition of such tax shall be in the same manner as proceedings for the initial imposition of the tax, but the newly authorized tax shall not be imposed until the expiration of the tax then in effect.

(b) The purpose or purposes for which the proceeds of the tax are to be used and may be expended include:

(1) Capital outlay projects for educational purposes.

(2) The retirement of previously incurred general obligation debt with respect only to capital outlay projects of the school system; provided, however, that the tax authorized under this Paragraph shall only be expended for the purpose authorized under this subparagraph (b)(2) if all ad valorem property taxes levied or scheduled to be levied prior to the maturity of any such then outstanding general obligation debt to be retired by the proceeds of the tax imposed under this Paragraph shall be reduced by a total amount equal to the total amount of proceeds of the tax imposed under this Paragraph to be applied to retire such bonded indebtedness. In the event of failure to comply with the requirements of this subparagraph (b)(2), as certified by the Department of revenue, no further funds shall be expended under this subparagraph (b)(2) by such county or independent board of education and all such funds shall be maintained in a separate, restricted account and held solely for the expenditure for future capital outlay projects for educational purposes; or

(3) A combination of the foregoing.
(c) The resolution calling for the imposition of the tax and the ballot question shall each describe:
  (1) The specific capital outlay projects to be funded, or the specific debt to be retired, or both, if applicable.
  (2) The maximum cost of such project or projects and, if applicable, the maximum amount of debt to be retired, which cost and amount of debt shall also be the maximum amount of net proceeds to be raised by the tax; and
  (3) The maximum period of time, to be stated in calendar years or calendar quarters and not to exceed five years.
(d) Nothing in this Paragraph shall prohibit a county and those municipalities located in such county from imposing as additional taxes local sales and use taxes authorized by general law.
(e) The tax imposed pursuant to this Paragraph shall not be subject to any general law limitation regarding the maximum amount of local sales and use taxes which may be levied in any jurisdiction in this state.
(f) The tax imposed pursuant to this Paragraph shall not be subject to any sales and use tax exemption with respect to the sale and use of food and beverages which is imposed by law.
(g) The net proceeds of the tax shall be distributed between the county school district and the independent school districts, or portion thereof, located in such county according to the ratio the student enrollment in each school district, or portion thereof, bears to the total student enrollment of all school districts in the county, or upon such other formula for distribution as may be authorized by local law. For purposes of this subparagraph, student enrollment shall be based on the latest FTE count prior to the referendum on imposing the tax.
(h) Excess proceeds of the tax which remain following expenditure of proceeds for authorized projects or purposes for education shall be used solely for the purpose of reducing any indebtedness of the school system. In the event there is no indebtedness, such excess proceeds shall be used by such school system for the purpose of reducing its millage rate in an amount equivalent to the amount of such excess proceeds.
(i) The tax authorized by this Paragraph may be imposed, levied, and collected as provided in this Paragraph without further action by the General Assembly, but the General Assembly shall be authorized by general law to further define and implement its provisions including, but not limited to, the authority to specify the percentage of net proceeds to be allocated among the projects and purposes for which the tax was levied.
(j) (1) Notwithstanding any provision of any constitutional amendment continued in force and effect pursuant to Article XI, Section I, Paragraph IV(a) and except as otherwise provided in subparagraph (j)(2) of this Paragraph, any political subdivision whose ad valorem taxing powers are restricted pursuant to such a constitutional amendment may receive the proceeds of the tax authorized under this Paragraph or of any local sales and use tax authorized by general law, or any combination of such taxes, without any corresponding limitation of its ad valorem taxing powers which would otherwise be required under such constitutional amendment.
  (2) The restriction and limitation of ad valorem taxing powers described in subparagraph (j)(1) of this Paragraph shall remain applicable with respect to proceeds received from the levy of a local sales and use tax specifically authorized by a constitutional amendment in force and effect pursuant to Article XI, Section I, Paragraph IV(a), as opposed to a local sales and use tax authorized by this Paragraph or by general law. (Source: Sec.St. 1997).

Section VII
Educational Assistance

Paragraph I. Educational assistance programs authorized.
(a) Pursuant to laws not now or hereafter enacted by the General Assembly, public funds may be expended for any of the following purposes:
  (1) To provide grants, scholarships, loans, or other assistance to students and to parents of students for educational purposes.
  (2) To provide for a program of guaranteed loans to students and to parents of students for educational purposes and to pay interest, interest subsidies, and fees to lenders on such loans. The General Assembly is authorized to provide such tax exemptions to lenders as shall be deemed advisable in connection with such program.
  (3) To match funds now or hereafter available for student assistance pursuant to any federal law.
  (4) To provide grants, scholarships, loans, or other assistance to public employees for educational purposes.
  (5) To provide for the purchase of loans made to students for educational purposes who have completed a program of study in a field in which critical shortages exist and for cancellation of repayment of such loans, interest, and charges thereon.
(b) Contributions made in support of any educational assistance program now or hereafter established under provisions of this section may be deductible for state income tax purposes as now or hereafter provided by law.
(c) The General Assembly shall be authorized by general law to provide for an educational trust fund to assist students and parents of students in financing postsecondary education and to provide for contracts between the fund and the purchasers for the advance payment of tuition by each purchaser for a qualified beneficiary to attend a state institution of higher education. Such general law shall provide for such general terms, conditions, and limitations as the General Assembly shall deem necessary for the implementation of this subparagraph. Notwithstanding any provisions of this Constitution to the contrary, the General Assembly shall be authorized to provide for the guarantee of such contracts with state revenues. (Authority: OLC, pages 128–129).

Paragraph II. Guaranteed revenue debt. Guaranteed revenue debt may be incurred to provide funds to make loans to students and to parents of students for educational purposes, to purchase loans made to students and to parents for educational purposes, or to lend or make deposits of such funds with lenders which shall be secured by loans made to students and to parents of students for educational purposes. Any such debt shall be incurred in accordance with the procedures and requirements of Article VII, Section IV of this Constitution.

Paragraph III. Public authorities. Public authorities or public corporations heretofore or hereafter created for such purposes shall be authorized to administer educational assistance programs and, in connection therewith, may exercise such powers as may now or hereafter be provided by law.

Paragraph IV. Waiver of tuition. The Board of Regents of the University System of Georgia shall be authorized to establish programs allowing attendance at units of the University System of Georgia without payment of tuition or other fees, but the General Assembly may provide by law for the establishment of any such program for the benefit of elderly citizens of the state.

Article IX
Counties and Municipal Corporations

Section I
Counties

Paragraph I. Counties a body corporate and politic. Each county shall be a body corporate and politic with such governing authority and with such powers and limitations as are provided in this Constitution and as provided by law. The governing authorities of the several counties shall remain as prescribed by law on June 30, 1983, until otherwise provided by law.

Paragraph II. Number of counties limited; county boundaries and county sites; county consolidation.
- (a) There shall be not more than 159 counties in this state.
- (b) The metes and bounds of the several counties and the county sites shall remain as prescribed by law on June 30, 1983, unless changed under the operation of a general law.
- (c) The General Assembly may provide by law for the consolidation of two or more counties into one or the division of a county and the merger of portions thereof into other counties under such terms and conditions as it may prescribe; but no such consolidation, division, or merger shall become effective unless approved by a majority of the qualified voters voting thereon in each of the counties proposed to be consolidated, divided, or merged.

Paragraph III. County officers; election; term; compensation.
- (a) The clerk of the superior court, judge of the probate court, sheriff, tax receiver, tax collector, and tax commissioner, where such office has been replaced the tax receiver and tax collector, shall be elected by the qualified voters of their respective counties for terms of four years and shall have such qualifications, powers, and duties as provided by general law.
- (b) County officers listed in subparagraph (a) of this Paragraph may be on a fee basis, salary basis, or fee basis supplemented by salary, in such manner as may be directed by law. Minimum compensation for said county officers may be established by the General Assembly by general law. Such minimum compensation may be supplemented by local law or, if such authority is designated by local law, by action of the county governing authority.
- (c) The General Assembly may consolidate the offices of tax receiver and tax collector into the office of tax commissioner.

Paragraph IV. Civil service systems. The General Assembly may by general law authorize the establishment by county governing authorities of civil service systems covering county employees or covering county employees and employees of the elected county officers.

Section II
Home Rule for Counties and Municipalities

Paragraph I. Home rule for counties.
- (a) The governing authority of each county shall have legislative power to adopt clearly reasonable ordinances, resolutions, or regulations relating to its property, affairs, and local government for which no provision has been made by general law and which is not inconsistent with this Constitution or any local law applicable thereto. Any such local law shall remain in force and effect until amended or repealed as provided in subparagraph

(b)This, however, shall not restrict the authority of the General Assembly by general law to further define this power or to broaden, limit, or otherwise regulate the exercise thereof. The General Assembly shall not pass any local law to repeal, modify, or supersede any action taken by a county governing authority under this section except as authorized under subparagraph (c) hereof.

(b) Except as provided in subparagraph (c), a county may, as an incident of its home rule power, amend or repeal the local acts applicable to its governing authority by following either of the procedures hereinafter set forth:

(1) Such local acts may be amended or repealed by a resolution or ordinance duly adopted at two regular consecutive meetings of the county governing authority not less than seven nor more than 60 days apart. A notice containing a synopsis of the proposed amendment or repeal shall be published in the official county organ once a week for three weeks within a period of 60 days immediately preceding its final adoption. Such notice shall state that a copy of the proposed amendment or repeal is on file in the office of the clerk of the superior court of the county for the purpose of examination and inspection by the public. The clerk of the superior court shall furnish anyone, upon request, a copy of the proposed amendment or repeal. No amendment or repeal hereunder shall be valid to change or repeal an amendment adopted pursuant to a referendum as provided in (2) of this subparagraph or to change or repeal a local act of the General Assembly ratified in a referendum by the electors of such county unless at least 12 months have elapsed after such referendum. No amendment hereunder shall be valid if inconsistent with any provision of this Constitution or if provision has been made therefore by general law.

(2) Amendments to or repeals of such local acts or ordinances, resolutions, or regulations adopted pursuant to subparagraph (a) hereof may be initiated by a petition filed with the judge of the probate court of the county containing, in cases of counties with a population of 5,000 or less, the signatures of at least 25 percent of the electors registered to vote in the last general election; in cases of counties with a population of more than 5,000 but not more than 50,000, at least 20 percent of the electors registered to vote in the last general election; and in cases of a county with a population of more than 50,000, at least 10 percent of the electors registered to vote in the last general election, which petition shall specifically set forth the exact language of the proposed amendment or repeal. The judge of the probate court shall determine the validity of such petition within 60 days of its being filed with the judge of the probate court. In the event of the judge of the probate court determines that such petition is valid, it shall be his duty to issue the call for an election for the purpose of submitting such amendment or repeal to the registered electors of the county for their approval or rejection. Such call shall be issued not less than ten nor more than 60 days after the date of the filing of the petition. He shall set the date for such election for a day not less than 60 nor more than 90 days after the date of such filing. The judge of the probate court shall cause a notice of the date of said election to be published in the official organ of the county once a week for three weeks immediately preceding such date. Said notice shall also contain a synopsis of the proposed amendment or repeal and shall state that a copy thereof is on file in the office of the judge of the probate court of the county for the purpose of examination and inspection by the public. The judge of the probate court shall furnish anyone, upon written request, a copy of the proposed amendment or repeal. If more than one-half of the votes cast on such question are for approval of the amendment or repeal, it shall become of full force and effect; otherwise, it shall be void and of no force and effect. The expense of such election shall be borne by the county, and it shall be the duty of the judge of the probate court to hold and conduct such election. Such election shall be held under the same laws and rules and

regulations as govern special elections, except as otherwise provided herein. It shall be the duty of the judge of the probate court to canvass the returns and declare the result of the election. It shall be his further duty to certify the result thereof to the Secretary of State in accordance with the provisions of subparagraph (g) of this Paragraph. A referendum on any such amendment or repeal shall not be held more often than once each year. No amendment hereunder shall be valid if inconsistent with any provision of this Constitution or if any provision has been made therefor by general law. In the event that the judge of the probate court determines that such petition was not valid, he shall cause to be published in explicit detail the reasons why such petition is not valid; provided, however that, in any proceeding in which the validity of the petition is at issue, the tribunal considering such issue shall not be limited by the reasons assigned. Such publication shall be in the official organ of the county in the week immediately following the date on which such petition is declared to be not valid.

(c) The power granted to counties in subparagraphs (a) and (b) above shall not be construed to extend to the following matters or any other matters which the General Assembly by general law has preempted or may hereafter preempt, but such matters shall be the subject of general law or the subject of local acts of the General Assembly to the extent that the enactment of such local acts if otherwise permitted under this Constitution:

(1) Action affecting any elective county office, the salaries thereof, or the personnel thereof, except the personnel subject to the jurisdiction of the county governing authority.

(2) Action affecting the composition, form, procedure for election or appointment, compensation, and expenses and allowances in the nature of compensation of the county governing authority.

(3) Action defining any criminal offense or providing for criminal punishment.

(4) Action adopting any form of taxation beyond that authorized by law or by this Constitution.

(5) Action extending the power of regulation over any business activity regulated by the Georgia Public Service Commission beyond that authorized by local or general law or by this Constitution.

(6) Action affecting the exercise of the power of eminent domain.

(7) Action affecting any court or the personnel thereof.

(8) Action affecting any public school system.

(d) The power granted in subparagraphs (a) and (b) of this Paragraph shall not include the power to take any action affecting the private or civil law governing private or civil relationships, except as is incident to the exercise of an independent governmental power.

(e) Nothing in Subparagraphs (a), (b), (c), or (d) shall affect the provisions of subparagraph (f) of this Paragraph.

(f) The governing authority of each county is authorized to fix the salary, compensation, and expenses of those employed by such governing authority and to establish and maintain retirement or pension systems, insurance, workers' compensation, and hospitalization benefits for said employees.

(g) No amendment or revision of any local act made pursuant to subparagraph (b) of this section shall become effective until a copy of such amendment or revision, a copy of the required notice of publication, and an affidavit of a duly authorized representative of the newspaper in which such notice was published to the effect that said notice has been published as provided in said subparagraph has been filed with the Secretary of State. The Secretary of State shall provide for the publication and distribution of all such amendments and revisions at least annually.

Paragraph II. Home rule for municipalities. The General Assembly may provide by law for the self-government of municipalities and to that end is expressly given the authority to delegate its power so that matters pertaining to municipalities may be dealt with without the necessity of action by the General Assembly.

Paragraph III. Supplementary powers.
(a) In addition to and supplementary of all powers possessed by or conferred upon any county, municipality, or any combination thereof any county, municipality or combination thereof may exercise the following powers and provide the following services:
 (1) Police and fire protection.
 (2) Garbage and solid waste collection and disposal.
 (3) Public health facilities and services, including hospitals, ambulance and emergency rescue services, and animal control.
 (4) Street and road construction and maintenance, including curbs, side-walks, street lights, and devices to control the flow of traffic on streets and roads constructed by counties and municipalities or any combination thereof.
 (5) Parks, recreational areas, programs, and facilities.
 (6) Storm water and sewage collection and disposal systems.
 (7) Development, storage, treatment, purification, and distribution of water.
 (8) Public housing.
 (9) Public transportation.
 (10) Libraries, archives, and arts and sciences programs and facilities.
 (11) Terminal and dock facilities and parking facilities.
 (12) Codes, including building, housing, plumbing, and electrical codes.
 (13) Air quality control.
 (14) The power to maintain and modify heretofore existing retirement or pension systems, including such systems heretofore created by general laws of local application by population classification, and to continue in effect or modify other benefits heretofore provided as a part of or in addition to such retirement or pension systems and the power to create and maintain retirement or pension systems for any elected or appointed public officers and employees whose compensation is paid in whole or in part from county or municipal funds and for the beneficiaries of such officers and employees.
(b) Unless otherwise provided by law,
 (1) No county may exercise any of the powers listed in subparagraph (a) of this Paragraph or provide any service listed therein inside the boundaries of any municipality or any other county except by contract with the municipality or county affected; and
 (2) No municipality may exercise any of the powers listed in subparagraph (a) of this Paragraph or provide any service listed therein outside its own boundaries except by contract with the county or municipality affected.
(c) Nothing contained within this Paragraph shall operate to prohibit the General Assembly from enacting general laws relative to the subject matters listed in subparagraph (a) of this Paragraph or to prohibit the General Assembly by general law from regulating, restricting, or limiting the exercise of the powers listed therein; but it may not withdraw any such powers.
(d) Except as otherwise provided in subparagraph (b) of this Paragraph, the General Assembly shall act upon the subject matters listed in subparagraph (a) of this Paragraph only by general law.

Paragraph IV. Planning and zoning. The governing authority of each county and of each municipality may adopt plans and may exercise the power of zoning. This authorization shall not prohibit the General Assembly from enacting general laws establishing procedures for the exercise of such power.

Paragraph V. Eminent domain. The governing authority of each county and of each municipality may exercise the power of eminent domain for any public purpose.

Paragraph VI. Special districts. As hereinafter provided in this Paragraph, special districts may be created for the provision of local government services within such districts; and fees, assessments, and taxes may be levied and collected within such districts to pay, wholly or partially, the cost of providing such services therein and to construct and maintain facilities therefor. Such special districts may be created and fees, assessments, or taxes may be levied and collected therein by any one or more of the following methods:
- (a) By general law which directly creates the districts.
- (b) By general law which requires the creation of districts under conditions specified by such general law.
- (c) By municipal or county ordinance or resolution, except that no such ordinance or resolution may supersede a law enacted by the General Assembly pursuant to subparagraphs (a) or (b) of this Paragraph.

Paragraph VII. Community redevelopment.
- *(a) The General Assembly may authorize any county, municipality, or housing authority to undertake and carry out community redevelopment, which may include the sale or other disposition of property acquired by eminent domain to private enterprise for private uses.*
- *(b) In addition to the authority granted by subparagraph (a) of this Paragraph, the General Assembly is authorized to grant to counties or municipalities for redevelopment purposes and in connection with redevelopment programs, as such purposes and programs are defined by general law, the power to issue tax allocation bonds, as defined by such law, and the power to incur other obligations, without either such bonds or obligations constituting debt within the meaning of Section V of this article, and the power to enter into contracts for any period not exceeding 30 years with private persons, firms, corporations, and business entities. Notwithstanding the grant of these powers pursuant to general law, no county or municipality may exercise these powers unless so authorized by local law and unless such powers are exercised in conformity with those terms and conditions for such exercise as established by that local law. The provisions of any such local law shall conform to those requirements established by general law regarding such powers. No such local law or any amendment thereto, shall become effective unless approved in a referendum by a majority of the qualified voters voting thereon in the county or municipality directly affected by that local law.* (Authority: OLC, pages 138–139).
- *(c) The General Assembly is authorized to provide by general law for the creation of enterprise zones by counties or municipalities, or both. Such law may provide for exemptions, credits, or reductions of any tax or taxes levied within such zones by the state, a county, a municipality, or any combination thereof. Such exemptions shall be available only to such persons, firms, or corporations which create job opportunities within the enterprise zone for unemployed, low, and moderate income persons in accordance with standards set forth in such general law. Such general law shall further define enterprise zones so as to limit such tax exemptions, credits, or reductions to persons and geographic areas which are determined to be underdeveloped as evidenced by the unemployment rate and the average personal income in the area when compared to the remainder of the state. The General Assembly may by general law further define areas qualified for creation of enterprise zones and may provide for all matters relative to the creation, approval, and termination of such zones.* (Source: Sec.St. 1997).

Paragraph VIII. Limitations on the taxing power and contributions of counties, municipalities, and political subdivisions. The General Assembly shall not authorize any county, municipality, or other political subdivision of this state, through taxation, contribution, or otherwise, to appropriate money for or lend its credit to any person or to any nonpublic corporation or association except for purely charitable purposes.

Paragraph IX. Immunity of counties, municipalities, and school districts. The General Assembly may waive immunity of counties, municipalities, and school districts by law.

Section III
Intergovernmental Relations

Paragraph I. Intergovernmental contracts.
(a) *The state, or any institution, department, or other agency thereof, and any county, municipality, school district, or any other political subdivision of the state may contract for any period not exceeding 50 years with each other or with any other public agency, public corporation, or public authority for joint services, for the provision of services, or for the joint or separate use of facilities or equipment; but such contracts must deal with activities, services, or facilities which the contracting parties are authorized by law to undertake or provide. By way of specific instance and not limitation, a mutual undertaking by a local government entity to borrow and an undertaking by the state or a state authority to lend funds from and to one another for water and sewerage facilities or systems pursuant to law shall be a provision for services and an activity within the meaning of this Paragraph.*
(b) *Subject to such limitations as may be provided by general law, any county, municipality, or political subdivision thereof may, in connection with any contracts authorized in this Paragraph, convey any existing facilities or equipment to the state or to any public agency, public corporation, or public authority.*
(c) *Any county, municipality, or any combination thereof, may contract with any public agency, public corporation, or public authority for the care, maintenance, and hospitalization of its indigent sick and may as a part of such contract agree to pay for the cost of acquisition, construction, modernization, or repairs of necessary land, buildings, and facilities by such public agency, public corporation, or public authority and provide for the payment of such services and the cost to such public agency, public corporation, or public authority of acquisition, construction, modernization, or repair of land, buildings, and facilities from revenues realized by such county, municipality, or any combination thereof from any taxes authorized by this Constitution or revenues derived from any other source.* (Authority: OLC, page 141).

Paragraph II. Local government reorganization.
(a) The General Assembly may provide by law for any matters necessary or convenient to authorize the consolidation of the governmental and corporate powers and functions vested in municipalities with the governmental and corporate powers and functions vested in a county or counties in which such municipalities are located; provided, however, that no such consolidation shall become effective unless separately approved by a majority of the qualified voters of the county or each of the counties and of the municipality or each of the municipalities located within such county or counties containing at least 10 percent of the population of the county in which located voting thereon in such manner as may be prescribed in such law. Such law may provide procedures and requirements for the establishment of charter commissions to draft proposed charters for the consolidated government, and the General Assembly is expressly authorized to delegate

its powers to such charter commissions for such purposes so that the governmental consolidation proposed by a charter commission may become effective without the necessity of further action by the General Assembly; or such law may require that the recommendation of any such charter commission be implemented by a subsequent local law.
(b) The General Assembly may provide by general law for alternatives other than governmental consolidation as authorized in subparagraph (a) above for the reorganization of county and municipal governments, including, but not limited to, procedures to establish a single governing body as the governing authority of a county and a municipality or municipalities located within such county or for the redistribution of powers between a county and a municipality or municipalities located within the county. Such law may require the form of governmental reorganization authorized by such law to be approved by the qualified voters voting directly affected thereby voting in such manner as may be required in such law.
(c) Nothing in this Paragraph shall be construed to limit the authority of the General Assembly to repeal municipal charters without a referendum.

Section IV
Taxation Power of County and Municipal Governments

Paragraph I. Power of taxation.
(a) Except as otherwise provided in this Paragraph, the governing authority of any county, municipality, or combination thereof may exercise the power of taxation as authorized by this Constitution or by general law.
(b) In the absence of a general law:
  (1) County governing authorities may be authorized by local law to levy and collect business and occupational license taxes and license fees only in the unincorporated areas of the counties. The General Assembly may provide that the revenues raised by such tax or fee be spent for the provision of services only in the unincorporated areas of the county.
  (2) Municipal governing authorities may be authorized by local law to levy and collect taxes and fees in the corporate limits of the municipalities.
(c) The General Assembly may provide by law for the taxation of insurance companies on the basis of gross direct premiums received from insurance policies within the unincorporated areas of counties. The tax authorized herein may be imposed by the state or by counties or by the state for county purposes as may be provided by law. The General Assembly may further provide by law for the reduction, only upon taxable property within the unincorporated areas of counties, of the ad valorem tax millage rate for county or county school district purposes or for the reduction of such ad valorem tax millage rate for both such purposes in connection with imposing or authorizing the imposition of the tax authorized herein or in connection with providing for the distribution of the proceeds derived from the tax authorized herein.

Paragraph II. Power of expenditure. The governing authority of any county, municipality, or combination thereof may expend public funds to perform any public service or public function as authorized by this Constitution or by law or to perform any other service or function as authorized by this Constitution or by general law.

Paragraph III. Purposes of taxation; allocation of taxes. No levy need state the particular purposes for which the same was made nor shall any taxes collected be allocated for any particular purpose, unless otherwise provided by this Constitution or by law.

Paragraph IV. Tax allocation; regional facilities. *As used in this Paragraph, the term "regional facilities" means industrial parks, business parks, conference centers, convention centers, airports, athletic facilities, recreation facilities, jails or correctional facilities, or other similar or related economic development parks, centers, or facilities or any combination thereof. Notwithstanding any other provision of this Constitution, a county or municipality is authorized to enter into contracts with: (1) any county which is contiguous to such county or the county in which such municipality is located: (2) any municipality located in such a contiguous county or the same county; or (3) any combination thereof. Any such contract may be for the purpose of allocating the proceeds of ad valorem taxes assessed and collected on real property located in such county or municipality with such other counties or municipalities with which the assessing county or municipality has entered into agreements for the development of one or more regional facilities and the allocation of other revenues generated from such regional facilities. Any such regional facility may be publicly or privately initiated. The allocation of such tax proceeds and other revenues shall be determined by contract between the affected local governments. Such contract shall provide for the manner of development, operation, and management of the regional facility and the sharing of expenses among the contracting local governments and shall specify the percentage of ad valorem taxes and other revenues to be allocated and the method of allocation to each contracting government. Unless otherwise provided by law, such a regional facility will qualify for the greatest dollar amount of income tax credits which may be provided for by general law for any of the counties or municipalities which have entered into an agreement for the development of the regional facility, regardless of the county or municipality in which the business is physically located. The authority granted to counties and municipalities under this Paragraph shall be subject to any conditions, limitations, and restrictions which may be imposed by general law.* (Source: Sec.St. 1997)

Section V
Limitation on Local Debt

Paragraph I. Debt limitations of counties, municipalities, and other political subdivisions.
(a) The debt incurred by any county, municipality, or other political subdivision of this state, including debt incurred on behalf of any special district, shall never exceed 10 percent of the assessed value of all taxable property within such county, municipality, or political subdivision; and no such county, municipality, or other political subdivision shall incur new debt without the assent of a majority of the qualified voters of such county, municipality, or political subdivision voting in an election held for that purpose as provided by law.
(b) Notwithstanding subparagraph (a) of this Paragraph, all local school systems which are authorized by law on June 30, 1983, to incur debt in excess of 10 percent of the assessed value of all taxable property therein shall continue to be authorized to incur such debt.

Paragraph II. Special district debt. Any county, municipality, or political subdivision of this state mat incur debt on behalf of any special district created pursuant to Paragraph VI of Section II of this article. Such debt may be incurred on behalf of such special district where the county, municipality, or other political subdivision shall have, at or before the time of incurring such debt, provided for the assessment and collection of an annual tax within the special district sufficient in amount to pay the principal of and interest on such debt within 30 years from the incurrence thereof; and no such county, municipality, or other political subdivision shall incur any debt on behalf of such special district without the assent of a majority of the qualified voters of such special district voting in an election held for that purpose as provided by law. No such county, municipality, or other political subdivisions shall incur any debt on behalf of such special district in an amount which, when taken together with all other debt outstanding incurred by such county, municipality, or political subdivision and on behalf of any such special district, exceeds 10 percent of the assessed value of all taxable property within such county, municipality, or political subdivision. The proceeds of the tax collected as provided herein shall be placed in a sinking fund to be held on behalf of such special district and used exclusively to pay off the principal of and interest on such debt thereafter maturing. Such moneys shall be held and kept separate from all other revenues collected and may be invested as provided by law.

Paragraph III. Refund of outstanding indebtedness. The governing authority of any county, municipality, or other political subdivision of this state may provide for the refunding of outstanding bonded indebtedness without the necessity of a referendum being held therefor, provided that neither the term of the original debt is extended nor the interest rate of the original debt is increased. The principal amount of any debt issued in connection with such refunding may exceed the principal amount being refunded in order to reduce the total principal and interest payment requirements over the remaining term of the original issue. The proceeds of the refunding issue shall be used solely to retire the original debt. The original debt refunded shall not constitute debt within the meaning of Paragraph I of this section; but the refunding issue shall constitute a debt such as will count against the limitation on debt measured by 10 percent of assessed value of taxable property as expressed in Paragraph I of this section.

Paragraph IV. Exceptions to debt limitations. Notwithstanding the debt limitations provided in Paragraph I of this section and without the necessity for a referendum being held therefor, the governing authority of any county, municipality, or other political subdivision of this state may, subject to the conditions and limitations as may be provided by general law:

(1) Accept and use funds granted by and obtain loans from the federal government or any agency thereof pursuant to conditions imposed by federal law.

(2) Incur debt, by way of borrowing from any person, corporation, or association as well as from the state, to pay in whole or in part the cost of property valuation and equalization programs for ad valorem tax purposes.

Paragraph V. Temporary loans authorized. The governing authority of any county, municipality, or other political subdivision of this state may incur debt by obtaining temporary loans in each year to pay expenses. The aggregate amount of all such loans shall not exceed 75 percent of the total gross income from taxes collected in the last preceding year. Such loans shall be payable on or before December 31 of the calendar year in which such loan is made. No such loan may be obtained when there is a loan then unpaid obtained in any prior year. No such county, municipality, or other political subdivision of this state shall incur in any one calendar year an aggregate of such temporary loans or other contracts, notes, warrants, or obligations for current expenses in excess of the total anticipated revenue for such calendar year.

Paragraph VI. Levy of taxes to pay bonds; sinking fund required. Any county, municipality, or other political subdivision of this state shall at or before the time of incurring bonded indebtedness provide for the assessment and collection of an annual tax sufficient in amount to pay the principal and interest of said debt within 30 years from the incurring of such bonded indebtedness. The proceeds of this tax, together with any other moneys collected for this purpose, shall be placed in a sinking fund to be used exclusively for paying the principal of and interest on such bonded debt. Such moneys shall be held and kept separate and apart from all other revenues collected and may be invested and reinvested as provided by law.

Paragraph VII. Validity of prior bond issues. Any and all bond issues validated and issued prior to June 30, 1983, shall continue to be valid.

Section VI
Revenue Bonds

Paragraph I. Revenue bonds; general limitations. Any county, municipality, or other political subdivision of this state may issue revenue bonds as provided by general law. The obligation represented by revenue bonds shall be repayable only out of the revenue derived from the project and shall not be deemed to be a debt of the issuing political subdivision. No such issuing political subdivision shall exercise the power of taxation for the purpose of paying any part of the principal or interest of any such revenue bonds.

Paragraph II. Revenue bonds; special limitations. Where revenue bonds are issued by any county, municipality, or other political subdivision of this state in order to buy, construct, extend, operate, or maintain gas or electric generating or distribution systems and necessary appurtenances thereof and the gas or electric generating or distribution system extends beyond the limits of the county in which the municipality or other political subdivision is located, then its services rendered and property located outside said county shall be subject to taxation and regulation in the same manner as are privately owned and operated utilities.

Paragraph III. Development authorities. The development of trade, commerce, industry, and employment opportunities being a public purpose vital to the welfare of the people of this state, the General Assembly may create development authorities to promote and further such purposes or may authorize the creation of such an authority by any county or municipality or combination thereof under such uniform terms and conditions as it may deem necessary. The General Assembly may exempt from taxation development authority obligations, properties, activities, or income and may authorize the issuance of revenue bonds by such authorities which shall not constitute an indebtedness of the state within the meaning of Section V of this article.

Paragraph IV. Validation. The General Assembly shall provide for the validation of any revenue bonds authorized and shall provide that such validation shall thereafter be incontestable and conclusive.

Paragraph V. Validity of prior revenue bond issues. All revenue bonds issued and validated prior to June 30, 1983, shall continue to be valid.

Section VII
Community Improvement Districts

Paragraph I. Creation. The General Assembly may by local law create one or more community improvement districts for any county or municipality or provide for the creation of one or more community improvement districts by any county or municipality.

Paragraph II. Purposes. The purpose of a community improvement district shall be the provision of any one or more of the following governmental services and facilities:
- *(1) Street and road construction and maintenance, including curbs, sidewalks, street lights, and devices to control the flow of traffic on streets and roads.*
- *(2) Parks and recreational areas and facilities.*
- *(3) Storm water and sewage collection and disposal systems.*
- *(4) Development, storage, treatment, purification, and distribution of water.*
- *(5) Public transportation.*
- *(6) Terminal and dock facilities and parking facilities.*
- *(7) Such other services and facilities as may be provided for by general law.*

Paragraph III. Administration.

(a) Any law creating or providing for the creation of a community improvement district shall designate the governing authority of the municipality or county for which the community improvement district is created as the administrative body or shall provide for the establishment and membership of an administrative body for the community improvement district. Any such law creating or providing for the creation of an administrative body for the community improvement district other than the municipal or county governing authority shall provide for representation of the governing authority of each county and municipality within which the community improvement district is wholly or partially located on the administrative body of the community improvement district.

(b) Any law creating or providing for the creation of a community improvement district shall provide that the creation of the community improvement district shall be conditioned upon:

(1) The adoption of a resolution consenting to the creation of the community improvement district by:

(A) The governing authority of the county if the community improvement district is located wholly within the unincorporated area of a county;

(B) The governing authority of the municipality if the community improvement district is located wholly within the incorporation area of a municipality; or

(C) The governing authorities of the county and the municipality if the community improvement district is located partially within the unincorporated area of a county and partially within the incorporated area of a municipality; and

(2) Written consent to the creation of the community improvement district by:

(A) A majority of the owners of real property within the community improvement district which will be subject to taxes, fees, and assessments levied by the administrative body of the community improvement district; and

(B) The owners of real property within the community improvement district which constitutes at least 75 percent by value of all real property within the community improvement district which will be subject to taxes, fees, and assessments levied by the administrative body of the community improvement district; and for this purpose value shall be determined by the most recent approved county ad valorem tax digest.

(c) The administrative body of each community improvement district may be authorized to levy taxes, fees, and assessments within the community improvement district only on real property used nonresidentially, specifically excluding all property used for residential, agricultural, or forestry purposes and specifically excluding tangible personal property and intangible property. Any tax, fee, or assessment so levied shall not exceed 2 1/2 percent of the assessed value of the real property or such lower limit as may be established by law. The law creating or providing for the creation of the community improvement district shall provide that taxes, fees, and assessments levied by the administrative body of the community improvement district shall be equitably apportioned among the properties subject to such taxes, fees, and assessments according to the need for governmental services and facilities created by the degree of density of development of each property. The law creating or providing for the creation of a community improvement district shall provide that the proceeds of taxes, fees and assessments levied by the administrative body of the community improvement district shall be used only for the purpose of providing governmental services and facilities which are specially required by the degree of density of development within the community improvement district and not for the purpose of providing those governmental services and facilities provided to the county or municipality as a whole. Any tax, fee, or assessment so levied shall be collected by the county or municipality for which the community improvement district is created in the same manner as taxes, fees, and assessments levied by such county or municipality. The proceeds of taxes, fees, and assessments so levied, less such fee to cover the costs of collection as may be specified by law, shall be transmitted by the collecting county or municipality to the administrative body of the community improvement district and shall be expended by the administrative body of the community improvement district only for the purposes authorized by this Section.

Paragraph IV. Debt. The administrative body of a community improvement district may incur debt, as authorized by law, without regard to the requirements of Section V of this Article, which debt shall be backed by the full faith, credit, and taxing power of the community improvement district but shall not be an obligation of the State of Georgia or any other unit of government of the State of Georgia other than the community improvement district.

Paragraph V. Cooperation with local governments. The services and facilities provided pursuant to this Section shall be provided for in a cooperation agreement executed jointly by the administrative body and the governing authority of the county or municipality for which the community improvement district is created. The provisions of this Section shall in no way limit the authority of any county or municipality to provide services or facilities within any community improvement district; and any county or municipality shall retain full and complete authority and control over any of its facilities located within a community improvement district. Said control shall include but not be limited to the modification of, access to, and degree and type of services provided through or by facilities of the municipality or county. Nothing contained in this Section shall be construed to limit or preempt the application of any governmental laws, ordinances, resolutions, or regulations to any community improvement district or the services or facilities provided therein.

Paragraph VI. Regulation by general law. The General Assembly by general law may regulate, redistrict, and limit the creation of community improvement districts and the exercise of the powers of administrative bodies of community improvement districts. (Authority: OLC, pages 147–150).

Article X
Amendments to the Constitution

Section I
Constitution, How Amended

Paragraph I. Proposals to amend the Constitution; new Constitution. Amendments to this Constitution or a new Constitution may be proposed by the General Assembly or by a constitutional convention, as provided in this article. Only amendments which are of general and uniform applicability throughout the state shall be proposed, passed, or submitted to the people.

Paragraph II. Proposals by the General Assembly; submission to the people. A proposal by the General Assembly to amend this Constitution or to provide for a new Constitution shall originate as a resolution in either the Senate or the House of Representatives and, if approved by two-thirds of the members to which each house is entitled in a roll-call vote entered on their respective journals, shall be submitted to the electors of the entire state at the next general election which is held in the even-numbered years. A summary of such proposal shall be prepared by the Attorney General, the Legislative Counsel, and the Secretary of State and shall be published in the official organ of each county and, if deemed advisable by the "Constitutional Amendments Publication Board," in not more than 20 other newspapers in the state designated by such board which meet the qualifications for being selected as the official organ of a county. Said board shall be composed of the Governor, the Lieutenant Governor, and the Speaker of the House of Representatives. Such summary shall be published once each week for three consecutive weeks immediately preceding the day of the general election at which such proposal is to be submitted. The language to be used in submitting a proposed amendment or a new Constitution shall be in such words as the General Assembly may provide in the resolution or, in the absence thereof, in the language as the Governor may prescribe. A copy of the entire proposed amendment or of a new Constitution shall be filed in the office of the judge of the probate court of each county and shall be available for public inspection; and the summary of the proposal shall so indicate. The General Assembly is hereby authorized to provide by law for additional matters relative to the publication and distribution of proposed amendments and summaries not in conflict with the provisions of this Paragraph.

If such proposal is ratified by a majority of the electors qualified to vote for members of the General Assembly voting thereon in such general election, such proposal shall become a part of this Constitution or shall become a new Constitution, as the case may be. Any proposal so approved shall take effect as provided in Paragraph VI of this article. When more than one amendment is submitted at the same time, they shall be so submitted as to enable the electors to vote on each amendment separately, provided that one or more new articles or related changes in one or more articles may be submitted as a single amendment.

Paragraph III. Repeal or amendment of proposal. Any proposal by the General Assembly to amend this Constitution or for a new Constitution may be amended or repealed by the same General Assembly which adopted such proposal by the affirmative vote of two-thirds of the members to which each house is entitled in a roll-call vote entered on their respective journals, if such action is taken at least two months prior to the date of the election at which such proposal is to be submitted to the people.

Paragraph IV. Constitutional convention; how called. No convention of the people shall be called by the General Assembly to amend this Constitution or to propose a new Constitution, unless by the concurrence of two-thirds of the members to which each house of the General Assembly is entitled. The representation in said convention shall be based on population as near as practicable. A proposal by the convention to amend this Constitution or for a new Constitution shall be advertised, submitted to, and ratified by the people in the same manner provided for advertisement, submission, and ratification of proposals to amend the Constitution by the General Assembly. The General Assembly is hereby authorized to provide the procedure by which a convention is to be called and under which such convention shall operate and for other matters relative to such constitutional convention.

Paragraph V. Veto not permitted. The Governor shall not have the right to veto any proposal by the General Assembly or by a convention to amend this Constitution or to provide a new Constitution.

Paragraph VI. Effective date of amendments or of a new Constitution. Unless the amendment or the new Constitution itself or the resolution proposing the amendment or the new Constitution shall provide otherwise, an amendment to this Constitution or a new Constitution shall become effective on the first day of January following its ratification.

Article XI
Miscellaneous Provisions

Section I
Miscellaneous Provisions

Paragraph I. Continuation of officers, boards, commissions, and authorities.
- (a) Except as otherwise provided in this Constitution, the officers of the state and all political subdivisions thereof in the office on June 30, 1983, shall continue in the exercise of their functions and duties, subject to the provisions of laws applicable thereto and subject to the provisions of this Constitution.
- (b) All boards, commissions, and authorities specifically named in the Constitution of 1976 which are not specifically named in this Constitution shall remain as statutory boards, commissions, and authorities; and all constitutional and statutory provisions relating thereto in force and effective on June 30, 1983, shall remain in force and effective as statutory law unless and until changed by the General Assembly.

Paragraph II. Preservation of existing laws; judicial review. All laws in force and effect on June 30, 1983, not inconsistent with this Constitution shall remain in force and effect; but such laws may be amended or repealed and shall be subject to judicial decision as to their validity when passed and to any limitations imposed by their own terms.

Paragraph III. Proceedings of courts and administrative tribunals confirmed. All judgments, decrees, orders, and other proceedings of the several courts and administrative tribunals of this state, heretofore made within the limits of their several jurisdictions, are hereby ratified and affirmed, subject only to reversal or modification in the manner provided by law.

Paragraph IV. Continuation of certain constitutional amendments for a period of four years.
- (a) The following amendments to the Constitution of 1877, 1945, and 1976 shall continue in force and effect as part of this Constitution until July 1, 1987, at which time said amendments shall be repealed and shall be deleted as a part of this Constitution unless any such amendment shall be specifically continued in force and effect without amendment either by local law enacted prior to July 1, 1987, with or without a referendum as provided by law, or by an ordinance or resolution duly adopted prior to July 1, 1987, by local governing authority in the manner provided for the adoption of home rule amendments to its charter or local act: (1) amendments to the Constitution of 1877 and the Constitution of 1945 which were continued in force and effect as a part of the Constitution of 1976 pursuant to the provisions of Article XIII, Section I, Paragraph II, of the Constitution of 1976 which are in force and effect on the effective date of this Constitution; (2) amendments to the Constitution of 1976 which were ratified as general amendments but which by their terms applied principally to a particular political subdivision or subdivisions which are in force and effect on the effective date of this Constitution; (3) amendments to the Constitution of 1976 which were ratified not as general amendments which are in force and effect on the effective date of this Constitution; and (4) amendments to the Constitution of 1976 of the type provided for in the immediately preceding two subparagraphs (2) and (3) of this Paragraph which were ratified at the same time this Constitution was ratified.
- (b) Any amendment which is continued in force and effect after July 1, 1987, pursuant to the provisions of subparagraph (a) of this Paragraph shall be continued in force and effect as a part of this Constitution, except that such amendment may thereafter be repealed but may not be amended.

(c) All laws enacted pursuant to those amendments to the Constitution which are not continued in force and effect pursuant to subparagraph (a) of this Paragraph shall be repealed on July 1, 1987. All laws validly enacted on, before, or after July 1, 1987, and pursuant to the specific authorization of an amendment continued in force and effect pursuant to the provisions of subparagraph (a) of this Paragraph shall be legal, valid, and constitutional under this Constitution. Nothing in this subparagraph (c) shall be constructed to revive any law not in force and effect on June 30, 1987.

(d) Notwithstanding the provisions of subparagraphs (a) and (b), the following amendments to the Constitution of 1877 and 1945 shall be continued in force as a part of this Constitution: amendments to the Constitution of 1877 and the Constitution of 1945 which created or authorized the creation of metropolitan rapid transit authorities, port authorities, and industrial areas and which were continued in force as a part of the Constitution of 1976 pursuant to the provision of Article XIII, Section I, Paragraph II of the Constitution of 1976 and which are in force on the effective date of this Constitution.

(e) Any person owning property in an industrial area described in subparagraph (d) may voluntarily remove the property from the industrial area by filing a certificate to that effect with the clerk of the superior court for the county in which the property is located, but only if the property is located on an island. Once the certificate is filed, the property described in the certificate, together with all public streets and public rights of way within the property, abutting the property, or connecting the property to property outside the industrial area will no longer be in the industrial area and may be annexed by an adjacent city. The filing of a certificate will be irrevocable and will bind the owners, their heirs, and their assigns. The term "owner" includes anyone with a legal or equitable ownership in property but does not include a beneficiary of any trust or a partner in any partnership owning an interest in the property or anyone owning an easement right in the property. (Source: Sec. St. 1997)

Paragraph V. Special commission created. Amendments to the Constitution of 1976 which were determined to be general and which were submitted to and ratified by the people of the entire state at the same time this Constitution was ratified shall be incorporated and made part of this Constitution as provided in this Paragraph. There is hereby created a commission to be composed of the Governor, the President of the Senate, the Speaker of the House of Representatives, the Attorney General, and the Legislative Counsel, which is hereby authorized and directed to incorporate such amendments into this Constitution at the places deemed most appropriate to the commission. The commission shall make only such changes in the language of this Constitution and of such amendments as are necessary to incorporate properly such amendments into this Constitution and shall complete its duties prior to July 1, 1983. The commission shall deliver to the Secretary of State this Constitution with those amendments incorporated therein, and such document shall be the Constitution of the State of Georgia. In order that the commission way perform its duties, this Paragraph shall become effective as soon as it has been officially determined that this Constitution has between ratified. The commission shall stand abolished upon the completion of its duties.

Paragraph VI. Effective date. Except as provided in Paragraph V of this section, this Constitution shall become effective on July 1, 1983; and, except as otherwise provided in this Constitution, all previous Constitutions and all amendments thereto shall thereupon stand repealed.

Bibliography

Books and Publications

ACCG, *1995 Survey of County Governments.*

Ammons, David N. and Campbell, Richard W. (1993). "County Government Structures" in Weeks, J. Devereaux and Hardy, Paul T., eds. *Handbook for Georgia County Commissioners.* Athens: Carl Vinson Institute of Government, University of Georgia.

Argyle, Nolan J. (1991). *New Federalism and Public Mass Transit: The Case of SCAT.* Discussion Paper 91-6. Atlanta GA: Institute of Public Administration, Georgia State University.

Allen, Lee M. (1989). "Civil Service Reform Act of 1978" in Vol. 11 *Encyclopedia USA.* Gulf Breeze, FL: Academic International Press.

Atlanta, City of. (1993). *The 1993 Annual Report,* (Atlanta: Atlanta City Council).

Atlanta, City of. (1993). *The 1993 Atlanta City Council,* (Atlanta: Atlanta City Council).

Banks, Carolyn L. *"Councilmembers marched to the Capitol in protest of unfunded mandates"* in *Council Contact* (In-house publication of the Atlanta City Council), Winter, 1994.

Barber, James D. (1965). *The Lawmakers.* New Haven: Yale University Press.

Blackmon, Douglas A. (1993). *"Council avoids risk, supports stadium"* in the *Atlanta Journal/Atlanta Constitution,* March 2, 1993.

Bullock, Charles S. III. (1991). *The Georgia Political Almanac: The General Assembly.* Decatur, GA: Cornerstone Publications.

———. (1993). *The Partisan, Racial and Gender Makeup of Georgia County Offices,* Public Policy Research Series, (Carl Vinson Institute of Government: The University of Georgia).

Burke, Edmund. (1967) "Address to the Electorate at Bristol" in *The Works of Edmund Burke.* New York: Harper.

Busbee, George D. (1981). *Proposed Constitution of the State of Georgia.* Atlanta, GA: Select Committee on Constitutional Revision, Georgia General Assembly.

Bibliography

Cason, Michael H. (1991). *City of Valdosta Approved Budget, FY 1992.* Valdosta, GA: Office of the City Manager.

Christianberry, George A. Jr. (1991). "The Facts: The Department of Administration" in *Georgia State Telephone Directory.* Atlanta, GA: Office of the Secretary of State, January.

Cleland, Max. (1991). *Constitution of the State of Georgia.* Atlanta, GA: Office of the Secretary of State, January.

———. (1991). *Georgia State Telephone Directory.* Atlanta, GA: Office of the Secretary of State, January.

Cooper, Philip J. (1988). *Public Law and Public Administration.* Englewood Cliffs, NJ: Prentice Hall.

Crutchfield, James A. (1990). *The Georgia Almanac and Book of Facts 1989–1990.* Nashville, TN: Rutledge Hill Press.

Current, Richard N.; Williams, T.H.; Fredal, Frank and Brinkley, Alan. (1983). *A Survey of American History.* 6th ed. New York: Alfred A. Knopf.

Dahl, Robert. (1967). *Pluralist Democracy in the United States.* Chicago, IL: Rand McNally.

Delk, Glenn. (1993). *"School choice law is common sense"* in the *Atlanta Journal/Atlanta Constitution,* September 26, 1993.

Dye, Thomas R. (1997). *Politics in States and Communities.* 9th ed. Englewood Cliffs, NJ: Prentice-Hall.

Elza, Jane L. (1991). "Teaching Research Skills in Administrative Law" in the *Preceedings of the 14th National Teaching Public Administration Conference.* Knoxville, TN: American Society of Public Administration.

Elazar, Daniel J. (1984). *American Federalism: A View from the States.* 5th ed. New York: Thomas Y. Crowell Company.

——— and Grodzin, Morton. (1966). *The American System.* Chicago, IL: Rand-McNally Press.

Eldersveld, Samuel J. (1964). *Political Parties: A Behavioral Analysis.* Chicago, IL: Rand-McNally.

Fleischmann, Arnold and Pierannunzi, Carol. (1997). *Politics in Georgia.* Athens: UGA Press.

Gold, Steven D. (1990). "Demystifying Those Scary Statistics" in *State Legislatures* (May/June).

Gray, Virginia and Jacob, Herbert. (1996). *Politics in the American States: A Comparative Analysis.* 6th ed. Washington, D.C.: CQ Press.

Gray, Virginia and Eisinger, Peter. (1997). *American States and Cities.* New York: Longman.

Grodzin, Morton and Elazar, Daniel J. (1966). *The American System.* Chicago, IL: Rand-McNally Press.

Friedman, Barry. (1991). *Regulations in the Reagan Era: New Procedures, New Results.* Unpublished Ph.D. Dissertation at the University of Connecticut.

Hardy (see Weeks and Hardy, Handbook for Georgia Mayors and Council members, 1993).

———. (1982). *The Georgia History Book.* Athens, GA: Carl Vinson Institute of Government, University of Georgia.
Henry, Nicholas. (1987). "Report on Evaluation of the 50 State Legislatures" in *Governing at the Grass Roots.* 3rd ed. Englewood Cliffs, NJ: Prentice-Hall.
Hepburn, Lawrence R. (1987). "Politics and Government" in *Contemporary Georgia.* Athens, GA: Carl Vinson Institute of Government, University of Georgia.
Holder v. Hall (No. 91202, 1994).
Hy, Ronn and Saeger, Richard T. (1976). "The Nature and Role of Political Parties" in *Mississippi Government and Politics in Transition,* edited by David M. Landry and Joseph B. Parker. Dubuque, IA: Kendall/Hunt Publishing Company.
Jackson, Edwin L. and Stakes, Mary E. (1988). *Handbook of Georgia State Agencies.* Athens, GA: Carl Vinson Institute of Government, University of Georgia.
Kirchner, Joan. (AP 2–12–1998). "Few Select Groups in the Running for Georgia Sales Tax Exemptions" in the Valdosta Daily Times. Valdosta, GA: February 12, 1998, at 3-A.
LWV. (1991). League of Women Voters of Georgia, Inc. *The Georgia Government.* Atlanta, GA: The League of Women Voters of Georgia, Inc.
Lasswell, Harold. (1936). *Who Gets What, When and How?* New York: McGraw Hill.
Lehan, Edward A. (1984). *Budgetmaking: A Workbook of Public Budgeting Theory and Practice.* New York: St. Martin's Press.
Lauth, Thomas P. and Reese, Catherine C. (1993). *"The Line-Item Veto in Georgia: Incidence and Fiscal Effects."* A scholarly paper presented at the Annual Meeting of the Georgia Political Science Association, Savannah, GA, February 25–27, 1993.
Lewis, Eugene. (1977) *American Politics in a Bureaucratic Age: Citizens, Constituents, Clients and Victims.* Cambridge, Mass.: Winthrop Publishing Inc.
Locke, John. Two Treatises of Government, any edition.
Lowi, Theodore J. and Ginsberg, Benjamin. (1991). *American Government: Freedom and Power.* New York: W.W. Norton & Company.
Machiavelli, Niccolo. (1952). *The Prince.* Translated by Luigi Ricci, Introduction by Christian Gauss. New York: Mentor Books.
Madison, James; Hamilton, Alexander and Jay, John. (1961). *The Federalist Papers.* (New York: New American Library).
Miller, Zell. Feb. 24, (1994). *"House Embraces Tax Cut"* in the *Atlanta Journal/ Atlanta Constitution,* at p. A1.
Mishou, Thomas E. and Ellinger, Ken. (1997). "An Analysis of Voter Turnout in Georgia's Presidential Elections 1960–96: Proposals for Electoral Reform," unpublished paper presented at the 1997 Annual Meeting of the Georgia Political Science Association, Savannah, Georgia, February 21–22, 1997.

Nachmias, David and Rosenbloom, David H. (1980). *Bureaucratic Government USA*. New York: St. Martins Press.
OLC. (1991). Office of the Legislative Council, *Official Code of Georgia, Annotated*. Charlottesville, Va.: The Michie Company.
———. (1991). *The Pocket Part*. The Michie Company.
Osinski, Bill. (1994). *"Law has towns fighting Oblivion"* in The Atlanta Journal/Atlanta Constitution, 03-28-94, p. B6.
Parenti, Michael. (1988). *Democracy for the Few*, 5th ed. Boston: St. Martins Press.
Parker, Jennifer F. (1993). *"Business owners worry about bus disruption"* in Atlanta Journal/Atlanta Constitution, August 29, 1993.
Pound, Merritt B. and Saye, Albert B. (1971). *Handbook on the Constitutions of the United States and Georgia*. 9th ed. Athens, Ga.: Department of Political Science, University of Georgia.
Rankin, Bill. (1993). *"Top judges say they need a pay increase"* in the Atlanta Journal/Atlanta Constitution, December 07, 1993.
Rousseau, Jean J. Du Contrat Social, St. Martins Press, 1978.
Saeger, Richard T. and Hy, Ronn. (1976). "The Nature and Role of Political Parties" in *Mississippi Government and Politics in Transition*, edited by D.M. Landry and J.B. Parker. Dubuque, IA: Kendall/Hunt Publishing Company.
Salter, Sallye. (1993). *"Nearby merchants excited about project"* in Atlanta Journal/Atlanta Constitution, August 29, 1993.
Salzer, James. (1994). *"State Flag Supporters Fire Angry Volley"* in Savannah Morning News, 2-25-94, Morris News Service.
Seabrook, Charles. *"State Lawmakers debate impact of reprimand"* in Atlanta Journal/Atlanta Constitution, Jan. 14, 1993.
Smith, Edward C. (1979). *Constitution of the United States, with Case Summaries*. New York: Harper and Row, Publishers.
Thomas, William R. and Prather, James E. (1993). *"Race, Politics and redistricting in Georgia: Analysis of the 1992 Congressional Election"* a scholarly paper presented at the Annual Meeting of the Georgia Political Science Association, Savannah, Georgia, February 25-27, 1993.
Tocqueville, Alexis de. *Democracy in America*. New York: Knopf.
Vickers, Robert J. (1994). *"Friends and contributors all"* in the Atlanta Journal/Atlanta Constitution, January 2, 1994.
Watson, Tom. (1993). *"Gay fight unfolds in Georgia"* in USA Today, August 23, 1993.
Weber, Max. (1958) *From Max Weber: Essays in Political Sociology*, edited by H.H. Gerth, and C. Wright Mills. New York: Oxford University Press.
———. (1961). *Basic Concepts in Sociology*. New York: Citadel, 1913, or see Amitai etzioni, ed. *Complex Organizations*. New York: Holt, 1961 at pp. 4-14.

Weeks, J. Devereaux and Hardy, Paul T., eds. (1993). *Handbook for Georgia Mayors and Council members.* Athens: Carl Vinson Institute of Government, UGA.
Whitt, Richard. (1994). *"Study commissions: Where bills go to die"* in the *Atlanta Journal/Atlanta Constitution,* January 10, 1994.
Wilson, J.Q. (1992). *American Government: Institutions and Policies.* Lexington, Mass.: D.C. Heath & Company.
———. (1980). *The Politics of Regulation.* New York: Basic Books, Inc.
Winder, David W. *"Governor Miller Drops Proposal to Change the Georgia State Flag for 1993"* in *Comparative State Politics* Vol. 14, (June 1993).
———. (1991). "The Powers of the Attorneys General: A Quantitative Assessment" in Vol. 19, *Southeastern Political Review.*
Wolfe, W.H. (1991). *Decatur County, Georgia: Past and Present.* (Roswell, GA: Historical Publications.
Wooten, Jim. (1993). *"I give up in the war on lottery"* in the *Atlanta Journal/Atlanta Constitution,* September 26, 1993.
Zanardi, David. (1994). *"Experts say mega-school is unwise"* in the *Tifton Gazette,* (September 17, 1993).

Journals and Newspapers

AJ/AC. (02–21–1992). Editorial. "Miller's Roads to Glory" in the *Atlanta Journal/Atlanta Constitution.* (February 21, 1992) at A12.
———. Jan. 13, (1994). *"A Greener Year for State Spending"* in the *Atlanta Journal/Atlanta Constitution,* at p. E4.
Associated Press. (03–29–1992). "300-pound Woman Sues in Bus Arrest" in the *Florida Times-Union, Georgia Section.* (Atlanta, GA: AP, March 29, 1992) at B8.
———. (04–29–1992). "Busted Bingo Players Pledge to Change Law" in the *Florida Times-Union, Georgia Section.* (Lavonia, Georgia: AP, April 29, 1992) at A1.
———. (01–01–1992) "Who Should Draw State's Districts? *Valdosta Daily Times.* (Valdosta, GA: January 1, 1992) at 5-A.
———. (02–23–1992). Paulding Ponders County Manager. *Florida Times-Union, Georgia Section.* (Dallas, Georgia: AP, February 23, 1992) at B4.
Associated Press. (1993). *"Bowers: Murphy threatened child protection funding"* in the *Tifton Gazette,* October 5, 1993.
Associated Press. (1993). *"Atlanta's archbishop urges support for voucher law"* in the *Florida Times-Union,* October 10–19–93.
Associated Press. (1993). *"State would need big-time bucks to take over Georgia education costs"* in the *Tifton Gazette,* 11–15–93.
Associated Press. (1994). *"Gov. gives lawmakers new agenda as he prepares for re-election bid"* in the *Tifton Gazette,* January 1, 1994.

Associated Press. (1994). *"Weeping Murphy growls over guide dog coverage"* in the *Tifton Gazette,* February 23, 1994.

Associated Press. (1994). *"How will Georgia House be ruled after Speaker Murphy"* in the *Tifton Gazette,* March 28, 1994.

Beer, Samuel H. (1978). "Federalism, Nationalism and Democracy in America" in *American Political Science Review.* (March, 1978).

Cook, Rhonda. (04–02–1992). "Feds Play 'Partisan Politics' with Re-districting, Miller says" in the *Atlanta Journal/Atlanta Constitution* (April 2 1992) at D3.

———. (10–14–1991). "Backlog of State Inmates Is Growing" in the *Atlanta Journal/Atlanta Constitution (*October 14, 1991), at D1.

Cook, Rhonda and Hendricks, Gary. (01–22–1992). "Black vote was 'minimalized,' so redistricting starts again today." *The Atlanta Journal/The Atlanta Constitution* (Wednesday, January 22, 1992) at A1, A8.

Froman, Lewis L. (1985). "Some Effects of Interest Group Strength in State Politics" in *American Journal of Political Science* Vol. 29, (February).

Gibson, James L. (1985). "Whither the Local Parties?" *American Journal of Political Science* Vol. 29 (February).

Harvey, Steve. (04–01–1992). "$8.2 Billion Budget OK'ed on Eve of Adjournment" in *The Atlanta Journal/The Atlanta Constitution,* April 1, 1992), at A1 and A8.

LoMonte, Frank. (04–02–1992). "Miller Proclaims Session a Success" in the Georgia Section of the *Florida Times-Union* (April 2, 1992) Georgia Section.

———. (04–02–1992) "Zell Miller to Sign New Ethics Bill Monday" in the Georgia Section of the *Florida Times-Union,* (April 2, 1992) Georgia Section.

Pettys, Dick. (06-26-1990) "Lobbying a Thriving Business in Georgia, Even IF IT Is Illegal" in the *Brunswick News* (June 26, 1990).

Roberts, Sylvia L. (01-24-1992). Letters to the Editor: Berrien Should Delay School Consolidation. *Valdosta Daily Times* (January 24, 1992) at 4-a.

Sherman, Mark. (01-22-1992). "Primary change boosts Ga.'s profile" in *The Atlanta Journal/The Atlanta Constitution* (Wednesday, January 22, 1992) page A1.

Staff Report. (04–01–1992). "Status of Major Bills in Legislature" in *The Atlanta Journal/The Atlanta Constitution* (Wednesday, April 1, 1992) at A1 and A8.

The World Almanac and Book of Facts 1997. Mahwah, NJ: World Almanac Books.

Walston, Charles and Cook, Rhonda. (01–22–1992). "Blame the Legislature, not Justice, Brooks says" in *The Atlanta Journal/The Atlanta Constitution* (January 22, 1992) at A-8.

General Index

Abernathy, Ralph David III, 51
Ad valorem tax, 104
Administrative Law Judge, 90
African-Americans, 20–21, 63
AIDS, 116
Alaska, state of, 133
Allen, Lee M., 65
Amending process, 8
American Legion (AL), 36
American Revolution, 36
Americans for Democratic Action (ADA), 36
Ammons, David N., 135
Annexation, 146, 159
Apple pie model, 63, 110–111, 147
Appalachian Mts., 1
Appropriation bills, 56–58
Arnall, Ellis, 11, 70, 89
Articles of Confederation, 10
Association of County Commissioners, 37, 135–136
Athens, City of, 146
Atlanta Braves, 112–113
Atlanta, City of, 3, 32, 63, 90, 100, 112–113, 139
    airport, 74, 141, 144
Attorney General, 28, 34, 61, 69, 75, 85, 99
Augusta, City of, 33, 146
Australia, 7

Baker, Thurbert, 34
Baldwin County, 55
Banks, Carolyn, 113
Barber, James D., 64
Barnes, Roy, 4, 61
Barr, Bob, 30
Beer, Samuel H., 2, 67
Bibb County, 33
Bibles, 106, 109
Bill of Rights, 4, 5, 13
Bingo, 23
Bishop, Sanford, 30
Bleckley County, 135
Blackburn, Ben, 30
Blackmon, Douglas, 113

Board of Education, 119, 120, 145
Board of Elections, 78
Board of Natural Resources, 62, 78, 83, 84
Board of Regents of the University System, 69, 119–120, 125–126, 145
Bonds, 103, 110
Bourbon Coup, 5
Bowers, Michael J., 34
Boy Scouts, 106
British Colonies, 10
British Parliament, 10, 39
Brooks, Tyrone, 55
Brunswick, City of, 146
Budgeting, 103–117
Bureaucratic Constitution, 5
Bureaucracy
    and activity, 75
    constitution, 76
    government, 73–87
    leaders, 78
    regulations, 84, 85
    workforce, 74
    workload, 75
Burke, Edmund, 129
Business, 2
Business Council of Georgia, 37

Callaway, Howard (Bo), 30
Campaign contributions, 40
Campbell, Bill, 140
Campbell, Richard W., 135
Carter, James, 64–65
Catoosa County, 32
Chambliss, Saxby, 30
Chatham County, 33
Checks and balances, 54
Chicago, City of, 122, 139, 144
Chief Justice of the Supreme Court,
Christenberry, George A., 75
Churchill, 143
Cities, 137–143
Civil Rights Act 1964, 33
Civil War, 5, 32, 61
Clayton County, 55

261

General Index

Clerk of the House of Representatives, 48
Cobb County, 6, 33, 55
Coca-Cola Company, 37
Collins, Mack, 30
Columbus, City of, 33, 146
Commissioner of Agriculture, 7, 28, 61, 70, 85
Commissioner of Insurance, 7, 28, 34, 61, 70, 83
Commissioner of Labor, 7, 28, 61, 70
Confederacy, 32
Connecticut, 133
Conservation, 84
Constitution of Georgia
    ten constitutions, 5, 11
    1983 Constitution, 6–8
Constitutional basis, 3–4, 151
Constitutional boards and commissions, 73–83
Constitutional bureaucracy, 76–77
Cook, Rhonda, 55
Cooper, Philip J., 76
County Commissions, 143
Courts, 70, 89–100
Coverdell, Paul, 30
Crimes, 90, 92–93, 158
Culture, 101, 130, 153
Current, Richard N., 54
CVIG—Carl Vinson Institute of Government, 192, 208

Deal, Nathan, 30
Debt, 103–104, 109
Dekalb County, 33, 56, 135
Delk, Glenn, 127
Delta Airlines, 37
Democratic Party, 30, 31, 35
Department of Transportation, 37, 81
Director of the Fiscal Division, 85
Dirksen, E.M., 1
Disability in Office, 67
District Attorneys, 100
Dougherty County, 55
Drug Abuse, 129–130
Dukakis, Michael, 28
Duke, David, 30
Dunne, J.R., 55
Dye, Thomas R., 9, 10, 37, 108

Eagle Forum (EF), 36
Echols County, 100
Edwards, Edwin, 30
Education, 112, 119–131, 153, 159
Elazar, Daniel, 9, 101
Eldersveld, Samuel, 35
Election turnout, 31
Electoral College, 7, 34
Ellinger, Ken, 31
Eminent domain, 24
Ethics, 40

Examining Boards, 79, 80
Executive Commission, 78–79

Families, 130
Fannin County, 32
Fayette County, 55
Federalism, 63
Felton, Rebecca, 19
Fiscal Year, 103
Fisheries Commission, 84
Flag dispute, 63–64
Fleischmann, Arnold, 74
Fletcher v. Peck (1810), 54
Florida, 10
Friedman, Barry, 76
Froman, Lewis, 36
Fulton County, 113

Galveston, 143
Gambling, 107
General Appropriations Bills, 56–58
General Assembly, 7, 15, 20, 23, 28, 39
    see also legislature
Georgia Association of Educators, 37, 38
Georgia
    Bureau of Investigation, 73
    Georgia State Finance and Investment Commission, 85
    Georgia Trial Lawyers Association, 37
    Municipal Association, Georgia
    Rebound Program, 65, 126
Gerrymandering, 55–56
Gibson, James L., 36
Gingrich, Newt, 30
Girl Scouts, 106
Glynn County, 33, 146
Gold, Steven D., 108
Goldwater, Barry, 33
Goldwater Republicans, 33
Good Hope, 138
Governor, 5, 6, 7, 28, 62, 85, 89, 98, 99, 154
    and appointments, 68
    powers of, 62
Gray, Virginia, 32, 62, 71, 108
Green, Mark, 76
Gwinnett County, 33

Hardy, Paul T., 142
Harris, Joe Frank, 138
Helms, Jimmy, 73
Henry, Nicholas T., 38
Hepburn, L.R., 1, 62
Hillhouse, Sarah P., 19
Historic Chattahoochee Commission, 84
Holder v. Hall (1994), 135
Homestead Exemption, 21
Home Rule, 133–134, 153

General Index

Hope Scholarship Program, 67, 126
House of Representatives, 48
Houston County, 55
Howard, Pierre, 46, 56, 67
Hrebenar, Ronald, 37, 41
Hy, Ronald J., 29

Ideology, 33
Impeachment, 48, 51, 54
Interest Groups, 36–41, 150–152
Intergovernmental interaction, 83–84
Intergovernmental relations, 83
Interim Constitution, 5
Islands, 146

Jackson, Edwin L., 77
Jefferson, Thomas, 4
Jewell, Richard, 16
Johnson, D., 56
Joint-Secretary of the State Examining Boards, 78
Judicial Power, 89–101
Judicial Qualifications Commission, 98–99
Junior Tuesday, 55
Jurisdiction, Court, 89–95

King, Martin Luther, Jr., 20, 21, 66
Kingston, Jack, 30

Lauth, Thomas P., 116
Lavonia, City of, 73
Layer cake, 63
League of Women Voters (LWV), 36
Legislature, state
    appropriations, 56–58
    bills, 49, 52
    committees 49, 50
    composition, 43
    majority leaders, 46
    powers, 53–58
    sessions, 43
Lewis, John, 30
Licensing boards, 79
Lieutenant Governor, 7, 28, 46, 65, 67, 85
Lincoln Plan, 5
Linder, John, 30
Lobbying, 39–41
Local government, 8, 112, 133–147
Local legislation, 8
Locke, John, 76, 149
LoMonte, Frank, 66
Lottery, 22, 107, 114, 158
Louisiana, 5, 30
Lowndes County, 33, 137

Machiavelli, 62
Macon, City of, 33, 73
Madison, James, 2, 8, 153

Magna Carta, 56
Managers (city), 142–145
Marble cake, 63
Massachusetts, 5
Mattingly, Mack, 30
Mayors, 139–142
Medical Association of Georgia (MAG), 37, 38
Mickey Code, 155
Miller, Zell, 4, 63, 65, 67, 93, 96, 106, 108, 116, 126
Miller v. Johnson (1996), 56
Moral Turpitude, 98
Moralistic culture, 9
    see also religion
Morality, 128
Muscogee County, 33
Motto (Georgia State), 89
Murphy, Thomas B., 46–48, 63

Nachmias, David, 11
National Association for the Advancement of Colored People (NAACP), 36
National Association of Chiefs of Police, 37
National Association of Counties, 37
National Council of Churches (NCC), 36
National Governors Association, 84
New Deal, 1
New York, City of, 139
Norwood, Charlie, 30

O'Neill, Tip, 33
Oglethorpe, James, 61, 76
OLC—Office of Legislative Counsel, 193
Olympic Committee, 6, 112, 140
Osinski, 138

Pardons, 158
Parenti, Michael, 40
Participation, 27–31
Paulding County, 73
Peach County, 55
Peach State, 41
Petty, Dick, 40
Political Action Committees (PAC), 14, 40
    Culture, 9–10
    Party Organization, 34–36
    Party System, 31–34
Porter, Dubose, 56
Pound, Merritt B., 11, 67
Precincts, 36
President of the Senate, 51
    see also Lt. Governor
President Pro Tempore, 46
Primary elections, 36
Prisons, 93
Public Service Commission (PSC), 34, 62, 74, 75
Public Utilities Commission, 11
Putnam County, 100

General Index

Quality Basic Education (QBE), 56, 122, 127
Queer Nation/Atlanta, 38

Radioactive Waste Management
    Commission, 84
Railroad Commission, 74
Reapportionment, 55
Reconstruction Era, 5
Redistricting, 55
Reese, Catherine C., 116
Religion, 127–128
Republican Party, 30, 32, 35, 105
Restoration Constitution, 5
Revenues, 114–116
Revolutionary War, 10
Rhode Island, 133
Richmond County, 33, 100
Riddleville, 138
Roberts, Sylvia L., 56
Roosevelt, F.D., 1
Rousseau, J.J., 76, 149
Run-off election, 28

Saeger, 129
Savannah, City of, 33
Saye, Albert B., 11, 67
Schools, 120–122, 125, 145
Sea Island, 33
Sears-Collins, L., 97
Secretary of State, 7, 28, 61, 70, 78
Senate, 7
    appropriations committee, 56
Sherman, Mark, 55
Sin taxes, 106, 115
Smith, George T., 96
Smyre, C., 55
Southeastern Interstate Forest Fire Protection
    Compact Advisory Committee, 84
Southern Growth Policies Board, 84
Southern States Energy Board, 84
Sovereign Immunity, 23
Sparticus, 17
Speaker of the House of Representatives,
    46–48, 85
Speaker Pro Tempore, 48
Special Authorities, 144–145
Special Legislation, 53
State
    Auditor, 85
    State Bar of Georgia, 100
    State Board of Education, State Board of
        Pardons and Paroles, 62, 78, 79
    Constitution, 3–8
    Ethics Commission, 40
    Financing and Investment Commission, 85
    Merit System of Personnel
        Administration, 82
    Municipal Associations, 37
    Personnel Board, 62, 78, 82

School Superintendent, 7, 28, 34, 61, 69
Supreme Court, 89, 91, 106
Transportation Board, 7, 62, 78, 80
Succession, 66
SunTrust Bank, 37
Super Tuesday, 55
Swindall, Pat, 30

Talmadge, Eugene, 70, 89
Talmadge, Herman, 89, 148
Taxes, 103–115, 145, 159
Taylor, Mark, 46, 67
Texas, 25, 27
Thomas, Clive, 37, 41
Thompson, M.E., 89
Traditions, 76
Treason, 18

Unified Court System, 90–92
Unruh, Jesse, 38
U.S. Justice Department, 27, 55

Valdosta, City of, 33
Valdosta State University, xiii
Vermont, 105
Venue, 92
Veterans Service Board, 62, 78, 82
Veto, 116, 154
Vickers, Robert J., 126
Virginia, 105
Virginia Bill of Rights, 4
Voter turnout, 29
Voting Rights Act, 27
Vouchers, 127–128

Wachovia Bank, 37
Walker, G., 56
Walston, Charles W., 56
Washington D.C., 2
Waskey, Jack, 152
Weber, Max, 76, 77
Weeks, J. Devereaux, 142
Weidenbaum, Murray, 76
Weltner, Charles, 97
Wesleyan College, 19
White, Leonard, 76
Whitfield County, 32
Whitt, Richard, 49
Wilson, James Q., 63, 149–150, 160
Winder, David, 63–64, 69
Wooten, Jim, 114
Wowen, 130
Wright, 83
Writ of Habeas Corpus, 17

Yazoo Land Grant Fraud, 39, 54
Zinardi, David, 127
Zoning, 138, 159